BLACK
IS
Beautiful
BUT IT FITS THE
DESCRIPTION

BLACK

IS

Beautiful

BUT IT FITS THE

DESCRIPTION

The Challenges of Living In A Melanin Skin In A Colorless World

vase
on
Table
Publishing

PRICELY D. FRANCIS

Author: Pricely D. Francis
Title: Black Is Beautiful but It Fits the Description
ISBN: 978-1-9992892-8-7
Category: Self-Help/Motivational/Politics and Social Sciences/Social Sciences/ Violence in society/Dreams

Publisher: Vase On Table Publishing
Toronto, Canada
Contact: +1 647 299 6181

Dedication

To those who died so we may live

**Black men died in North Africa,
fighting the Germans! Black men died at
Anzio Beach at Palermo at Naples to free
Rome, to free Paris, to free Europe! Dam
it! We died to build America and America
has rebuilt Germany and Japan, and the
Nigga is still suffering and dying in the
streets of America!**
- Louis Farrakhan

Contents

Introduction

Black Fits the Description

The hard, cold steal clamped shut on the man's wrists. The five cops, one of whom gave the handcuffs a final tug to ensure they held fast, had him caged in like a dangerous animal who might break loose at any moment.

He was once a lawyer who defended innocent people. After that he was a Judge who upheld the law for close to 30 years[1] and no doubt sentenced law breakers to years of confinement. As a distinguished Jury, he had made significant contributions to judicial, legal education, and the development of the law in British Columbia and Canada. He was voted by B.C. lawyers as one of the four best Provincial Court Judges in the province in 1991. In 2008, he received a distinguished service award from the Black Law Students Association of Canada and upon his retirement in 2015, he was honoured by the City of Vancouver, and a gala held for him by the Canadian Association of Black Lawyers.[2]

But now here he stood, his arms twisted behind him and a handcuff biting into his flesh. Humiliation washed over him, but he felt even more diminished by the gawking spectators who only saw a common criminal.

His heart thudded in his chest as a haze of disbelief totally engulfed him. He was ringed by five threatening Vancouver police officers, because as Constable Tania Visintin later said, he was "possibly violent and could potentially severely hurt an innocent person."[3]

Moments before, the 81-year-old, mild-mannered, retired Judge, Selwyn Romilly, was enjoying a leisurely stroll on Vancouver's seawall. The clement weather buoyed his spirit while the warm, gentle sun caressed his black skin. Of course, I do not know for sure the Judge's state of mind on that fateful day, but if he and the other citizens were out for a pleasant stroll, he must have been feeling sunshiny. But in the next moment he was arrested and detained like a two-bit criminal because he fit the description of a dark-skinned man, 40 to 50 years old, who screamed, shouted at people, and attempted to kick and punch them.

If retired Judge Selwyn Romilly was possibly two times the age of the suspect, why was he arrested by the police? Because the reported offender was dark-skinned. **That was all the police needed to know to arrest the first Black person that materialized in their crosshairs.**

"Without much ado," the Judge told *Vancouver Sun*, "They told me to turn around and put my hands behind my back and put me in handcuffs. The place is packed with people, and they're seeing a Black man placed in handcuffs. ... They didn't ask me my name or questions. They put the handcuffs on in indecent haste."

Black Is Beautiful But. . .

Black is beautiful, according to Song of Solomon 1:5, but what the author of that Bible verse was never inspired to say was black also "fits the description." Your physical appearance does not matter: You may be male or female, a child[4] or an adult, young or old, fat or slim, bald head or dreadlocks; if you are black, you fit the description.

"Anybody else, they'd ask the name, ask a few questions before they decide to put them in handcuffs," Romilly said when asked if he thought he was racially profiled. "I was no threat to them. I had no firearms on me. It was a new experience for me being put in handcuffs.

"I thought things had changed, and they haven't," Romilly told *Global News* of the incident. "I hate to say racial profiling, but I can't help but think if it was an 81-year-old white man, regardless of the description, they wouldn't have put him in handcuffs for 'officer safety.'"[5]

When the police saw the Judge, was he "running around English Bay, screaming and shouting at people" and trying to "kick and punch" those around him? Or was he taking a leisurely stroll or just standing and soaking up the beautiful morning? I bet your bottom-dollar retired Judge Romilly was NOT "running around, screaming and shouting at people" and trying to "kick and punch" them, **but he was BLACK! And black fits the description - always.**

Constable Tania Visintin insisted the 81-year-old Mr. Romilly "matched the description" of the suspect, described as "a dark-skinned man, about 40 to 50 years old."[6]

Vancouver Mayor, Kennedy Stewart, said he was appalled by the incident and apologized to the Justice. He is quoted by the *Vancouver Sun* as saying:

*This is not something anyone should
be forced to go through. Incidents like
this can be a very damaging experience, especially for those in the Indigenous, Black and Person
of Colour communities who already face multiple barriers
and discrimination.*

*I want to say again, all of our institutions are based on colonialism
and, as such, are systemically racist. This includes the City of
Vancouver and the Vancouver Police Department. We must
continue to acknowledge this reality and do our best to
combat racism — especially in our government
institutions.*

Talk about striking the nail on the head!

The Vancouver Police officers thought an eighty-one-year-old Black man matched the description of a 40 to 50 year-old violent offender only because he was "a dark-skinned man."

Black people always fit the description.

Weird Looking Kids

The first time I saw the pictures of Chinese children, I thought they looked weird. I do not know precisely how old I was, but I do remember that it was before I had learnt to read. At that stage of my life, I only looked at pictures in books and was able to deduce only the meaning the pictures were willing to surrender.

I first learned to read in the summer months before I entered grade three. The prescribed reading book for that grade had just arrived. The crisped, clean pages and their new-book-smell held me spellbound, and I was eager to look at the lively, colorful pictures because I had still not mastered the art of reading - or so I thought.

When I opened the book to the story of the fox and the rabbit caught in the brier, (the rabbit caught in the brier, not the fox) the words which had, until the day before, withheld their meaning like mean, malicious misers, generously flooded my consciousness with their essence. I can still remember the rapture and the euphoria as I joyfully and hungrily decoded the story.

But I digress. If I were about eight years old, in grade three, I am guessing I was about four or five when I first saw pictures of Chinese children. Although I cannot be precise about my age, I can remember my thoughts and emotions when I saw those pictures. I thought the Chinese children looked strange and felt sympathy for people who looked like that.

Pray, do not judge me. I was only a small boy, a relative newcomer to earth and had not seen any other physical human being except Black people and the picture of White people, chief of whom were two White kids in my grade two (or was it grade one?) reading book. Their names were Dick and Jane (and their dog, Spot. How could I forget Spot?), who did nothing unless they did it at least twice, and you read their names and their activities in a sing-song manner:

Come, Spot.
>*Come see Jane fall.*
>>*Oh, Spot*
>>>*Come and see.*
>>>>*See Jane ride.*
>>>>>*See Dick run.*
>>>>>>*Come, come, come.*

Self-Denigration

What may intrigue you even more than the fact that the four or five-year-old me thought Asian kids looked weird is that I thought White Dick and Jane appeared normal, perhaps even beautiful. When I reach back into the archives of my memory to try and explain my cognitive dissonance, I can only come up with two possible explanations. The first is that only White people were represented in all the picture books I had seen. Also, the picture scrolls my church used for Sabbath school had a White God, Jesus, angels, patriarchs, and apostles. The only dark figure in those picture scrolls was the crooked, scraggly-winged Satan.

The second explanation is more insidious and way more consequential. Babies and small children who are rapid learners by nature and propensity ensured that I would subconsciously imbibe my mother's inherited colonial assertion that "anything black no good." On the other hand, my mother held White people in high esteem. Mr. and Mrs. Crooks were mainly to be blamed for that. They were my young mother's employers, and they were very lovely people. They treated my mother well. She delighted in regaling us (her children and grandchildren) with stories about how wonderful it was to work for the couple.

The one thing she liked best about Mr. Crooks was his nose. "Him nose so straight, you coulda tek it and juck dumpling outa pot." Translated into the Queen's English, (Oh! Sorry, the Queen died since I first wrote this. It's now the King's language) she literally said, "His nose was so straight, (pointed) it could spear a boiled dumpling and take it from a pot."

Without any consideration given for the agony Mr. Crooks' nose would have had to endure if used to spear a hot, scalding flour dumpling from a pot, my mother wanted our noses to be as straight as Mr. Crooks'. Occasionally, she would call one of us who happened to be within sight and earshot. "Come ya boy (or gal). How y'u nose so flat?" She then proceeded to "straighten" our imperfect appendage by squeezing it between her index and middle fingers.

Beauty for my mother was white skin (anything black no good) and a straight nose (how y'u nose so flat?). I guess you can see how the stable and steady diet of White superiority from my church (powerful White God, Jesus, angels, etc., black devil) and my mother's relentless message of black ugliness would condition me to see Dick and Jane as beautiful. I would have been as sorry for myself as I was for those "weird looking" Asian kids if I were compared with those two fictitious White children.

Things a Little Black Boy Could Not Have Known

Now, having taken the time to outline my innate, puerile prejudice against Chinese children and my self-denigration in comparison to White children, I must hasten to tell you that by and large, as a child, I assumed that I, the people I knew, my way of living and culture (except I did not as yet know the word or its meaning) were normal and the only way to be in the world. I was so convinced of this that any time I discovered there were other ethnic groups with a totally different (and bizarre) way of life, I suffered violent and discomforting paradigm shifts. In my childish mind, I wondered why those people did not live like "normal" people.

The four or five-year-old me could not have known that a Chinese child several thousand miles across the globe may have looked at my picture and thought I was ugly. I could not have known that, possibly at the same time I judged Chinese children less handsome than me, people with my skin color were being brutalized and dehumanized in America (I had not yet heard about that country), a so-called civilized nation.

My judgement on Asian children may have happened at the same time Governor George Wallace, with State troopers by his side, was blocking two Black students,

Vivian Malone and James Hood, from entering the University of Alabama to enroll in classes.[7] It might have been the same time Mississippi NAACP Field Secretary Medgar Evers was assassinated,[8] and his family would not have guessed that Byron de la Beckwith, a Ku Klux Klan member arrested for the crime the following year, would have walked free until 1990![9]

Perhaps my less than favourable regard for my Asian counterparts happened about the time of the march on Washington; or when Ku Klux Klan members bombed the Sixteenth Street Baptist Church in Birmingham, killing four girls—Addie Mae Collins, Denise McNair, Carole Robertson, and Cynthia Wesley—between the ages of 11 and 14 and injuring many more.[10] It could have been the same day on which three civil rights workers involved with the Freedom Summer project—James Chaney, Andrew Goodman, and Michael Schwerner—were abducted and killed in Mississippi by members of the KKK.[11] Who knows?

The first indication that wearing black skin could be dangerous to your health was when my mother read a book on Dr. Martin Luther King Jr. My mother wept as she read of the injustice, cruelty, imprisonment, and humiliation visited upon Dr. King. I felt her distress keenly and wondered why she persisted in reading the book through. Still, I could not have appreciated the magnitude of the evil Black people endured because as of yet, I knew nothing about the oppressive and murderous South Africa's apartheid system of government, nor had I heard about the centuries of enslavement of Africans.

I could not have guessed, as the age-old saying goes, the half has never been told, even from my mother's copious crocodile tears while reading about the abuses directed at Dr. King, the intensity of the hate and the brutal and debased treatment White Americans dished out to their Black counterparts! I was well into my late teens before I knew there were once black and white water fountains, places of businesses that Black people dared not set foot in, or that the back of the bus was the designated place for Black commuters.[12] I still did not know of the frequent lynching of Black people and that such savage acts were celebrated on postcards! I had heard nothing about the high rate of Black unemployment and its generational ill effects - incomes below the federal poverty threshold or no incomes, all of which were due to racially discriminatory employment practices. I was an adult, well past middle age, before I heard about Black Wall Street and how White people burned that community to the ground and murdered its citizens en masse.[13]

The point I am making is simply this: At the very moment the four or five-year-old me judged Chinese children as looking funny, I could not have known that other people in the world would have seen me as ugly, loathsome, less than an animal, unless I was a monkey, of course. I could not have known they would gleefully hang me from a tree, burn my body for good measure, and kill my mother, who believed that White people were beautiful!

Everyone Thinks They're All That

It is the nature of humans to believe they are superior to others. The tiny version of me, unaided by any adult prejudice or malice, assumed I was more handsome than Chinese children and that my way of living and being in the world was the only normal and sane reality. I was still unaware of my mother's dislike for anything black, so naturally, I had an inflated, though innocent, view of myself. I later came to believe I was ugly because of my thick lips when I was about nine, and it was sometime after that I discovered my ears were too small. Just imagine a child's internal turmoil from the creeping conviction that his lips were too big for his face while his ears were too small for his head!

I eventually lost my discomfiture over my thick lips after my older sister kissed me goodbye and exclaimed how soft my lips were. My pride in my thick, now "soft," lips was reinforced when in my college years, I learnt that a female student (I never found out who) loved, perhaps even lusted for my lips. With time, I completely forgot about my tiny ears except occasionally when I see them in the mirror for a few fleeting seconds.

Although I had self-esteem issues and suffered the indignity of being scornfully looked down upon because of my ill-fitting church clothes, attending elementary school barefooted and my poverty, I confess that I caught myself on many occasions looking down my nose on others I judged inferior to me or less fortunate.

People think they are superior by virtue of their religion, social and economic fortune, education, gender, culture, ethnicity, caste or skin color. This glitch in human nature is what accounts for John 4:9 - "For Jews do not associate with Samaritans," or Acts 11:2, 3 - "So when Peter went up to Jerusalem, the circumcised believers criticized him and said, 'You went into the house of uncircumcised men and ate with them.'" It is what accounts for Adolf Hitler and the notion of a superior Aryan race. It explains why men suppressed women for centuries and denied them the right to own property or vote. It accounts, in part, for the enslavement of other people, plundering of their resources, and slaughtering them. It accounts for the rabid racism in South Africa and America's segregation laws, injustices and abuses of Black people who still suffer from the stubborn vestiges of this evil baked into the very foundation of that nation.

Everyone thinks they are "all that." It is difficult not to conclude that this tendency in humans is innate, automatic - a reflex tendency judging from the preponderance of historical and current evidence. The absurdity of this fault in humans is so monumental that we have imposed a stratification of caste or class upon others of our fellowmen and exalted ourselves on nothing more than the accidental occasion of our social standing, wealth, birth or color of our skin!

Many people eventually overcome their instinctive leaning to look with disfavour at their fellowmen. The evolution may come through maturity, education, observation, experience or religious conviction. In my case, I came to accept other people as "normal" as myself by reading, watching TV, and later in life, living and working with people of different ethnic and cultural backgrounds. My religious upbringing helped in this respect. My Sabbath School teacher taught me this little chorus:

> *Jesus loves the little children*
> *All the children of the world*
> *Red and yellow, black and white*
> *They are precious in his sight*
> *Jesus loves the little children of the world.*

My Church later taught me that Jesus died for all peoples and that around the throne of God in heaven, there will be a "great multitude . . . from every nation, tribe, people and language, standing before the throne and before the Lamb" (Revelation 7:9 NIV). Even as a boy, I eventually accepted that everyone, including Chinese children, was my coequal - and beautiful. However, later in life, I discovered that other "Christian" people who got the same religious instruction I got treated Black people with contempt. Imagine my surprise when I discovered that my Church's headquarters and health institutions were once segregated!

The Washington Sanitarium and Hospital, in 1943, turned away Lucy Byard because she was a Black woman.[14] Prior to 1943, Black parishioners were treated at the Sanitarium, but on a "limited, selective and subpar basis." Only a certain kind of Black person was admitted in emergency cases and the patient had to be treated "in an inconspicuous way" in the basement of the Sanitarium by off-duty hospital staff.[15]

On April 6, 1944, Dr. Robert Hare of the institution wrote to Elder W. E. Nelson:

> *I cannot feel that the Sanitarium should be called upon to carry a mixed*
> *clientele. We have persons of high degree and low degree of the white race and*
> *no question exists with regard to their presence here, but were colored patients*
> *seen in our buildings there will immediately rise numerous complicating*
> *questions and certain groups of our patients . . . would be expected to take a*

degree of offense at their presence. I would just as willingly minister to the need of a colored patient as anyone else, but mentally, emotionally and in certain psychological respects, they differ from the white and I do not favor mixing them.[16]

Elder W. E. Nelson replied to Dr. Hare: "It would be absolutely disastrous for the Washington Sanitarium to carry a mixed clientele." He agreed with Dr. Hare that the membership of the Church from a wide swath of America would "strenuously" object to having Black people in the Sanitarium and that "the Psychology of these black people is so different from the white that it would be impossible for us to mix them." He went on to say that as he saw the issue, it was not that colored people wanted "a little sanitarium for their own where they can get attention" but what "they want is racial and social equality."

He talked about training "Negro girls as nurses." Regarding education, there was more freedom to engage Black people. Still, he warned, using his experience gained at Pacific Union College, "We must not permit a very large percentage of Negro enrollment if we are to maintain proper standing."[17]

Understand, this was the leadership of the worldwide Church putting their raciest bias in black and white (pun intended) for posterity. These were the same people who supplied the Sabbath School picture scrolls depicting a Black Satan but a White God and a White Jesus in heaven surrounded by White children and one token little Black child. These were the same people who, like me, read Revelation 7:9 all the time.

Even the pious have a problem with black skin!

Who You Calling Black?

"Go away. You Black!" The old lady in the wheelchair hurled her words at me with violent, vehement aggression. Her wrinkled face twisted into an angry, contemptuous mass, and her slitted gray eyes burned like two tiny glowing coals. In a fraction of a second, I became as defensive as if she had accused me of stealing her money or raping her granddaughter. I almost shot back at her, "Who you calling black!" But the next instant, I remembered, I was black!

Whenever I tell my friends about this incident, they never cease to have a few good belly lol.

Black Is Beautiful

"I am black, but comely." The dark-skinned woman of Song of Solomon (1:5) found it necessary to say she was beautiful (Dark am I, yet lovely. NIV) despite her skin color. For centuries, since then, Black people have found it necessary to call attention to their beauty, sometimes to reassure even themselves.

In the 70's, in my pre-teen years, there was a sudden explosion of the affirmation that "Black is beautiful!" I remember the statement took me by surprise because by then, my self-denigration had hardened from my mother's barrage of negative messages about blackness and the scarcity of Black faces in magazines, books and on television.

As a small boy, I had never seen a Black person at the tax office or the banks. Only very light-skinned Jamaicans, descendants of raped African slave women and White slave masters, held those positions. But now, suddenly, about my eleventh or twelfth birthday, there was this brazen assertion that Black people were beautiful.

I did not know at the time that the phrase "Black is beautiful" was a 1960s, 1970s wholehearted embracing of black culture and identity by Black people. The expression, "Black is beautiful" was a call for an appreciation of black history as a worthy legacy, as delineated on the National Museum of African American History and Culture website. "In its philosophy, 'Black is beautiful' also focused on emotional and psychological well-being. The movement affirmed natural hairstyles like the 'Afro' and the variety of skin colors, hair textures, and physical characteristics found in the African American community.'"[18]

Emotional and psychological well-being was what I lacked as a teenage boy convinced that "anything black not good." The affirmation of Black beauty could not have come at a better time for me because the boy version of me struggled to embody the idea that black was beautiful. My subconscious perception of beauty, as a budding artist, was limited to a straight nose, thin lips, and white skin. Tried as I might, I lacked the skill to draw Black features. And to make matters worse, tried as I might, I could never grow an Afro like my peers did! I was sorely disappointed.

The "Black is beautiful" movement aimed to dispel the racist notion that Black people's natural features such as skin color, facial features and hair were inherently ugly. I suspect my dear mother was never aware of the "Black is beautiful" movement until the day she died in 2007. (Remember, she tried to make my nose as straight as Mr. Crooks'). Yet, my mother was a beautiful, voluptuous woman (if I can describe my mother thus).

Eventually, I imbibed the truth of Black beauty, and today I consider myself lucky to be a Black individual. I am proud of my skin color. I do admire the beauty of White and Asian people, but I no longer disdain my blackness or African features.

Sadly, however, many Black Jamaicans (and other Black people) still have not gotten the "Black is beautiful" memo more than sixty years later! In a blog post, 18karatreggae, there is an article, "I Know Why Jamaicans Bleach Their Skin." The post claims that Jamaica has the most bleaching per capita in the world. Just under 17 percent or more than one out of ten Jamaicans use some form of skin-lightening product. "The country that says "wi likkle but wi tallawah" is proud of their accomplishments despite the island's size, but they are not too proud of their African skin tone," the post observed. "More than 90% of Jamaicans are of dark complexion," the post continued, "yet more than 90% of the contestants they send to represent the country in beauty pageants look almost white." A picture on the blog compares the Japanese and Jamaican contestants. Miss Japan was darker than Miss Jamaica! What is the reason for this? "The system teaches them to see themselves as less beautiful."[19]

It is still the reflex tendency of my Black Jamaicans and perhaps many other Black people to retort, "Who you calling black?" It is therefore necessary for the lady of Song of Solomon to remind people of every race, including people of African descent, she is black but comely.

How Black Is the Biblical Beauty?

I am black, but comely,
O ye daughters of Jerusalem,
as the tents of Kedar, as the
curtains of Solomon.

How black is the lady of Song of Solomon? As the tents of Kedar. How beautiful is she? As the curtains of Solomon.

The footnote in the New English Translation enhances our understanding of Song of Solomon 1:5. The tents of Kedar (Qedar in NET) were the rugged tents, made from the wool of black goats, of an ancient Arabian tribe of Bedouin of Northern Arabia. These tents were not beautiful to look at for they were rough, rustic, rugged, and weather-beaten. But never judge a book, (tent or woman) by its cover because, the Sister of Song of Solomon said, even though she was Black, she was as beautiful as the decorative inner tent-curtains of King Solomon.

It is a safe bet that a large part of the world's population care nothing for Arabs or anything black, except their dresses, cats and cars, but they would dote, whoo and ahhh at the beauty and luxury of the inner curtains of King Solomon's tent, especially if they believe he was a White man, as was (and probably still is) depicted in my Sabbath School picture scroll.

The Beloved of Song of Solomon was first to coin the phrase "Black is beautiful," and "do not judge me by the color of my skin but by the content of my character."

Don't Look at Me Like That!

The King James Version's rendition of Song of Solomon 1:6 is "Look not upon me, because I am black." The New International Version's rendition uses the word "stare." Generally, the "look" or "stare" Black people get is not friendly; it is not admiring or fawning attention. Sure, there are exceptions to this rule as I can attest, but usually it is the kind of look the old lady in the wheelchair gave me. It is the kind of look the "Karens" in America give Black people walking in their communities, BBQing in the park, operating a lemonade stand, watering the neighbour's flowers, swimming in the pool, entering their apartments buildings, or doing their jobs.

It is the kind of look that many police officers and White people give Black people who somehow always "fit the description" or "look suspicious," even if all they are doing is walking home from the store as law-abiding, unarmed citizens like Elijah McClain.[20]

It is the kind of look bank managers and tellers give blue and white-collar Black workers when they cash a cheque or try to withdraw money from their *own* accounts!

The dark-skinned woman in Song of Solomon was not mistaken about the nature of the look. When she said "Look not upon me, because I am black" what she meant was, "Do not look at me like *that*; with the anger and scorn and loathsome disregard distorting and contorting your hateful features. She also knew why they looked at her like that: It was because she was black!

Made for Men

The dark-skinned lady of Song of Solomon was hurt from the betrayal by her family. "My mother's children were angry with me" (1:6b). Is it not true that the other races have not regarded Black people as brothers and sisters and have treated them as less than human? In the wake of George Floyd's murder in broad daylight as if he were a wild animal, a friend sent me a WhatsApp video of a West Indian woman of Indian extraction, and by her accent, a Trinidadian, angrily berating all Black people as criminals and monkeys. The hate and contempt that gushed from this human being like hot volcanic rage alarmed me.

We hold these truths to be self-evident, that all men are created equal, that they are endowed by their Creator with certain unalienable Rights, that among these are Life, Liberty and the pursuit of Happiness.

Let me be the first to admit the quote above is not a great segue from the Caribbean East Indian's tirade against Black people, but let us move on.

The words above are the lofty pronouncement of the July 4, 1776, unanimous Declaration of the thirteen United States of America. In making such a declaration, Americans were assuming;

the powers of the earth, the separate and equal station to which the Laws of Nature and of Nature's God entitle them.[21]

But even as America's Founding Fathers framed this Declaration of Independence, they held Africans in brutal bondage!

If Americans crafted a document that gave "all men" equality, recognized the stamp of the Creator God on such men and affirmed their right to life, liberty and happiness, for the sole reason that those men were simply claiming what was natural in Nature's law and Nature's God, while they enslaved Black people, **it stands to reason that Black people are not "men" - humans, and AMERICA'S GOD DID NOT CREATE AFRICANS.**

The Dred Scott v. Sandford 1857 landmark decision of the United States Supreme Court convincingly proved that the fledgling America did not see Black people as included in the category of "all men." **The Court held that the United States Constitution was not meant to include American citizenship for people of African descent, regardless of whether they were enslaved or free.**[22] Five years earlier, Frederick Douglass had asked, "Are the great principles of political freedom and of natural justice, embodied in that Declaration of Independence, extended to us?" In 1857 the Supreme Court answered with a resounding, "**NO!**"

Deep in the collective psyche of America (and all colonial powers) lurks the lingering doubt that Black people are humans - an exalted and sublime status they unreservedly ascribe to frozen embryos.[23] During slavery, they counted their slaves among their livestock. They denied the Black population the fundamental right to vote. Even when they amended their constitution (the Fifteenth Amendment, ratified in 1870 and the Twenty-fourth Amendment, ratified in 1964) to afford Black people this right, forces among them employed every trick in the book (state constitutions and laws, poll taxes, literacy tests, the "grandfather clause," and outright intimidation) to cancel the right to vote.

From 2021 to the present, there has been a slew of voter restriction laws designed to undermine the election process and deny primarily Black and Brown people the right to vote.

The Second Amendment to the United States Constitution protects the right to keep and bear arms, but once again, that is not a right meant for Black people. Tamir Rice, twelve years old, was playing with a toy gun when he was shot and killed in cold blood by a White police officer in Cleveland, Ohio, seconds after arriving on the scene.[24]

John Crawford, a twenty-two-year-old man, was shot and killed by Beavercreek police officer Sean Williams in a Walmart store in Beavercreek, Ohio while holding an un-packaged BB/pellet air rifle from inside the store's sporting goods section.[25] Ohio is an "open carry" state in which the open carrying of firearms is legal with or without a license![26]

Philando Castile, a licensed gun owner who told the officer he was carrying, was gunned down in the presence of his girlfriend and baby daughter.[27]

Amir Locke was a legal gun owner. The Minneapolis police executing a "no-knock" search warrant, barged in on him while he was sleeping and killed him while he was still rousing from sleep. An ABC News online report said Amir was dead in less than 10 seconds after police invaded his room. Locke, although he had his gun with him, was not a suspect in the crime for which the warrant was issued and was not named in the document.[28]

In the same article, advocates lamented the dangers of legal gun ownership for Black Americans due to "racism and implicit bias." Bryan Strawser, the chair of the Minnesota Gun Owners Caucus, a non-profit gun rights advocacy group, is quoted to have said, "Black men, like all citizens, have a right to keep and bear arms. Black men, like all citizens, have the right to be secure in their persons, houses, papers and effects against unreasonable search and seizure."

Nope! Remember, Mr. Strawser, the rights and privileges of the American constitution were meant for "men." In the history of America, there has never been a consensus that Black people are "men."

Police interaction with open carry Black gun owners confirms the reluctance of America to afford constitutional rights to its Black citizens. At a protest in Dallas in 2016, police quickly arrested an armed open carry member of the Huey P. Newton Gun Club.[29] They released a photograph of another Black man in a camouflage T-shirt with a gun slung around his body, calling him a suspect. As it turned out, that Black open carry citizen had not broken any law.[30] But being Black and carrying a gun in an open-carry state made him a suspect.

In a July 8, 2016, online article, "Police Shootings Highlight Unease Among Black Gun Owners," *The New York Times* quotes Yafeuh Balogun, owner of a 12-gauge Mossberg 500 he carries over his shoulder. "Here I am telling black people: 'Hey, bear arms legally. You'll have a better opportunity to protect yourself. Maybe the law will respect you more.'" Mr. Balogun made that comment after he learnt that Philando Castile, a Black gun owner, was shot to death after declaring he possessed a legal firearm.

In September 2016, police officers in Charlotte, North Carolina, an open carry state, shot and killed 43-year-old Keith Lamont Scott, a Black man. The police said he refused repeated orders to drop a handgun.[31]

The incidents cited above raised the question of whether the Second Amendment is applied evenly across races. If all men are created equal, but the United States Constitution was not meant to include American citizens of African descent, regardless of whether they were enslaved or free, then it is obvious the Second Amendment cannot be applied evenly across races.

Am I Not a Man and a Brother?

"My mother's children were angry with me." Black people accept everyone, regardless of race, as their brothers and sisters. It cannot be said that everyone accepts people of African descent as brothers and sisters.

Being Black in France

On the day George Floyd was buried, hundreds of people in France knelt, in solidarity, for nine minutes. "In France, we say we are all equal, but we are not all treated equally. If you're a young Black or an Arab man, you're targeted and harassed by the police," a 22-year-old Black man tells Deutsche Welle (DW), a German international broadcaster and international media outlet. Dina Sanches Tavares, a Black woman, concurs. Her 16-year-old brother is "constantly stopped and controlled by the police, even when he's just coming home from the gym." She said she was terrified for his safety. "Can you imagine how scary it is to be treated like a criminal simply because of the way you look?"

Black people in France also turn up dead in police custody, as was the case of 24-year-old Adama Traoré. And as in America, they call for justice and accountability only to have the justice system rule that "officers who arrested Traoré had no involvement in his death and that he died due to underlying health conditions and heart failure."[32]

Being Black in England

In a YouTube video, (TYTSports, 2022), cops in England racially profiled and searched a young Black man simply because he was wearing a coat.[33]

Dale Semper, a Black bank manager, (Channel 4 News, 2022), was wrongfully targeted by officers and faced accusations of money laundering, terrorism and trafficking in an investigation which lasted more than two years before being dropped with no apology. He was arrested in 2017 by 15-20 officers for firearm possession. Police raided and ransacked his home. The investigation switched from firearms to money laundering when they found money in his safe. During the interrogation, they wanted to know how he could afford the things he had in his house.[34] Hello! He's a bank manager!

"Get out of the car! Get out of the car, now!" The police officer who had rushed up to Ricardo Dos Santos' Mercedes had his police-issued baton raised above his shoulder as if he was about to smash the driver window.

Olympian athletes, Dos Santos and Bianca Williams and their son were returning from a training session and had just pulled up in front of their home.

The officer with the elevated baton fumbled over something about section 1 and continued to shout, "Get out of the car!" Four other officers swarm the car and a female voice can be heard contributing to the bellowed orders.

Dos Santos got out of his car and the baton - touting officer rushed him as he backed away and asked, "What did I do?" Two other officers grab hold of him, pushed him up against a wall and handcuffed him. "What did I do! My kid's in the car," he shouted.[35]

Another video showed police officers, one a female, trying to get the panicked Williams out of the car. "Just get out of the car," the female officer said. "You gonna be detained for a search, ok, under section 1." Williams was whining and protesting, but soon the officers had her out of the car and handcuffed, as the female officers informed her that under section 1 they will search for weapons.[36]

In the Dos Santos video, the officers have him jammed up against the wall while he loudly demanded to know why he was being detained and complained about his discomfort. Dos Santos told the officers he knew they were following for no reason.

Mr. Dos Santos, for what reason? Section 1. Section 1 of the Security Service Act 1989 defines the function and duties of the Security Service (MI5) in relation to *national security and crime prevention*[37] and Section 1 of the Police and Criminal Evidence Act 1984 grants the power to constables to stop and search persons, vehicles and anything in or on them for *stolen or prohibited articles.*[38]

So, Mr. Dos Santos, even though you and your partner bring glory to England through your athletic endeavours, you are both Black and fit the description.

They stopped you under Section 1 just to see if they would be lucky enough to find **stolen or prohibited articles** or better yet, to see if you were a **threat to national security,** you know, just like they slanderously accused bank manager Dale Semper.

Two police officers, Jonathan Clapham and Sam Franks, were dismissed because they lied about smelling cannabis when they accosted Dos Santos and Williams in front of their home.[39] The "smell of cannabis" is just as effective a trigger as "calm down," "gun!" "Stop resisting!" "Why are you getting so worked up?"

I was driving to the airport to pick up a friend at 5 a.m. one day when I ran into a police roadblock. An officer approached my car. "Do you know the driver behind you?"

"No, officer," I replied, thinking about the chances of knowing the random driver behind me or the one ahead of me.

"Are you sure?"

"Yes! I am sure." A surge of frustration welled up in my breast. I was tempted to say, "Huummm! Am I sure? Let me see."

"I smell alcohol on your breath." I regarded the assertion as a low-down, dirty lie. I do not drink, smoke, use drugs or gamble. (Okay, I buy lottery tickets sometimes).

"That must be the toothpaste I used just a while ago." The edge in my voice was evident. He waved me through, and I went on my way, very annoyed.

But that is the police for you. They try to set you up with trigger words so they can search your car, shoot or slam your face down into the hard ground.

That is what the British cops tried with British world championship medallist Bianca Williams and Portugal Olympic sprinter Ricardo Dos Santos. They went one step further to report Dos Santos was driving in an "appalling" and "suspicious" manner.[40] But note that they did not say he drove through traffic lights, drove around corners at high speed, swerved across the road and endangered the lives of pedestrians. Police often lie on their report, especially if their victim is black.

Those cops ganged up on the couple for one reason and one reason alone. Dos Santos said it well: "DWB." Driving While Black.[41] How can anyone deny that since Dos Santos was stopped nine times within four weeks after buying a new car in 2018?

Being Black in Israel

Black people in Israel are also compelled to protest police brutality. Ethiopian Jews in Tel Aviv protested violently on May 3, 2015, after a video of police beating a young Ethiopian Israeli soldier in uniform. A *Time* online article, "Why the Latest Protest Against Police Brutality is Happening in Israel," reported the concerns of

Black Jews: discrimination in all sectors of society, including housing, education and the workplace.[42]

Tadello Blilin, her husband and their children had waited nine years to fulfill their lifelong dream of making Aliyah—the right of every Jew to move to Israel and become an Israeli citizen. Tadello's parents and siblings had already moved there in previous waves of Ethiopian immigration. At the last minute, Israeli authorities told her that her two older daughters, who were married, would need to take a separate flight with their husbands. Tadello didn't want to fly to Israel without all of her children, but the authorities assured her that her two daughters would be on the next flight. "The government promised us it would take a week, a month, two months tops," Tadello tells Yardena Schwartz of Daily Beast through tears. "It's been almost 13 years."[43]

In her article, Schwartz wrote that Israel is home to over 145,000 Ethiopian Jews who call themselves Beta Israel, or the House of Israel. It is believed they descended from the lost tribe of Dan, or as others say, their ancestry is tied to Emperor Menelik I, the son of King Solomon and the Queen of Sheba, who ruled Ethiopia around 950 B.C. "Yet today's Israeli government rejects the notion that many Ethiopian Jews are in fact Jewish."

Ethiopian Jews need special permission from the Israeli government to make Aliyah, unlike Jews from Europe, the U.S. and other countries. Their Judaism is questioned by religious authorities because when Jews were persecuted under Soviet rule, many abandoned their religion or became Christians. Nevertheless, White Jews of the former Soviet Union were not prevented from becoming citizens, and nearly 1 million immigrated to Israel in the '90s. "If we were white, we wouldn't have this problem," says Sefi, Tadello's 23-year-old daughter. "No one has the right to say I'm less Jewish because of the color of my skin."

Rabbi Menachem Waldman, a leading scholar of Ethiopian Jewry, notes the Jewish community of Ethiopia maintains a religious lifestyle, complete with Sabbath observance, prayers three times a day, religious study, and a kosher diet. "Whoever says they're not Jews either doesn't understand, or they're lying," says Waldman. "How are they different from the Jews from Spain and Portugal who were forced to convert and then returned to Judaism?" Waldman continues. "This is the only time we have refused Jews who returned to our people. We have never had this in our history. Only for the Jews of Ethiopia."

How does one account for the difficulties Ethiopian Jews endure? Racism, say Activists. That is the only "explanation for Israel's refusal to grant Ethiopian Jews the right of return that is given to every other Jewish community. Israel's treatment of Ethiopian Jews stands in stark contrast to the welcome embrace it gives to the tens of thousands of Jews who immigrate each year from America, France, the U.K., and elsewhere."

Being Black in China

In 2020, Human Rights Watch demanded that China end the discriminatory treatment of Africans related to the Covid-19 pandemic. The complaint was that Chinese authorities in the southern city of Guangzhou, Guangdong province, where China's largest African community lived, began a campaign to forcibly test Africans for the coronavirus, and ordered them to self-isolate or to quarantine in designated hotels. Landlords then evicted African residents, forcing many to sleep on the street. Hotels, shops, and restaurants refused African customers. Other foreign groups have generally not been subjected to similar treatment.

There was no evident scientific basis for the policy. Furthermore, most imported cases of Covid-19 to the province were Chinese nationals returning from abroad. Many Africans had already tested negative for coronavirus, had no recent travel history, or had not been in contact with known Covid-19 patients.

Africans in other parts of China reported police and local officials had harassed them, and hospitals and restaurants turned them away. The article on the Human Rights website said that Africans in China have long experienced racial discrimination. Police frequently target Africans, often linked on Chinese social media with violent crimes, overstaying their visas and for immigration enforcement. Some job advertisements specifically exclude "heiren," or blacks, or set a lower salary for African applicants. Some Africans report being paid less than their White colleagues for the same job. Many also said they were turned away by taxis, restaurants, or shops. In 2018, a sketch aired during the annual Lunar New Year Gala on state TV featured a Chinese actress in black face saying things such as "China has done so much for Africa," and "I love Chinese people! I love China!" A Chinese laundry detergent brand advertisement showed a Black man being pushed into a washing machine, getting "cleaned," and emerging as a lighter-skinned Asian.[44]

Being Black Ukrainian Refugees

In the aftermath of Russia invading Ukraine, we hear the mournful tones of the Black but comely woman cataloging her betrayal by her mother's children. The United Nations High Commission for Refugees confirmed discrimination in admitting Black refugees.[45] A Congo native was refused admittance when he tried to board a train. Instead, he was told he would be given a weapon so he could fight for Ukraine. He said the Rzeszow, Poland's border guards, were aggressive toward

Black people. This hyper aggression is on full display in another YouTube Video. Guards blocked a stairway, repeatedly shouting, "Move!" at a group of people trying to ascend the steps. Someone can be heard saying, "They are pushing her; they're not letting her go. Is it right? They are not letting the Black girl go."[46]

In the same video, a Ukrainian guard points a gun at a group of African males holding their hands high as they shout, "We don't have arms! We don't have arms." The next shot is of a group of Black people standing among railway tracks and a male voice, with an apparent African accent saying, "These people left without taking the Blacks. None of the Blacks, man."

A Back young woman says, "It seems like there is a hierarchy of Ukrainians first, Indians second, Africans last."

Two African medical students, one of them a brain surgeon resident, were told by Ukrainian border guards that only one foreigner for every ten Ukrainians was allowed through.[47] They trekked to the Hungarian border, where a Channel 4 News Correspondent caught up with them. They told the Correspondent about Ukrainian's policy of separating large groups of Black people from Ukrainians.

Democracy Now! reported that non-white people who fled Ukraine were held in long-term detention centers in Poland and Estonia! African students were held in long-term detention centres outside Warsaw. An African student held in Lesznowola Guarded Centre for Foreigners told an activist that he was worried about his mental health. He said he was scared. After escaping Ukraine, he was now being held in a detention centre. "At the beginning, I thought I was kid-napped."

One African student who waited at the Ukrainian border for three days was told by police he had to go back into Ukraine to fight. He ran away after the police confiscated his bag with his laptop and his documents. After getting into Poland, he immediately reported to the police there. What did the Polish police do? Took him to a camp![48]

To be fair, the Ukrainians and Polish discriminated against other racial groups such as the Indians, and Europe, as a whole, have Syrian refugees languishing in refugee camps throughout the winter for years while they fling open their doors for White Ukrainians. However, it is doubtful whether those people who bore the brunt of discrimination alongside Black people from Africa and the Caribbean would treat the Black, beautiful woman in Song of Solomon any better if she found herself in their country. Black people are always at the bottom of the barrel.

Look At Me! I Am a Person!

The daughters of Jerusalem (people of other races) have long denied the humanity of the sun burnt damsel of Song of Solomon. Long she has lamented the betrayal of her brothers and sisters who refuse to grant her "unalienable Rights, Life, Liberty and the pursuit of Happiness," and in the case of Ukraine, sanctuary. In vain, she has been crying out, "Look at me! I am a person."

Not all the daughters of Jerusalem denied the humanity of Black people. In 1787, a group of Quakers in London formed the "Society for Effecting the Abolition of the Slave Trade." As part of the creation of the Society, several members designed a distinctive seal for its use, emblematic of its mission and belief system. They created an image of a kneeling African male, shackled at the wrists and ankles, bound by chains, bearing the caption "Am I not a man and a brother?"[49] Ironically, these well-meaning "daughters of Jerusalem" did not depict the African man standing upright, strong and proud but as helpless, servile and making a pitiable plea to his heartless, oppressive brothers and sisters for his "unalienable Rights, Life, Liberty and the pursuit of Happiness." But, as they say, it is the thought that counts.

Indeed. Am I not a man and a brother? Black people have had the need to pose the same question to people who deny their humanity and their connection to the God they claim to worship. During the Civil Rights Movement at the Memphis sanitation strike in 1968, Black American men carried signs that simply read, "I Am a Man!"[50]

One hundred and ninety-two years after the US Second Continental Congress ratified its Declaration of Independence,[51] America still did not consider Black people as "men." In 1968, Black men in Memphis were hauling trash, a taxing, filthy job, dragging heavy, leaking tubs of garbage onto trucks. When these men got home and pulled off their clothes, maggots fell out of them.[52]

These men worked long hours, even in inclement weather, for 65 cents an hour, yet the federal hourly minimum wage rate at the time was $1.65![53] They got no overtime pay and no paid sick leave. If they got injured on the job, they could get fired. If they didn't work, they didn't get paid.[54] Can someone say, slavery?

On February 1, 1968, torrential rain flooded the streets and caused the sewers to overflow. Still, the Memphis public works department required its sanitation workers — all Black men of course — to continue to work in the downpour. Two sanitation workers, Echol Cole and Robert Walker, took shelter in the back of a garbage truck because America did not consider them "men" who could shelter in buildings designated for "Whites only."

As Cole and Walker rode in the back of the truck, an electrical switch malfunctioned, and the compactor crushed the two men to death.[55] The public works department refused to compensate their families!

America still treated their dogs and horses better than Black people almost 200 years after it declared "all men are created equal."

The Memphis sanitation workers went on strike, protesting horrible working conditions, abuse, racism, and discrimination by the city and demanding a wage increase.[56]

Memphis' mayor, Henry Loeb III, refused the demands of the sanitation workers union. He refused to take malfunctioning trucks off routes, pay overtime and improve conditions. At a news conference, Loeb pronounced, like his slave master ancestors would have done, "It has been held that all employees of a municipality may not strike for any purpose. Public employees cannot strike against your employer. I suggest to these men you go back to work." On February 14, Loeb issued an ultimatum, telling the men to return to work by 7 a.m.[57]

In response to Henry Loeb's slave master declaration, the Rev. James Lawson said at a news conference:

> *When a public official orders a group of men to 'get back to work and then we'll talk' and treats them as though they are not men, that is a racist point of view. And no matter how you dress it up in terms of whether or not a union can organize, it is still racism. At the heart of racism is the idea 'A man is not a man.'*

One hundred and sixteen years after Frederick Douglass said it was plain that a Black slave was a man, Rev. Lawson still found it necessary to assert that the descendants of slaves were men. That point was still not conceded, because the progeny of the slave master Founding Fathers, Henry Loeb III, still doubted it.

In this context, in 1968, One hundred and ninety-two years after America ratified its Declaration of Independence, more than 200 Black sanitation workers marched, under the watchful eyes of bayoneted gun-toting National Guard and tanks, draped in signs that read, "I Am a Man."

Fifty-Five years later, Black Americans still need to say they are humans, using different verbiage. "Black Lives Matter!" has been the cry since 2013. It began with the use of the hashtag #BlackLivesMatter on social media after the acquittal of George Zimmerman in the shooting death (murder as far as I am concerned) of a Black teen, Trayvon Martin, in February 2012.[58]

Many Americans choke on the phrase. Try as they may, they cannot say "Black Lives Matter," but that is because they do not believe Black people are brothers and sisters. Some Americans can say, "All Lives Matter," but we know that when they say that, they have their figurative fingers crossed behind their figurative backs because, like their Founding Fathers and their Constitution, they do not genuinely believe "all lives" include "Black lives."

Donald Trump and his cohorts are well practiced in denouncing the Black Lives Matter organization. Trump told Fox and Friends it was "a Marxist group that is not looking for good things for our country."[59] On a Fox News interview, former Mayor Rudolph Giuliani called on President Trump to declare Black Lives Matter a domestic terror organization that wanted to overthrow the Government, which, as it turned out, was a case of the "pot calling the kettle black!"

Arizona Republican Representative Paul Gosar called for the hanging of General Mark Milley, the chairman of the Joint Chiefs of Staff, who he described as the "homosexual-promoting-BLM-activist."[60] Understand this one thing: In Gosar's mind, homosexuality is contemptible, detestable, loathsome and revolting and he associated the concept of "Black Lives Matters," and by extension, Black people as just as vile. Like his slave master and Jim Crow forefathers, and the 1857 United States Supreme Court, the status of "men" does not apply to Black Americans and in this case, same-sex people.

So it is. If Black people dare to advocate for their humanity in the face of racial discrimination, violence and murder, they are terrorists! The unkindest cut inflicted upon the Black beauty of Song of Solomon by her mother's children!

Keeper of Vineyards

"They made me the keeper of the vineyards; but mine own vineyard have I not kept."

Indeed, the melaninated woman of Songs of Solomon tended the vineyard of everyone, and certainly not by choice. All the daughters of Jerusalem got in on the act of domination and exploitation of this beautiful Black woman.

Over 14 centuries, the Muslim world enslaved 28 million Africans, sexually exploiting the women as concubines for their harems, and forcing the men into military service.[61] A Wikipedia submission informs us that Europeans shipped 12 million to 12.8 million Africans across the Atlantic over 400 years to work on their coffee, tobacco, cocoa, sugar, and cotton plantations, gold and silver mines, rice fields, the construction industry, cutting timber for ships, as skilled labour, and as domestic servants.

Think about it: For almost 2000 years, the sister of Song of Solomon was wickedly exploited, constantly tending the vineyards of others but never her own. She must be exhausted by now!

The Black and beautiful woman was eventually emancipated, but some daughters of Jerusalem schemed with sinister subterfuge to enslave her again. They passed vagrancy laws and exploited the "slavery" and "involuntary servitude" loophole in the 13th Amendment, which ended slavery in the United States in 1865. Using those two provisions, they incarcerated as many as 200,000 Black Americans, including children! "They were forced into back-breaking labour in coal mines, turpentine factories and lumber camps. They lived in squalid conditions, chained, starved, beaten, flogged and sexually violated. They died by the thousands from injury, disease and torture."[62]

They terrorized the ebony sister, murdering her by lynching and burning her body. They burned down her towns and flooded others with enough water to make several lakes. They redlined her by denying her mortgages to buy a home in certain neighbourhoods or getting a loan to renovate her house.[63]

They assassinated her champions like Martin Luther King. Jr., Malcolm X (and jailed innocent people for the crime.[64]) Their colonial brothers and sisters hanged Paul Bogle, George William Gordon and Samuel Sharpe of Jamaica.[65] (Consulate General of Jamaica. National Heroes. n.d.), and stole South Africa from native Africans and India from the Indians!

Then, after millennia of tending other people's vineyards, the sun burnt sister of Song of Solomon is accused of being lazy and wants to live on welfare, food stamps, and commit crimes for reparations! "They are not soft on crime," Sen. Tommy Tuberville bellowed like a fire breathing dragon. "They're pro-crime. They want crime. They want crime because they want to take over what you got. They want to control what you have. They want reparations because they think the people that do the crime are owed that."[66]

But the most outrageous insult thrown at the dark-skinned woman of Song of Solomon is that she fits the description no matter who does the crime. It matters not what is her age, physique, or gender; she always fits the description, even if a White person is said to have committed the crime!

Chapter 1

19-Year-Old Girl for A 170lbs Bald Male

The police were looking for a machete-wielding suspect, a 25 to 30-year-old man, bald, about 160 - 170 pounds, standing at 5 feet 10 inches, when they attacked and set their dog on Tatyana Hargrove, a 19-year-old girl, 5 feet 2 inches tall and weighing 115 pounds.[1] Do you think Judge Selwyn Romilly or any other Black person would have fared better? Think again.

On June 18, 2017, Hargrove was walking home when an officer approached her. She claimed he drew his gun as soon as he got out of his patrol car. The arresting officer, Christopher Moore, said in his police report that he didn't know Hargrove was a woman until after she was handcuffed. He mistook her for a machete-wielding suspect who had come out of the Grocery Outlet Bargain Market on Ming and Ashe Avenues after threatening several people. Black is beautiful, but it fits the description.

Hargrove said she had stopped to take a sip of water from one of her water bottle containers when she looked behind her and saw three cop cars. One of the officers al-

1

ready had his gun drawn, Hargrove related. "They asked me was I inside the store, and I told them no. And then they asked me if I was sure and I was like, 'Yeah!'"

At this point, she asked another officer what was going on. He told her to give him the backpack. Tatyana asked if he had a warrant. The officer pointed behind her, indicating the K9. Tatyana said she got scared and said, "Just take the backpack."

The officer suddenly grabbed her by the wrist and neck, punched her in the mouth and threw her onto the ground. That was when the dog attacked and began to bite her legs. "He put his other knee on my head, and I told him, 'I can't breathe, I can't breathe' and I started yelling out: 'Somebody help me, somebody help me, they're going to kill me.'"

After the cops tied her hands and feet and "threw" her in one of their cars, Tatyana Hargrove said she heard somebody said, "That's not the guy! That's not the guy."

The man the police were looking for was described in multiple police reports from June 18 as a 25- to 30-year-old man, bald, about 170 pounds, standing at 5 feet 10 inches. He was wearing a white t-shirt, dark jeans and a pink or red backpack that contained the machete. When Moore found Hargrove behind the Grocery Outlet Bargain Market, the 115-pound teen, who stands 5 feet 2 inches, was wearing a baggy white shirt, blue jean shorts and a black hat. She was straddling a bicycle, a red and black backpack slung over her shoulder. In it were three cold water bottles.

The police report said that Hargrove did not cooperate and appeared as if she was going to ride away. After Officer G. Vasquez arrived, Moore told Hargrove she matched the description of a man who had just threatened people with a machete, and he ordered her again to get off her bike and put her hands up. Hargrove's response, according to Moore was "This isn't happening. I'm leaving."

Moore retrieved his K9, Hamer, and while Vasquez was handcuffing Hargrove, she spun her left shoulder into him and knocked him off balance. He fell to the ground, his legs tangled in the bicycle. Hargrove fell backward on top of him, then spun around into "a mounting position" astride the officer. Vasquez punched her in the mouth, pushed her off, but she got back on top of him.

Because Hargrove was within arm's reach of her backpack, which Moore suspected contained a machete, he released his dog. Hargrove fought the dog, grabbing his muzzle. "She thrashed back and forth, screamed obscenities and kicked at the officers as they subdued her."

According to his report, Officer Moore did not ask the young woman for her name until she was beaten, bitten, restrained and locked in his car. Did the

2

Vancouver police officers ask Judge Selwyn Romilly for his name before they cuffed him like a common criminal?

Hargrove called her parents from the hospital. Tatyana's mother described her as a responsible young lady, but what does that matter when Black always fits the description?

Chapter 2

Bald or Deadlocks - It Doesn't Matter

Retired Judge Romilly of
Vancouver was an 81-year-old bald man. Clarence Evans
of Harris County, Texas, wore dreadlocks. But both of them were
Black men, so they both fit the description.

A police officer tried to arrest a Black father, Clarence Evans, in front of
his own home after incorrectly identifying him as a suspected criminal from
another state. Apparently, this police officer was driving by and saw this Black
family hanging out on their driveway. The whole thing was caught on camera and
published on UGET Tube.[1]

When the video began, the police officer had the Black man against a car,
which I assume was the family car. Clarence is protesting that the officer doesn't
even know his name, but he was telling him he had an open warrant. All this
time, the cop was trying to hustle him towards the cop car and calling
him Quintin from Louisiana.

Mr. Evans and a female, off-camera, were protesting strongly
(Mr. Evans loudly at times and with some choice swear
words thrown in) for a good five minutes that
Clarence is not Quintin and

does not live in Louisiana.

That did not persuade the officer one bit, because the most important thing about Clarence Evens was his black skin and, in this case, as we will later see, his dreadlocks.

Did I tell you that Clarence Evans was chilling in front of his home with his family when this cop happened to drive by his house? The cop stopped, asserted that the dog in Mr. Evans' yard was not his, and began to harass the Black man, trying to arrest him as Quintin, who had an open warrant in Louisiana. So now, it doesn't matter what you look like (male or female, a child or an adult, young or old, fat or slim, bald head or dreadlocks), and it also doesn't matter where you are and how long you've been there, if you are Black, you fit the description.

The officer insisted that Evans go to his car, where he had a photo on his phone that would prove Evans was a fugitive from the law. However, Mr. Evans, knowing full well the low odds of coming home alive after being falsely arrested, loudly and stubbornly declared that he was not getting into that cop car because he was not going to be the "next ni**** you kill. F*ck that sh*t."

As I watched the video, it became apparent that Mr. Evans had decided that it would be preferable to die on his doorsteps than to get in that police cruiser.

Eventually, another officer appeared on the scene and got the arresting cop's cell phone with the photo ID of "Quintin" from his car. "Here is the deal, doesn't that look like you?

"No! No! That don't look like me!" Evans bellowed with supreme confidence.

"That's not him!" the female voice off-camera chimed in.

"What the f*uck is wrong with you man?" Mr. Evans stared back at the cop holding the phone in his right hand.

"Calm down!" the cop ordered.

"What you trying to say?" challenged Mr. Evans, "'cause I got dreads and I am black, that's me?"

"No," the cop replied.

"That's not him," called the female voice behind the camera.

"She can see that's not me from over there." My Evans pointed towards the camera. He looked again at the picture and said, "No way!"

The would-be arresting officer said he wanted to see Mr. Evans' ID.

(At this point, a written narration appeared on the screen: "Evans said the picture was of a black man with locs in his fifties.")

There is a lot of shouting from Evans and the woman operating the camera. The two officers were still trying to convince Evans the picture of the wanted man was him. They make as if to take a firm hold of Evans, who declared, "It's gonna take a lot more than two of y'all." The officers continued to arm-wrestle Evans. At the same time, the now panic-stricken female voice cried out repeadedly, "Please! Stop! That's not him!"

The first officer pried Evan's wallet from his hand and looked at his ID. From this point on, the officer seemed satisfied that Clarence Evans was not "open warrant" Quintin from Louisiana. With that, Evans got really angry and loud. He told the two officers to get the f*uck out of his yard, and "You just said I am somebody named Quintin because he got dreads and he Black. What the f*ck is that sh*t?"

Ahhh! Mr. Clarence Evans. I thought you knew the rules by now. If you are Black, you fit the description. That is the point, the end all and be all.

Chapter 3

A Minor on His Way to McDonald's

Peel police officers and members of the Toronto Police Emergency Task Force were looking to apprehend 21-year-old Kwami Garwood who was wanted on suspicion of kidnapping in Peel Region and in connection with an unrelated murder in Toronto. Who do you think they took down? A 17-year-old teen on his way to McDonald's.[1]

Police boxed in the teen's car, smashed the window with a hammer, fired a stun grenade into the car, dragged the teen from the vehicle, and cuffed him. Video of the incident captured by a bystander shows the boy being held to the ground by heavily armoured officers. A bystander who shot the video said she was concerned that the teen couldn't breathe and said she saw him patting his chest when he was pressed against the car. "That's how George Floyd died," she said in a video on toronto.ctvnews.ca. She said she would have been "traumatized for life" if she had been the subject of the arrest she witnessed.

Dave Bosveld, the teen's godfather, said the minor suffered lacerations to his face and a leg injury. Even after police realized their error, they charged his godson with breaching a court condition not to drive because he was caught driving without a license when he was younger. "The fact that they persisted in laying charges after they got the wrong guy for something entirely unrelated just goes to show what we're dealing with out here."

It doesn't matter how you appear, as long as you are Black, you fit the description? Judge Selwyn Romilly was about 81 when he was mistaken for a 40 to 50-year-old man! Tatyana Hargrove was a girl, 19, 5ft 2in, 115 lbs. but mistaken for a 170 lbs. bald, 5ft 10in male suspect! A 17-year-old teen on his way to McDonald's was mistaken for a 21-year-old guy, whose picture I am assuming the police must have had since he was so well known as a lawbreaker.

In June of 2022, statistics released by the force's Equity, Inclusion and Human Rights Unit alongside outside data experts and a 12-member community panel, revealed that in 2020, Black, Indigenous and Middle Eastern people were all overrepresented in the number of "enforcement actions" taken against them relative to their total population in Toronto. For Black residents, it was by a factor of 2.2 times. That meant that Black people made up about 10 percent of the city's population that year but faced 22.6 percent of police enforcement, which included arrests, provincial offences tickets, cautions and diversions.

Black, Latino, East/Southeast Asian and Middle Eastern people were overrepresented by factors of 1.6 times, 1.5 times, 1.2 times and 1.2 times, respectively, when it came to use of force. Police also tended to use more force against racialized groups more often compared to White people, especially when it came to officers drawing their firearms. Black people were greatly over-represented in Toronto enforcement population use of force and strip searches.

Interim Toronto Police Chief James Ramer apologized for the report. "As an organization, we have not done enough to ensure that every person in our city receives fair and unbiased policing," he said. Ramer went on to say the release of the data would cause pain for many and admitted that the data from 2020 disclosed that there was a systemic discrimination in policing and that there was a disproportionate impact experienced by racialized people, particularly those of Black communities."[2]

It is just as Dave Bosveld said: "It just goes to show what we're dealing with out here."

Black is beautiful but who cares? You fit the description.

Chapter 4

Black Fit the Description When the Criminal is White

The ethnicity and skin color of the criminal matters not to the police. If you are Black, you (always) fit the description. Let me tell you about Shane Lee Brown, a 25-year-old Black man who was arrested in January 2020 and jailed for six days by two Nevada police agencies that misidentified him as a White ex-felon almost twice his age.[1]

Shane Neal Brown is the guy the police wanted. He was a 51-year-old White man with a bushy white beard and taller than Shane Lee Brown. The White Neal Brown was arrested two days after they falsely threw the Black Lee Brown in prison.[2]

How could law enforcement in the 21st Century make such a blunder? We can all agree with E. Brent Bryson, Brown's attorney, that police and corrections officers could have easily seen the difference between a Black man and a wanted White Felon if they had a comparison of physical descriptions, fingerprints, photos, dates of birth, or criminal ID numbers following his client's arrest. Ah! And did I mention that Lee Brown kept telling Henderson and Las

Vegas police repeatedly that he was not the White "Shane Brown" named in the felony warrant?

"It felt like every word I said was falling on deaf ears. No one gave me the time of day, or even listened to what I was trying to explain to them," Lee Brown told CNN. His protests went ignored for days. "Most of the time I didn't even get a response," he said, adding that at the time, he didn't know the other Shane Brown was White.

Ah, Lee Brown, what good would any of the above common sense verification processes have done when your skin color is black? It's just as your lawyer said. The police were indifferent to you. Do you know why? The color of your skin.

The police justified their incompetence and their locking up Lee Brown because his driver license was suspended, and he had traffic warrants. You know what. Life is hard.

Once, Peel police pulled me over for driving with an expired license. My car could not pass the Drive Clean Test which was a must to renew my license. I could not pay for the necessary mechanical repairs that would make my car burn cleaner because a year before that, a divorce scrubbed my entire life of all I had worked for. I had a twenty-thousand-dollar debt from the marriage to take care of, child support that took half of my pay cheque, unpaid bills, and hunger in my belly most days.

If I could not drive my car, I could not work. If I did not work, my financial situation would worsen: My overdue bills would grow into a bigger mountain, child support would go unpaid and result in threatening calls from Accountability Office and aggressive, demeaning phone calls and messages from my Ex.

When my car could not pass the drive clean test and the license could not be renewed, I had to decide what I would do. And so, I drove my car for a whole month beyond my birthday. Eventually, I got pulled over and given a $180 ticket. I could just barely put enough gas in the tank to drive to work let alone pay that punitive ticket.

I went to court and begged the judge who gave me a suspended sentence. Luckily for me, by the date of my court appearance, my mechanic had given me an old Ford Tempo which passed the emissions test.

Like I said, life is tough. I do not know why Lee Brown was driving with a suspended driver license, but I am going to guess it was not because he was a Maverick. However, the police did not lock him up for that crime, but for the more serious crimes of Neal Brown.[3]

Lee Brown's Experience Is Not a One Off

Do you suppose the 25-year-old Shane Lee Brown's experience was a one-off? Not by the hairs of your chinny-chin-chin. An article on blAck Americaweb. com, raw bodycam of West Chester Police footage and a YouTube video of news coverage tell a typical tale that a regular Black person can encounter on a typical day of the week.

"How are you doing?" Officer Mintkenbaugh said, walking toward Eric Lindsay. "Take your hands out of your pocket for me. How you doing?"[4]

Eric Lindsay of Liberty Township, Ohio, had walked into a Meijer grocery store to pick up a few items, (am guessing a few items because he did not have a shopping cart). He pulled his hands from his pockets, "I'm doing well until I got stopped," he responded a little on edge. "What's up?"

Officers Mintkenbaugh, and his understudy, Csendes, were responding to a call from a grocery store worker who called the police and reported that a White man in his 30s, wearing a dark green/gray jacket with a red hoodie, was stealing inside the store. A police dispatcher also described a Caucasian male, maybe late 30s, wearing a dark green slash, gray type colored Carhartt coat, a red hoodie and possibly had a cutting device.

A few minutes after Mintkenbaugh and Csendes entered the store, they spotted Lindsay. "Is this him right here walking up to us?" Csendes wondered. "Yeah, looks like a Carhartt... never mind it's not Carhartt."

"It doesn't look anything like him," Mintkenbaugh said. However, the two officers approached Lindsay, the only Black person in the store, according to attorney Fanon Rucker. Csendes later alleged that Lindsay looked at him and mirrored him, according to a WCPO 9 coverage of the incident. Zack Linly, reporting on the incident for blAckamerica.com wrote in his article: "In my Black experience, police look for any excuse to find a Black person suspicious. If a Black person looks at cops, then attempts to walk away once eye contact is made, that's reason enough for said cops to suspect said Black person has done something."[5]

While the two officers started their approach to the Black shopper, who was two times the age of the White suspect, a police dispatcher on the body camera video told them the real suspect was at a different part of the store (WCPO 9 coverage). But they persisted in their approach to Lindsay because, although beautiful, he was a Black man, and black fits the description, even if the suspect is White and is in another part of the store.

Mintkenbaugh and Csendes got to where Lindsay was standing. "LP called and said you were concealing some items inside your jacket," Mintkenbaugh informed Lindsay.

"Eh!" Lindsay echoed in complete shock. He stood dumbstruck for a moment, sighed and turned towards shelves burdened with grocery items. He turned back to Mintkenbaugh . "Who do I sue, aah? Who do I sue when you don't find shit?" Lindsay spoke forcefully and took what looked like an earbud from his left ear. He pointed to someone (possibly the store manager) out of the camera shot. "Hey, come get this on film," he called, looked again at Mintkenbaugh and demanded, "Who do I sue?"

"No worries, we just trying to figure it out," Mintkenbaugh said calmly.

"We got a call from somebody who say he got a brown jacket on," Officer Csendes butted in. (It sounds like he said brown jacked, but the WCPO 9 report said Csendes said tan. Tan is a pale tone of brown. Later on, Lindsay said his jacket was not tan).

"I walk in here five minutes after you guys walked in. I saw you walked in, so how could they see me stealing?"

"Sir, I don't....I have no idea," replied one of the officers.

"Get this on film, please!" Lindsay again pointed animatedly at the person out of camera range.

"That's why we are here trying to figure it out," cooed one of the officers.

"So, what do you want? What do you want me to do?" Lindsay said loudly and angrily.

Mintkenbaugh began, "If you have things to. . .."

"What did they say? A Black man did it?" Lindsay cut off the officer.

"No."

"Well, what did they say? Because I walked in here after you guys," Lindsay pointed aggressively toward the cops.

"Listen! Listen!" Csendes said.

Lindsay tugged at his jacket "This isn't tan! What am I listening to?" He looked towards Csendes. "What am I listening to?" Lindsay kept tugging at his jacket. "This isn't tan!" he said, getting louder with each 'this isn't tan'. He was now talking over Csendes, who tried in vain to get in a few words. "This is orange &%@*&$!" Lindsay yelled, looking directly at Csendes.

Csendes said, "Okay, okay."

"It's not okay! Lindsay yelled and looked back at Mintkenbaugh.

"Sir. . .," Mintkenbaugh began.

"It's not okay!" Lindsay ejaculated once more. "This is orange as &%@*&$!."

Mintkenbaugh asked Lindsay, "Do you have items in your jacket?"

"Hell yeah, I got items in my jacket."

"Okay,"

"Items that I walked in here with behind you guys," Linday continued and pointed accusingly at Mintkenbaugh.

"Okay," Mintkenbaugh responded, "but that's not we being told."

"I don't care about $$%%^#@@** told!" Linday bellowed, taking a step back. "Alright man, I'm getting this on film." He pulled his phone from his pocket moments after what sounded like a police dispatch communication. Mintkenbaugh is seen responding to the dispatch and turned away from Lindsay.

"Exactly!" Lindsay echoed triumphantly. "Exactly, get it straight man!"

"Okay. . .," said Mintkenbaugh.

"It's not okay!" Lindsay said loudly.

"We'll come back and talk to you," Mintkenbaugh said.

"No! You won't! I'm getting the fuck (indistinct) what I need to get."

At this stage of the encounter, a Black man who appeared to be the store manager can be seen on Csendes's camera. "Okay sir (indistinct) okay."

"It's not okay!" Lindsay insisted. "They got the wrong mother f%^$%er. Admit it! Admit it!" Lindsay yelled over the appeasing tone of Mintkenbaugh. "Admit it! I'm listening!"

"My name is officer Mintkenbaugh."

I'm listening!" Lindsay interrupted.

Mintkenbaugh reached for his business card, "I'll give you my business card." Csendes and the store manager were walking away from Mintkenbaugh and Lindsay at this point. Mintkenbaugh handed his card to Lindsay who grabbed it from his hand in apparent revulsion and disgust.

"Okay?"

Lindsay swore again. Mintkenbaugh said it was fine if Lindsay wanted to call and complain. "No problem at all."

"It's a problem! It's a problem!"

"I understand, sir."

"No, you don't! You don't understand a thing till you get the skank that I got!" (Uncertain about the last few words in this line).

A different officer arrested a White man who matched the suspect's description while Mintkenbaugh and Csendes were unlawfully harassing Lindsay.

Later, according to the WCPO 9 report, Lindsay said he was sorry for his anger and loud cursing at the officers. But as Lindsay said, since college and throughout his life, police officers in different communities have stopped and questioned him for no good reason. "You reach a boiling point, and I guess that was mine," Lindsay said.

Why do Black men like Eric Lindsay get stopped by the police all their lives for no reason? Black fits the description even if the suspect or criminal is White.

White never fits the description. The WCPO 9 YouTube video says West Chester police charged the suspect, Tyler Brewer with theft. Court records showed that he failed to report for a hearing. A judge issued a bench warrant for Brewer's arrest "nine months ago."[1] According to court records, Brewer has not been arrested on that warrant! Why? Because only Black people fit the description.

---

1   Eric Lindsay's Black fits the description incident took place on January 29, 2021 and the WCPO 9 YouTube video and article on *www.wcpo.com* by Craig Cheatham are dated February 24, 2022.

Chapter 5

I Am Responding to Somebody Who Has a Firearm Who Matches Your Description!

"Step out!"

"I work here."

The body cam faced the sun, which appeared low in the sky and gave the appearance of late afternoon or early evening with the darkened lawn, shrubs, trees and walls in the background.

"You work here?"

"I was keeping the door closed." A figure with his hands up and face blurred by @imposter edits (I assume) appeared in the video.

"Okay, pu..., turn around," the police officer ordered.

"I work here," insisted the figure, who appeared to be a young Black man in his twenties. He turned to his left with his back almost to the officer.

"That's fine. Step this way," the cop instructed. The Black male stepped back and turned slightly towards the cop and began to speak again, but the cop shouted over him impatiently and angrily. "Hey! Listen to me! Listen! Okay!"

"I got my hands up," the young man interjected.

"I'm responding to somebody with a firearm who matches your description.

15

You understand that?"[1]

On August 29, 2020, Officer Kerzaya went to the Hawthorn Suites hotel near Loop 101 and Southern Avenue on a call reporting a man with a gun, Black Enterprise.com reported.[2] The hotel manager told Kerzaya the suspect was a White man wearing a black T-shirt and tan pants.

Rebel HQ YouTube video from which the opening dialogue was taken, showed the body cam of officer Kerzaya in the hotel lobby earnestly and impatiently asking, "Is he a White male, a Black male? Come on!"

A voice responded: "White male. Uhhh. . .. He's going to be wearing a, uhh, black shirt and tan pants."

A man in a red shirt appeared on camera, pointed and told the cop where he thought the White male in the black shirt and tan pants would exit.

A voice I assume to be the officer's said, "Ten-four. He's probably going to be poking out on the west exit. The officer began to walk briskly to an exit. "He's walking out now," he said and hurried towards the double glass doors.

On his way to the west side of the hotel, officer Kerzaya had his gun drawn. He hurried past two White people, a male and a female.

Kerzaya went to the west side of the building, where he encountered a Black employee wearing a light gray shirt and black pants. Kerzaya held this innocent Black man dressed in a light gray shirt and black pants at gunpoint and declared impatiently that he "matched the description."

Jeff Wiggins, who narrated the Rebel HQ YouTube video, made a profound observation. He observed that the Officer passed two White people on his way to the west exit but did not engage them. Playing Devil's advocate, you could say the Black man could have changed his shirt, but so could the White male the cop passed on his way to the west side of the building. Jeff said he did not want the cop to point his gun at an innocent bystander, but he wanted to know why the cop chose one innocent bystander over the other. Was it because of the door?

Okay Jeff, I know you are being sarcastic, but we know what it's all about and it's not the door. Black, not White, fits the description. Do you still think any other Black person, young or old, male or female, bald head or dread, retired Black Judge or seventeen-year-old Black girl would have been treated any better than this Black hotel employee?

Yes, the suspect could have changed his clothes, but what about his skin color? True, White people have a history of blackening their faces but even office Kerzaya would have known, logically, such a transformation could not have happened so quickly and thoroughly. But in the officer's mind, Black always fits the description even when he knows the suspect is White!

Chapter 6

You Fit the Description. You Fit the Description. You Fit the Description.

T he car door clicked open as the officer's body cam showed him getting out of his cruiser. "Hey, buddy!" The officer's lips and a part of his nose appeared in the top left-hand corner of the frame. The car door gently closed.

"You are not in any trouble or anything." The officer walked around the front of his cruiser toward the curb. He addressed a Black man in a white tank top with a bold "HEEiST" on his chest and what appeared to be a pair of black jogging shorts. "There is a burglary that happened. **You kind of fit the description.**"[1]

I bolded "you kind of fit the description" not because the officer's attitude was aggressive. In fact, the officer was very nice about telling this random Black man that he fit the description. Those words are in bold font for a reason that will soon make itself evident.

The Black man who was obviously out for his evening run looked like someone who was into fitness; he was well built, his chest and shoulders prominent in his white tank top. Suddenly,

17

a White police officer had stopped him dead in his tracks with the usual "you fit the description."

"Really," a percipient smile (or a "I know what this means") adorned his face.

"Let me just make sure you are not him, okay, alright, ahaam. . . ."

"I'm a vet. I have my ID," the "you fit the description" random Black jogger said calmly.

"Okay, can I see your ID?"

The Black man produced his ID. "You look literal. . . They said white tank top, black shorts," the officer gesticulated towards the Black man. He took the man's ID. "And they said you had a beard, all right? So, I'm not saying it's you . . ., (the Black man nodded, stepped back and said "alright,") I'm not saying it's you," the officer emphasized, "It's a Black male, again not saying it's you, buddy."

"Alright," replied the Black man once more and looked down at his phone and appeared to activate an app with his fingers. A grey car with an adolescent vehicular boom rushed by, followed by a muted white van.

"Does the male have tattoos on him?" The officer inquired of someone on his communication device. Traffic sped by on the opposite side of the road, and the young Black male mopped his face with the top end of his jogging tank top. "And white beard, correct? (It sounded like he said white beard, but I must be mistaken). A faint voice responded and seemed to confirm that a beard was a part of the description.

"We got a male over here (muffled) right now on 2034 (muffled) North Normady **fitting the description.** I'm verifying him right now to make sure it's not him." Vehicles continued to speed by as the officer described the Vet he stopped because he fit the description. The indistinct responses came back over the radio.

"He was jogging," the officer spoke into his radio, "look like he was going for a run, just verifying muffled."

If a burglary took place while you are out jogging and you are Black, you will fit the description although you have your ID and you are a Veteran.

After some back and forth on his radio, the officer informed the random Black man that his superior instructed him to detain him. "Bear with me, okay, **'cause you fit the description.** I'm not saying you're guilty. My Sergeant told me to detain you."

And thus, it came to pass that this innocent Black man was placed in handcuffs although he was not under arrest, but he **"fit the description. Okay?"**

By this time, two other police officers had arrived on the scene. And then a third. **"Literally, you fit the description,"** the officer said for the fifth time.

The officer chitchatted courteously with the Black man who fit the description and promised to cut him loose if he was not the suspect. He even apologized for the inconvenience and expressed appreciation for his cooperation.

"I'm not trying to get shot over this," laughed the Black man nervously. The officer said things did not escalate because he cooperated. "You did exactly what we told you to do." He asked if the Black man honestly thought the police wanted to be killing people.

"If I was White, I wouldn't have fit the description." Exactly. All Black people fit the description even if they do not fit the age, gender, skin color or wearing the clothing of the suspect, as we shall also see in this case.

"If the guy was White, white tank top, black shorts, yes, he would," the officer assured the detained jogger.

Eventually, the officer announced the good news; he said the witness said the jogger's clothes did not fit the description. The officer assured the now-freed Black Vet that "this is not a race thing" and that "there were serious consequences for (police) racial discrimination." Yeah! Right! However, the officer immediately went on to say, "... **you literally match the description.**" Did you catch that? The witness said the jogger's clothes did NOT fit the description, however the police officer said in the next breath, "you LITERALLY match the description." If his clothes did not match but he LITERALLY fit the description, which part of the random Black jogger literally fit if not his ebony skin?

Another officer approached the Black Vet and admitted it was clearly not him but his "**clothes and description really match.**" (Oh my God!). He also said the picture from the video surveillance showed it was not him. Yet he still fit the description, - LITERALLY!

Do you doubt any random Black man walking or jogging or standing on 2034 (muffled) North Normady would not match the description? The YouTube video Imbalanced Status posted began with a handcuffed Black man surrounded by police officers. He had on a T-shirt, not a tank top jogging shirt. He was bald from the middle of his head down to his forehead and wore what looked to be grey shorts. But the random sweaty Black man who was out for a run, who was a Vet with identification, wearing white tank top and black shorts and a full head of hair and had no stolen items on him, LITERALLY fit the description.

Do you think a retired 81-year-old Black man would have fared any better? Well, if you think so let me tell you about another random Black man who fit the description and was shackled like a slave.

He Just Had Lunch

19

In California, on January 21, 2021, police officers walked up to Jamaal Williams' car, opened his door, asserted he "matched the description of someone who committed a burglary in the area," and ordered him to step out of the car. In the meantime, another officer was at the other door getting ready to charge in. "You are being detained for a burglary investigation." Look, the first Black person they ran into fit the description.

The officers dragged Williams out of his car, handcuffed him and shackled his legs just like their forefathers did Williams' ancestors.

The description of the real burglary suspect was a "Black male, about 20 years old, 6' 1" to 6' 2", wearing a blue hat, wearing all black, and possibly wearing a red shirt underneath." Williams was 40 years old at the time "he fit the description." He was wearing a maroon sweater, dark grey T-shirt underneath, and dark blue pants.[2]

Understand this, any Black person standing, walking, or sitting in their car on that corner would have fit the description regardless of clothing, gender or age.

Panhandler

Police in Valdosta Lowndes County, Georgia, received a call about a Panhandler. An officer got to the scene and accusingly accosted Antonio Smith, the first Black person he saw walking down the street. He told Smith he was there about suspicious activity. The officer would have approached any random Black person in this manner.

Smith told the officer he was waiting for someone and produced his ID upon request. But guess what? Another officer crept up on Smith from behind, grabbed him in a full-body hug with Smith's hands pinned to his sides and commanded him to place his hands behind his back! In the next instant, he slammed the defenceless and innocent Black man into the hard ground!

Now, other officers rushed into the milieu and helped to handcuff Smith, one of whose wrists was now broken. Smith said something and an officer responded, they had a warrant for his arrest. They had not bothered to ascertain whether Smith was the Panhandler because he was a Black man and Black people always fit the description.

Smith's lawyer said, "We want to be able to walk down the street, jog in the neighbourhood, fall asleep in a car without having the police kill us or injure us."[3] Ahh! But my dear lawyer, if all Black people LITERALLY fit the description, how can that be?

Chapter 7

Are You Doing Anything Wrong?

In September 2019, Aasylei Loggervale of Nevada drove her two daughters to California for college. She stopped at a Starbucks in Castro Valley, California, to rest when Alameda County sheriff's deputies approached her car.

A KTVU Fox 2 San Francisco YouTube video showed the entire encounter.[1]

"Hi," a deputy called out after knocking on the car window. He sounded friendly.

"Hi," replied Loggervale after she turned on the engine and rolled down her window.

"How are you?" The deputy still sounded friendly.

"Fine."

"What you guys doing here?"

Whoops! Not a friendly question. Any Black American would immediately know they were in a Black-fits-the-description situation.

Loggervale explained

21

that they were going into Starbucks in a few seconds and asked if there was a problem.

The deputy told the mother of two why he had approached her. Every morning there were auto break-ins at "this time."

"Thank you very much," Loggervale replied politely. Now, if I were the one sitting in Loggervale's seat, I would have said, "What! Those darn thieves! Officer, I am so glad you are here because I would hate to find my car broken into or stolen when I come out of Starbucks with my coffee."

But I may not have had time to interject because even before Loggervale had finished saying thank you very much, the deputy had rushed on with his reason for approaching the trio. "So, I've been driving around here, okay, and I notice that you guys aren't doing anything but hanging out."

Relax

Loggervale could barely get in, "Yeah, we just got here. I've been driving all night," before the deputy continued to charge into his racist and criminal insinuation. "Relax, that's my reason why I am talking to you."

Now, any time a police officer tells a Black citizen to relax or stop resisting when they, like Loggervale are calm, or like many unfortunate detained Black people who were not resisting, you know they have already decided you are going down!

In 2015, an Alabama police officer slammed a docile grandfather of 57 into the ground.[2] Sureshbhai Patel from India was visiting his family and went for a morning walk. He was returning home when somebody called 911 and reported that "'a skinny black guy' he had never seen before was walking around the neighborhood." White Americans do that all the time. They look out their window and see a Black person, male, female, old, young - as in a nine-year-old girl - and call the police.

That is how John Crawford lost his life. Ronald Ritchie reported that a man was "walking around with a gun in the store . . . . like, pointing it at people." He said Crawford loaded the gun, waved it back and forth and pointed it at two children. The truth was, Crawford mindlessly picked up an unloaded BB/pellet air rifle while he chatted with the mother of his children on the phone. Ritchie later admitted that "At no point did he (Crawford) shoulder the rifle and point it at somebody."[3] **My guess is that Ronald Ritchie knew that in America, the Second Amendment was not meant for Black citizens and gambled police would kill John Crawford.**

Okay, back to the unfortunate Sureshbhai Patel. When the police cruiser pulled up behind the Indian man, he was walking, unaware that he was being followed.

Both police officers apprehended the man. They handcuffed him, after which one or both officers said several times, "Do not jerk away from me." Then one of them said, "Relax." And the next instant he slammed the man face down into the ground as if he (the officer) were a UWW champion.

That word "relax" is a harbinger of police brutality! And now, Aasylei Loggervale was told to relax, although she was speaking in a normal tone. Can you guess what will happen to her and her kids next?

ID, Please

Loggervale emphasized that she drove all night and, beginning to sense that she was under suspicion, mentioned that her car was a rental and stated where she was from. It was at this moment the deputy asked if she had ID. A few seconds after she started rummaging around for her ID, it occurred to her that the officer had no credible reason to want to see her ID. From here on, the interaction got sparky.

"Okay, so wait a minute, why are you asking me for my ID. You just explained to me about the break ins. . .."

"Right," the cop replied.

"So why do you want to see my ID? What's that about?"

What's that about, Aasylei? You are Black, and although beautiful, you fit the description.

"What did I do? What kind of crimes did I commit?" Aasylei continued to ask the deputy.

"What kind of crime did you commit?"

"Yeah! You asked me for my ID."

"Yeah. You have to give me your ID."

"Why do I have to give you my ID?"

"Why?" The deputy sounded tentative.

"I don't have to give you my ID because I haven't done anything. You started talk about a break-in. . .."

"Okay."

"I thank you for informing me." Lady, did you really think he was looking out for *your* safety when he told you about the break-ins!

"Right."

"I'm going to. . . I'm resting because I'm about to go into Starbucks, right."

"Hummm." It was a kind of "Hummm" that said the deputy knew that nothing this woman said would make a difference. The mother reiterated that she told him she had been driving all night.

"But Starbucks has been open for about two hours."

What! In America, if a store is open for two hours, it's a crime not to have gone in an hour and 45 minutes earlier! Darn!

Aasylei said something about her GPS in response to Starbucks been open for two hours.

At this juncture, the deputy asked Aasylei, "Are you doing anything wrong?"

"No, I'm not!"

I would have said, "Am I, officer?" Now, I could have been tased, arrested for resisting arrest or shot in the face for such an impertinent question, but I would have injected a little surprise and alarm in my tone.

"Are you doing anything wrong?" was a stupid question asked by a dumb cop because before the deputy engaged this Black woman and while he was harassing her, she was sitting in her car. Just sitting.

"So, what's the big deal?"

Aasylei Loggervale doggedly insisted that she was not handing over her ID because she had done nothing wrong. At this point, it sounded like she started her engine. The cop said she was behaving in a manner that led him to believe she might be doing something wrong. Aasylei again strongly refuted the charge. "Don't try to chump up no charges." Cops are experts at that. Aasylei told her daughter to start recording.

"Why are you getting so worked up?" Another question that betrays the police's intention was to harm her and her family. The next question that betrayed the fact that the cops meant to make life difficult for the family was, "Why are you making this a big deal?" Understand that police officers lay down markers - *stop resisting, he's reaching for my gun, relax, why are you getting so worked up, there is a strong smell of marijuana coming from your car*, etc - when they unlawfully engage you to rationalize and sanitize their criminal behaviour.

The deputy then asked Aasylei if she had a driver's license. She replied she did, and she could not rent a car without one. The cop retorted that he did not know if she had rented the car. Do you see where this is going?

Aasylei told the cop to call his supervisor. He said he did not have to do that. Aasylei told him she would make a report at the Sheriff's department and asked for her tormentor's name and information. He said he would give her a card when they were done.

Aasylei's daughters began to reason with the cop, but that was futile. Their fate was sealed long before the trio had opened their mouths - **way back when the Officers saw that they were Black people.**

By now, you may have guessed I am rushing through this encounter, but I am attempting to hit the high notes, one of which was Aasylei's declaration she was calling the police! What girl! You gonna call more of the same upon yourself and daughters! You are either brave or deluded! But she did. She told someone on the line that she was being harassed by a police officer and did not even know if he was the police.

How Do You Think This is Going to End?

At this point, one of Aasylei's daughters seemed to have gotten out of the car to go to the restroom, but she was threatened with handcuffs if she did not return to the car. Things started to really heat up. The second daughter was out of the car, and Mother and daughters loudly protested about being victimized.

Over the animated protest, the officer was heard speaking into his radio. "We've got two (muffled) out of the car running around and filming us."

By this time, the person who the mother was speaking to had hung up on her. Lady, did you think you could report the police to the police?

About six minutes after the deputy knocked on the lady's car window, he gave the order to "detain these two" (the daughters who were still outside the car, looking to use the restroom and persistently asking what they had done wrong). Mom protested loudly and tried to get out of the car, but the officer pushed her door shut. In a few seconds, however, he opened the door and aggressively ordered the protesting mother out of the car while he pulled her out. Now the women were being assailed by both cops.

The mother refused to get out of the car, but the cop insisted. She was handcuffed after she got out while the other cop tried to do the same to the daughters, who appeared to be still filming (at least one of them). More police officers came and assisted with the detention of the trio.

All the time, the mother was shouting about how the cops would get into trouble, she would sue them, they would be fired, and she wanted an attorney. (The family was awarded 8.25 million dollars).[4]

Okay, this video is tiresome to narrate. It is 20 minutes long, and at minute eleven, the cop can be seen searching the mother's bag. All this time, the daughters were loudly protesting and giving the other cops a warm time as any proud Black person should do to crooked cops. Whoops! I shouldn't have said that. They could tase or shoot you to death for standing tall and proud.

The leading cop agitator asked the mother where in her car her ID was, and several other cops searched their car and bags in the trunk without the consent of the detained female family. The video went on without audio because the cop turned it off. I do not know what the law in California says about that, but you can understand if I find that suspicious, if not criminal.

Black always fits the description regardless of any other factors. Here was a Black family sitting in their car outside a Starbucks. They can be seen by anyone in the parking lot and possibly by people sitting in the coffee store and looking out. When the deputies rolled up on them, they were still sitting in their car. The mother had her seat reclined when the cop knocked on the car window. They were NOT, I repeat, they were NOT scoping out cars to break into. But they **FIT THE DESCRIPTION.**

They Never Committed a Crime

A CBS News online article by Brooks said, "The Loggervales were never accused or charged with a crime. ... Their attorneys also said the incident was inappropriate because a police report later indicated that **the car thief suspects were men.**" The bold emphasis is supplied because the truth is, Black people, whether male or female, young or old, teenager or nine-year-old-girl catching bugs on her street, standing on your driveway or having an evening run, baldhead or dreadlocks, a veteran of the armed forces or an ordinary civilian, never fail to fit the description.

Another KTVU Fox 2 video itemized the injustice done to Aasylei and her daughters.

1. Unlawful search (You know they were looking for something to lock up these ladies who should thank their lucky stars those cops didn't plant evidence)
2. False arrest
3. Invasion of privacy
4. Violation of constitutional rights.

Add racial profiling to that, because, as the ladies insisted, **they were stopped and searched because of the color of their skin.** How could anyone deny that when the deputies knew the criminals were men?

Here is another thought. If the cops reasonably thought the ladies sitting placidly in their car were the suspects, why wouldn't they hang back and wait to catch them in the act? Wouldn't law enforcement want solid evidence? But no. When they deal with a Black person, they know he or she fits the description, and therefore they can never be punished for unlawful searches, false arrests, invasion of privacy and violation of their constitutional rights. Who wants to be the next innocent Black person to run into those cops?

Do you remember the Alabama cop who slammed the 57-year-old face down into the ground? His name was Eric Parker. He partially paralyzed the Indian man and faced charges[5] for federal civil rights violations but was acquitted by a federal judge in 2016 following two hung juries.[6] **This cop returned to work. And the cops who harassed three Black ladies who they thought fit the description of male suspects were promoted.**

Who else taking a walk or sitting in their car wants to run into those cops?

You fit the description if you are Black (or Brown or look like "a skinny black guy" walking around the neighborhood), or a teen-age boy, or an old, retired judge taking a leisurely walk in a Canadian city. Recall that Constable Tania Visintin insisted 81-year-old Romilly fit the description of a dark-skinned man, about 40 to 50 years old. And three Black ladies also fit the description of male suspects!

Chapter 8

I Don't Know Who I Am Looking for Yet

Vice News reported on a May 2019 incident when Los Angeles police officers arrested a Black man outside his Hollywood home because he was "probably" a domestic violence suspect![1]

A Good Morning America YouTube video replayed the cops' body cam's audio.

"Is this the dude?"

"Probably," his partner answered.[2]

Antone Austin, a music producer known professionally as Tone Stackz, was putting out his garbage when the officers approached him and ordered him to turn around. In the body camera footage that showed the confrontation between the Los Angeles police officers and Antone Austin, Austin is shouting in alarm, saying he was not the guy they were looking for.

"Okay man, I don't know who I am looking for yet," one of the officers said as they tried to cuff Austin. The officers had no physical description of the suspect, but a random Black person would do just fine.

Austin's attorney

confirmed with the *Los Angeles Times* the police had no description of the suspect. "They literally saw the first Black man, and they arrested him." He could have added, "because Black fits the description even when there was none."

Austin's neighbour had called 911 about her ex-boyfriend who was White. Sounds familiar? According to a NBC News report, the suspect escaped during Austin's arrest! The innocent Black man could not escape the injustice even after the caller of the initial complaint could be seen in the officers' bodycam video desperately trying to tell them Austin was not the perpetrator. The NBC report, referencing the lawsuit Austin brought against the police, said "they continued to unlawfully seize Mr. Austin, placing him in a choke hold and tackling him to the ground and twisting his arms in positions causing extreme pain."

Austin's girlfriend, Michelle Michlewicz, rushed out to intervene, and was disrobed and pushed to the ground. They were taken to jail and held before they posted bail after midnight. Austin was charged with felony resisting arrest and assault on a police officer; his bail was set at $7,000. Michlewicz was charged with felony lynching, a California law against "the taking by means of a riot of another person from the lawful custody of a peace officer." "Peace" officer! Right! That charge carries a maximum of four years in prison. Her bail was set at $50,000!

Austin had to fight in court to have police body camera video made public to prove allegations he was racially profiled before his arrest, according to an online report on the *Los Angeles Sentinel's* site. Eventually, a settlement of two million dollars was tentatively reached with the city of Los Angeles, and a federal judge ordered the suit dismissed after learning of the pending settlement.

All the charges against the two were dropped. However, in court filings, the Los Angeles City Attorney's Office argued that the "couple's claim was without merit and should be dismissed and that Austin and his girlfriend were to blame for the incident." Attorneys for the city also maintained that the two LAPD officers were "immune from liability."

An interviewer asked Austin what his reaction was when he saw the video and heard what the officers said before they got out of their car.

"In your mind, you wanna say to yourself, this happened to me because I'm Black. And then you don't want to be that petty. You don't want to be that small. You don't really want to believe that. You don't want to think on that low of a scale. And then when you watch the footage, and you hear the guy in the car . . ..

"You know, like the girl in the 911 call sent them to a restaurant that was three blocks away from my house.

"It's crazy that they can just convict you, and they are supposed to be there as mediators. They are supposed to serve and protect, find out what's going on. But they, in their minds, are judge and jury, and they can convict you on the spot based on what you look like."

Isn't it interesting that this noble Black man did not want to feel petty for acknowledging he was falsely arrested and brutalized simply because of his skin color, but the corrupt cops and the Los Angeles City Attorney's Office felt no such diminution? Black people, you can't deny it. If you are Black, you fit the description, including times when there is no description, the suspect is White and is three blocks away from your house.

Chapter 9

You Stole Your Own Car!

"I'm not saying I don't like police. I'm not saying that. I'm saying I'm just scared of them. Nothing wrong with that.

"Sometimes we want to call them too. Somebody broke into my house once. This is a good time to call, but I don't. . . hummmm, hummmm, (laughter). House is too nice. It ain't a real nice house, but they wouldn't believe I live there anyway. 'He's still here!'" Chappelle smashed his mike into the mike stand. (Raucous laughter and applause).

"Open and shut case, Johnson. I saw this once before when I was a rookie. Apparently, this Nigga broke in and hang up pictures of his family everywhere." (Prolonged laughter).[1]

Dave is a Comedian, so I thought he was just clowning around. But in June 2018, Samuel Scott Jr. called Miami Police Department to report that his 2006 black Jeep was stolen from outside his aunt's house in Buena Vista. However, half an hour later, Scott was handcuffed by five Miami PD officers.[2]

Police arrived on the scene to find Scott waiting for them, but instead

31

of taking his statement about the stolen vehicle, police arrested Scott for stealing his own car! According to the police report, says Newsone.com, officers said Scott fit the description – Black male, bald, about 6' 2" and heavyset, with a white tank top.

And I thought Dave Chappelle was only being a comedian.

The officer's bodycam showed Scott pleading with the officers, trying in vain to persuade them that he was the one who called the police. An officer was heard telling Scott, "The description of the guy who took off in your car is just like yours."

Okay, how many times do I need to say it? Black is beautiful, but it fits the description even when someone steals your car or, like Chappelle noted, you are the victim of a burglary.

Scott was arrested and charged with leaving the scene of an accident, false reporting of a crime, failure to carry a concealed-weapon license, and possession of marijuana. He was searched unlawfully, wrongfully imprisoned, and racially profiled.

The *Miami New Times* reported that MPD officer Jonathan Guzman spotted the Jeep Compass being driven by a suspect who crashed the vehicle when Guzman attempted to stop it. The driver, who fled on foot, was described as a "Black male, bald, about 6' 2" and heavy set, with a white tank top." Scott was wearing a black shirt over a white undershirt — not a white tank top and was four inches shorter than the suspect's description. (We can excuse the four inches disparity). However, the arrest report states that the person reporting the stolen vehicle matched the description of the offender that fled the hit-and-run scene.

"Yeah, that's him," an officer says on the body-worn camera footage. "He's sweating, he has a black shirt on top of the tank top shirt."

If you are Black and someone steals your car, you fit the description, no matter what.

The charges against Scott were later dropped.

You Can Steal Your Own Car in Canada, Too

In November of 2022, Brice Dossa wanted some McDonald's fries, but when he tried to return to his vehicle, Montreal police officers rushed him and handcuffed him in a jiffy for stealing, guess what? His own car!!!

CBC.ca reported it was only after Dossa was in handcuffs that police scanned and identified the vehicle was his. And then they couldn't get him out of the handcuffs because they didn't have the key![3]

Police said Dossa's Honda CRV SUV had "typical and obvious attempted theft marks on one of the locks (damage)" CTV News, Montreal reported.[4]

GlobalNews.ca quoted Alain Babineau, the racial profiling and public safety director at anti-racial profiling group Red Coalition and a 27-year veteran of the RCMP, as saying he "worries the officers handcuffed the man because they perceived him as potentially violent. One element of racial profiling is the notion that Black males are 'perceived as being intrinsically violent and so that's why the question of racial profiling has to be raised."

Babineau said, "There's something within the culture of policing that says, 'we're never wrong,' and that is what is wrong with our culture and that has to change." Remember, Constable Tania Visintin insisted 81-year-old Romilly fit the description of a dark-skinned man about 40 to 50 years old. Antone Austin and his girlfriend were charged and imprisoned although they had broken no laws and the lady who called the police desperately tried to tell them Austin was not the perpetrator. The Los Angeles City Attorney's Office tried to keep the body camera footage of the initial incident hidden, arguing it would "interfere with the officers' expectation of privacy and cause risk to both the cops and their families." Indeed, the police are never wrong!

The police affirmed Babineau assertion when the union representing Montreal police officers said the comments by politicians risk fueling "police disengagement." Ahh! You see, in the psyche of the police, it is not their racial profiling of Black, beautiful people that causes "police disengagement." The Fraternite des policiers et policieres de Montreal continued its sulking in a post on Twitter: "In a society governed by the rule of law, elected officials should refrain from sharing their impressions on the character of a police operation until all the facts are known." Ahh! But are police officers governed by the rule of law and don't we already know the facts: Brice Dossa did not steal his car. The police were wrong about him and Black fits the description.

Fo Niemi, executive director of the Montreal-based civil rights organization Center for Research-Action on Race Relations, said he hopes the man will file a complaint with the police ethics commissioner so an investigation can be conducted into what happened before the interactions captured on film.

"This incident once again shows that Black drivers in Montreal cannot feel safe and be free to drive their own car without being subject to some kind of police control and profiling," Fo Niemi said. "This is what all the people who have turned to us for help told us: it's the violation of that sense of freedom and security that makes them lose trust in the police."

Black people, you're all beautiful, but you all fit the description.

Chapter 10

Banking While Black

In April 2021, police dragged Linda Stephens, a 70-year-old retired teacher, from the MidFlorida Credit Union, arrested her, fractured her nose during the arrest and locked her in a hot police car in 90-degree heat for 15 to 20 minutes. In all this time, none of the MidFlorida employees said anything in Stephens' defence or tried to explain the situation to the police officers.

Whoops! It was the MidFlorida Credit Union who called the police on this lady who was their client for just shy of 50 years!

The bank called the police on 70-year-old Linda Stephens because she was "irate and . . . yelling and arguing with employees," and "disturbing the other members and employees working in the branch." "Stephens continued to yell and scream while arguing with the teller manager. The police report said the "disturbance was so loud that the branch manager heard it from her office where the door was closed. But even when the branch manager tried to assist Stephens, she continued to scream and yell until the branch manager warned that the police would be called if she did not calm down."

After a police officer arrived, he witnessed Stephens' continued aggression toward the credit union employees, although the bank assured Stephens that her money was being digitally processed. She yelled that law enforcement was there to shoot and tase her.

After a second officer was dispatched to the credit union, the employees warned Stephens she may be charged with trespassing, but she refused to leave, even though they made multiple requests. At this point, the 70-year-old woman raised her voice and began screaming about a gun. "She ... immediately raised her voice (became louder) and began to repeatedly scream 'gun, gun, gun ...' over and over."

Tell me you know by now you cannot trust a police report for accuracy and truth? Do you see the trigger words, "gun, gun, gun"?

Well, let's ask Linda Stephens, a Black senior, to tell her side of the story.

Who is Linda Stephens?

Linda Stephens[1] is a retired educator who taught school for many years, 12 of which she was an assistant principal. She supervised the health curriculum for Polk County middle and high school. She's active in her church. She is the immediate past president of Polk County retired educators. She is a Community Activist and cares about people.

The Deposit

Linda Stephens deposited $600 (four one-hundred-dollar bills and ten twenty-dollar bills) for her mortgage at a MidFlorida Credit Union ATM. The money, however, was not credited to her account. She returned the following morning and told her story to a cashier who asked her for a receipt which she showed him. He told her he could do nothing to help her and that she needed to speak to his supervisor.

Stephens again shared her story with the supervisor and showed him the deposit receipt. The supervisor pointed to a technician who happened to be working on the machine because something had gone wrong with it. He told Stephens she needed to fill out a dispute form, but she said she was not disputing with herself that she deposited the money in the machine. The supervisor said that was the policy.

The Theft of Linda Stephens' Deposit (My Categorization)

She returned to MidFlorida at 9 o'clock and once again told someone what had happened. The lady photocopied her receipt and filled out a dispute form which

Stephens signed. The lady assured Stephens that everything would be in order within *two to three hours* in her account. But by the end of the day, her money was not deposited.

Stevens returned to the bank the following day and spoke to the teller she had seen the day before. Once again, the supervisor came to talk to Mrs. Stephens, who asked where her money was and mentioned that the day before, he had said the Technician was fixing the bank machine and promised she would have her money. Mrs. Stephens said the supervisor turned his back on her and walked away.

The head teller came and offered to help her in her office. She asked what was happening, and Stephens told her story all over again and showed her receipt. The head teller said, "Ma'am. You know how bureaucracy is." "No, I don't. I only want my money," the frustrated Linda Stephens replied.

The Po-Po

The head Teller called the Technician again to verify he had found the money. He affirmed he had; four one-hundred-dollar bills and ten twenties. Yet when the head teller got off the phone, she told Stephens she had to give them two or three days to get her money.

At this point, the manager and another lady and a police officer came over to the office where she was. The manager told her to leave and that they would get her money straightened out. Stephens insisted she wanted her money because she needed to pay her bill, and she wanted cash because she didn't put a cheque in the machine.

The manager threatened that if Stephens didn't calm down, they would "have to call the po-po." (I assume "po-po" is Stephens' choice of word).

After this, another police officer came into the office with his hand on his gun and said he thought he heard Stephens said she had a gun, and she was going to shoot somebody.

Did you notice the colossal trigger words so far? "Calm down," and now "gun." By now, I know you know when the police or the system tells a Black person to calm down or say the word gun, they intend to harm that Black person.

In telling her story, Linda Stephens emphasized that at this stage of the unfolding event, neither the first police officer, manager, head teller or the other lady who came with the manager said anything in her defence. Stephens said she thought her life was in danger.

In response to the second police officer, she said that she didn't have a gun, never owned one or knew how to shoot one. "What in the world are you talking about? Are you crazy?" Stephens asked the second cop, who appeared to be trigger-finger ready.

The Arrest

The second cop told Stephens if she said the word "gun" one more time, he would arrest her.

Stop here for a moment. We have already seen in the Introduction that America was founded on the assumption Black people were not "men" or were protected by the Constitution even if they were free. We also saw a few examples of how the second amendment was not meant for Black Americans. But now, this cop had up the ante. A Black American could not even say the word "gun," **even if she was only declaring she does not possess or knows how to use one.**

Well, what did Mrs. Linda Stephens do? She turned to him and said, "gun." And for that crime, the cop ordered her to stand up, snatched her purse, handcuffed her, placed her in a squad car standing in the hot, broiling sun for fifteen to twenty minutes.

The Abuses

Stephens heard the first officer tell the second she was never in trouble. "She's clean," Stephens quoted the officer. By now, we all know the arresting officer who made saying "gun" a crime was looking for something to justify his act of injustice. But wait! The police need no justification to lock up innocent Black people. And so, he carted off the innocent lady to jail, where they terrorized her - smashed her face against the seat, dragged her handcuffed along the floor, pinched her, treated her like a lunatic, left her completely naked, locked her in an unsanitary cell with very little bedding to sleep on and offered her no phone calls.

In telling her ordeal, Linda Stephens kept emphasizing that all the indignities heaped upon her were only because she asked MidFlorida to return her money. **You see, if your skin color is black and they steal your money, you still fit the description.**

MidFloridia Credit - We Were Wrong

A MidFlorida representative contacted Linda and confessed their people were wrong. How did they know that? They looked at the video feed. She conceded that if they had done what they told her they would do the day before (deposit her money in her account), Linda would not have needed to return to their branch. She then told Linda they, including the President of MidFlorida wanted to know "how she felt and how she was feeling."

"If you want to know how I feel," Linda told the representative, "think about the fact that if it was your Mama. Tell the President to think about the fact if it was his Mama or somebody that they knew and loved or something like that, that had come in just to ask for their money."

You see, Linda Stephens, those people do not think of you as a Mama, a grandmama or even a human, even after you had banked with them for nearly fifty years! They and their ancestors have always doubted that the Black and beautiful woman of Song of Solomon is human, worthy of the "unalienable Rights" of "Life, Liberty and the pursuit of Happiness," as a natural and self-evident phenomena of "the Laws of Nature and of Nature's God" dictate. That is why they stole your money and jailed you for good measure.

The Good Doctor

Upon completing her residency, Dr. Malika Mitchell-Stewart took her $16, 780.16 bonus cheque ("check" in American English) to a JPMorgan Chase branch in Sugar Land, Texas. However, two employees decided her cheque was not authentic and accused her of fraud.

Dr. Mitchell-Stewart's lawsuit against the bank said the employee who first assisted her challenged the "validity of the check (okay, let's use the American word), and her employment as a physician." The employee said she had to get the branch manager to verify the check, but she returned with another associate banker who told the newly minted Dr. Mitchell-Stewart her check was fraudulent.

Dr. Mitchell-Stewart was reminded she was a "Black woman attempting to deposit $16,000 in a predominantly white affluent suburb."

Black always fits the description even if you bust your chums to become a medical doctor, unlike those lazy, sorry Black people, according to Marjorie Taylor Greene.[2] The doctor's attorney said what his client endured is part of a bigger pattern of discrimination Black people face while banking.[3]

Canadian Black Banking Experience

Keshna Spalding is a TD Bank customer who works in painting and construction. He is often paid with cheques (Canadian spelling). He described his banking experience in Ottawa's East-end as an "uphill battle," "frustrating," "degrading," and "sleepless nights." The tellers always ask "pointed questions" and put a hold on his cheques no matter the amount. Spalding said his banking experience brings back "ugly memories" and describes it as racism.

Spalding is not alone in this Canadian "Black fits the description" banking experience. Charline Grant, Business Owner of Woodbridge, Ontario, said whenever she must go to the bank, she feels tension and have knots in her stomach.[4]

About half of Toronto Black business owners say accessing financing was a massive concern, according to a 2020 online article, "Banking barriers: How the Canadian financial sector excludes Black entrepreneurs, stifling innovation," by Falice Chin on cbc.ca/radio. Chin enumerated the "Banking While Black" experiences of Black Canadians.[5]

Black business owner, Tanya Reddick, who runs a burrito stand at the Halifax Forum Farmers' Market, conducts business on the phone as much as possible to avoid interacting with bank employees in person because she gets better customer service when the representative on the other end thinks she's White. "When you sound that way, [then] you show up at the bank, literally the smile comes off a person's face, and you get dealt with in a different way," Reddick said.

Ben Kisimolo runs a music and apparel startup in Calgary. He showed up in person after booking a business loan application appointment with a major financial institution, but when the banking associate saw him, she said, "Oh, are you Ben?" Kisimolo said she was happy when they talked on the phone, but when she saw him, "Her vibe completely changed. I knew already I wasn't going to get anything. And for sure, I was right." Kisimolo was born in Congo but raised in Montreal. People in Western Canada often misidentify his accent as French Canadian over the phone. "Many people think the business is owned by a white person," he said. "They're like, 'Oh, you're a Black person who's 26? You cannot be doing something like this.'"

Black business owners in Nova Scotia said one solution they have had to employ is "white fixers." They hire White lawyers or have other White representatives within their company conduct business on behalf of or represent Black entrepreneurs.

In the same article, Caroline Shenaz Hossein, associate professor of Business and Society at York University in Toronto, is quoted to have said, "poor customer service and cultural insensitivity are common barriers facing Black entrepreneurs who turn to commercial banks for financing. It's kind of an interrogation of questions that really does make them feel badly or feel that the kinds of business they are doing are not worthy of financing."

When Prime Minister Justin Trudeau announced Ottawa would partner with eight major financial institutions to introduce a $221-million loan program aimed at helping Black entrepreneurs, Hossein broached the all-important question: How are the banks going to be reformed by working with the government to provide more money for Black business owners? Hossein understands that the program will not address the "existing culture within banks that perpetuates financial exclusion" upon Black-owned businesses, whose owners are Black and will always fit the description even when they are law-abiding, tax-paying, ambitious people who are helping to strengthen the Canadian economic fortune and future.

Jailed for Returning His Own Money to His Account

In 2014, Frantz St. Fleur tried to deposit a $9,000 cheque at the Scotiabank location at Scarborough Town Centre, but bank staff called the police, who came and arrested him.

St. Fleur had banked with Scotiabank for almost 10 years (not anywhere close to Linda Stephens' almost 50 years with MidFlorida, but all the same) and had "all (his) accounts with them." Those accounts included a chequing, savings, a U.S. dollar account, a line of credit, Visa card and tax-free savings.

He had withdrawn from his (get this) Scotiabank tax-free savings account money he used as a deposit paid to Re/Max towards a condo. The deal fell through, so Re/Max returned St. Fleur's funds, and he returned it (or tried to return it) to his Scotiabank tax-free savings account. But what happened? A Banking while black experience!

St. Fleur said the only reason the bank called the police on him was because he was Black. "I'm black, and in the bank with a $9,000 cheque." It is difficult not to agree with St. Fleur because Re/Max said it was first contacted by Toronto police (not by the bank) about St. Fleur's attempt to cash the cheque. Phone records show the bank had NEVER called the real estate company. "We were first made aware of this issue by the Toronto police on the day of the incident. When we learned about the issue, we responded to the inquiry in a timely manner to clarify any concerns that were brought forward. We have always taken the position that the cheque was valid," said a statement given by Re/Max.[6]

Why would the bank bother contacting Re/Max to ascertain the validity of St. Fleur's cheque when he was a Black man who always fits the description and is not supposed to possess so much money at any one time?

Jailed for Depositing Check Issued by Bank

The word "Check" above should alert you that this next "Banking While Black" happened in the good old U.S. of A.

In June 2010, Chase mailed Ikenna Njoku a bank-issued cashier's check and then had him jailed for an entire weekend after he tried to cash the check. The next day, Friday, Chase realized it had made a big mistake and had someone call the Auburn Police detective handling the case. However, the detective was off that day and the agent never bothered to call anyone else at the police station. The detective didn't get the message until Monday morning.

Did you guess Ikenna Njoku was Black? Sure, you did!

Okay, let's back up a little. Njoku received a $8,463.21 tax-refund check which was deposited in his closed Chase account by the government. Chase deducted past overdraft fees and sent the victim the difference and then had him arrested for a felony charge of trying to cash a forged check!

While Njoku was in jail, his car was towed and impounded, and he was fired from his job. When he finally got out, Chase still wouldn't give him his check immediately, which he needed to cover things like the impound and tow fees that his car had racked up. Njoku's car was eventually auctioned off. A year later, Njoku got no answer or compensation from Chase until he finally lawyered up and talked to the press.[7]

The bank issued this statement: "This is a very unfortunate and unusual situation. We apologize to Mr. Njoku and deeply regret what happened to him. We are working quickly to understand all the details so we can reach a fair resolution."

Yeah! Yeah! Yeah!

If you are Black, they can give you a check, say it's fake, lock you up, embarrass you in public, dehumanize you, say you are crazy, refuse to alert your family that they unlawfully imprisoned you and ignore you like forever.

Chapter 11

It Doesn't Matter Who You Are

"There's a little Black woman walking, spraying stuff on the sidewalks and trees on Elizabeth and Florence," Lawshe told the police dispatcher. "I don't know what the hell she's doing. Scares me, though," Lawshe added.[1]

Gordon Lawshe is a White man and a former Caldwell Borough Council member. The "little Black woman" was Nine-year-old Bobbi Wilson who was collecting spotted lanternflies — an extremely invasive species that is harmful to over 70 different plant species. Bobbi was doing her bit to comply with the state's "Stomp it Out!"[2] campaign, which urges New Jersey residents to help eradicate the spotted lanternfly infestation. She learned about the pest at school and made her own version of an insect repellent she had seen on TikTok. She was going from tree to tree, spraying the bugs, plucking them from the trees and dropping them into a plastic bottle.

It Doesn't Matter If It's a Child

If you are a Black child, you still fit the description. An Associated Press investigation found that children as young as six have been treated harshly and, in some cases, brutally by police officers. They've been handcuffed, tased, taken down and pinned to the ground by officers often far bigger than they were.[3] More than half of the children handled forcibly by police were Black even though they make up just 15% of the child population.[4] A 2014 study published by the American Psychological Association found that Black boys as young as 10 may not be viewed with the same "childhood innocence" as their White peers and are more likely to be perceived as guilty and face police violence. Other studies have found a similar bias against Black girls.

"Hi, can you unlock this please?" A Sacramento police officer said respectfully at the door of an African American family. He and other officers were there to do a probation check on a verified gang member. One of the officers off-camera swore like a sailor, evidenced by the bleep that camouflaged the obscenity.

"Can you open this screen door, the Police Department," the officer framed in the bodycam said calmly. The dark-stained door stood ajar, displaying a framed picture or mirror (it's difficult to tell which) that reflected a dull yellow glow. "Can you open this?"

"Hey! Sacramento Police Department. Come to the door!" bellowed another officer, possibly the foul-mouth sailor, but I am only guessing. A sustained bleep sprang into auditory existence. "Come to the door!" the off-camera cop shouted again.

A child's voice echoed from the heart of the house. "Can you open this?" the officer at the door continued in his calm mannerism, but a shouted "Come to the door!" whooshed over his shoulder from the off-camera bellower. "Come to the door right now!" he blared once again.

"Listen, we're going to kick the door down, and we don't want to do that." This voice sounded different than that of the calm officer and the clamorous cop.

"Come to the door right now! Open the door!"

A blur appeared in the slit of the ajar door. "I'm a baby," a child's voice said.

"Open the door! Open the door!" one cop ordered.

"You're not a baby if you're not listening," said a cop who had never seen or heard of a "terrible two." The screen door swung open.

"Open the door! Come outside!"

"Come outside right now!" said the voice that asserted she was not a baby because she wasn't listening.

A blurred-out image of a girl in a red dress with broad black horizontal bands appeared in the doorway, her hands up. Two rough, adult cop hands grabbed and pulled her out of the house.

"Who is here? Who is here?" one cop demanded as he twisted the girl's arms behind her back and handcuffed her. It sounded like another cop said, "You're going to jail."

The child started to cry and said something inaudible. "No, you don't get to go and hide and turn off the lights," said a cop as the cuffs clicked around her wrists. "That's not how that works." The little girl cried loudly. "OK, but you're going to be in handcuffs," the cop said as he hustled the girl down the walkway.

"Mummy! Mummy!" At least it sounded like she was calling for her mummy through her wailing, and a desperate plea for her mother would be a natural desire for a Black child being terrorized by White cops.

"Why are you running and hiding?" the cop asked the wailing little girl.

"I'm scared. I don't. . ., I don't know what to do." The child is turned around and put to sit down. "I don't know what to do."

"How old are you?"

"I'm ten."

It was at this point the cop took the cuffs off the child.[5]

Childhood Denied Black Children

"America does not extend the fundamental elements of childhood to black boys and girls," wrote Stacy Patton after Officer Darren Wilson killed unarmed Michael Brown. "Black childhood is considered innately inferior, dangerous and indistinguishable from black adulthood. Black children are not afforded the same presumption of innocence as white children, especially in life-or-death situations."[6]

Patton noted that the officer described the unarmed Black teenager as a "demon," "aggressive," and said that Brown had taunted him by saying, "You are too much of a p---y to shoot me."

Stacy Patton's contention that "America does not extend the fundamental elements of childhood to black boys and girls" and that they were regarded as "innately inferior, dangerous and indistinguishable from black adulthood" was on shameful and undeniable exhibition in February 2022 when a Sacramento police officer could not discern that the Black American he had handcuffed and belittled for hiding and turning off the light was a child. He had to ask the child how old she was, and he would not have clued in that he was traumatizing a little girl if she had not said, "I'm scared. I don't know what to do. I don't know what to do."

This police officer could not tell he had handcuffed a child even though he heard her girlish voice. He treated her like an adult, although she said in timid tones, "I'm a baby." He reprimanded her for hiding and turning off the lights while she was wailing as a little, scared child would. In the eyes of the police and White

44

citizens like Gordon Lawshe, Black children do NOT have the luxury of the "fundamental elements of childhood" and are often seen and treated as "innately inferior, dangerous ... black (adults)."

In 2014, Peel police (Ontario) handcuffed a six-year-old girl by her hands and feet because, according to the officers, she posed a threat to her classmates and to herself.[7]

On December 27, 2020, Ottawa Police surrounded five Black teens with guns drawn and took them to the ground before handcuffing them. They were released without charges.[8]

In February of 2020, a 15-year-old boy in Halifax who objected to being questioned on the sidewalk was tackled to the ground and injured by police. The boy was released later that day without charge.[9]

Community activist, Rocky Coward, commenting on the case of the law enforcement harassment of the 15-year-old boy in Halifax told a reporter, the incident was "indicative of the meagre-minded, thug, bandit-type treatment that specifically young Black people have been subjected to over the past 40 or 50 years."[10]

Where can a Black child just be a child and be safe? Police officers in Hackney, east London used their van to ram a thirteen-year-old who was riding his bicycle, knocked him to the ground, and armed police officers pointed their firearms at him and had him arrested on suspicion of possession of a firearm.

The boy was having a water gun fight with his younger sibling. One gun was blue and white, and the other pink and white. Yet a police officer on patrol reported a potential firearms incident. The Alliance for Police Accountability (APA) condemned the boy's treatment by the police and asserted that the water pistol was unmistakably a toy.[11] Can a Black child get a break anywhere?

Black children are six times more likely to be shot to death by the police than their White counterparts.[12] Twelve-year-old Tamir Rice can attest to that. He was playing with a toy gun by himself in an open park, when an adult (I am guessing, White), signed his death warrant by telling police dispatcher, "The guy keeps pulling out a gun out of his pants. It's probably fake, but you know what? It's scaring the %$#^* out of me."[13]

This accomplice to twelve-year-old Rice's murder called him a "guy" and said he was scared just like Gordon Lawshe was terrified of the "Little Black woman," whose death he no doubt hoped to engineer by calling what Indisputable Dr. Rashad Richey refers to as "calling a gun" to the situation.

The police officer who shot down the child, Tamir Rice, in cold blood, reported, "Shots fired. Male down. Black male. Maybe 20." Are you kidding me!

Do you remember 16-year-old Ralph Yarl? Andrew Lester shot him in his head and arm for ringing his doorbell. Lester claimed he thought Ralph was trying to break into his home and he was "scared to death" due to the boy's size. Ralph's aunt says he is less than 6 feet tall and probably under 170 pounds.[14] Of course, Andrew Lester has never seen a White teenager less than 6 feet tall and under 170 pounds and he would shoot a White kid who, in error, rang his doorbell instead of testing his windows or crashing into his front door.

"You're messing with my kid psychologically. That's all I'm saying," an irate father said assertively.

A police officer with his back to an onlooker's camera made an inaudible response.

"This is a perfect kid," the distraught father pointed towards his still-handcuffed child. "Why you put him in handcuffs? Why put him in handcuffs? Why a Black kid have to go through trauma like this at all times?"

The officer's reply was still inaudible, but you can guess what he said by the father's response.

"You always use that as an excuse, man!"

The officer said something while he gesticulated toward a nearby dumpster.

"It doesn't matter," interjected the peeved-off father. "Once you're Black, you match any description. Bottom line."[15]

Black 12-year-old Tashawn Bernard was also subjected to the "meagre-minded, thug, bandit-type treatment reserved for young Black people" when he took trash to the dumpster.

A White gun touting police officer (his gun unholstered and held in front of him) arrested and handcuffed him. Why? The officer thought he was the suspect "in a string of car thefts"![16] Like the little Black 10-year-old girl who was handcuffed and reprimanded like a dangerous Black adult, Tashawn Bernard was now being arrested for being an adult member of a gang of car thieves. But all he was guilty of was doing his household chores.

The Michigan Lansing Police Department's explanation of this travesty also confirmed that Black children are considered dangerous adults. They said it was an "unfortunate case of 'wrong place, wrong time.'" **Notice that nothing was said about Tashawn Bernard being a child!** Therefore, to the Michigan Lansing Police Department, the 12-year-old Bernard resembled the description of an adult suspect involved "in a string of car thefts." It was only an unfortunate case of "wrong place at the wrong time." But never forget that Black people, even children, are ALWAYS in the wrong place, whether in the park, on the job, standing by the side of the road, sitting in their car, sitting in a public space, delivering a parcel, standing in their front yard or taking a nap in their dormitory.

A statement from Police Chief Ellery Sosebee referred to the 12-year-old child as a "young man" repeatedly. "A different officer was in the area and saw the **young man** pictured in the viral video wearing a very similar outfit and made contact with him. The initial officer was able to respond and clarify the **young man** in the video was not the suspect who fled earlier. Once this information was obtained, the **young man** was released, and officers continued to search the area.[17]

Twelve-year-old Tashawn Bernard was a "young man" just as 12-year-old Tamir Rice, killed in cold blood, was "Male down. Black male. Maybe 20," and Nine-year-old Bobbi Wilson was a "little Black woman." Even the Police Chief was wrapped up into the attitude that denies the "fundamental elements of childhood to black boys and girls!"

Furthermore, "another officer saw the child in 'a very similar outfit'" to the one the escaped suspect was wearing. Remember I told you, it doesn't matter who you are - male, female, young, old, adult, or child. If you are Black, you fit the description. That was why a child putting out the garbage and wearing "a very similar outfit" looked to a White police officer like an adult involved in a string of car theft. If Aasylei Loggervale and her two daughters of Nevada (Chapter 7) were putting out the trash, they, too, would have been cuffed for being members of a ring of car thieves!

You match the description, even if you are a Black child.

It Doesn't Matter If You're a Paying Client

Jermaine Massey was a guest at the DoubleTree by Hilton Portland in Oregon, when hotel officials summoned police after seeing him talking on his phone in the lobby.[18]

Massey asked the security personnel why the police were coming. "To escort you off the property," the security personnel Massey called Earl, said.

"Because why, because am staying here?"

Earl shook his head. "Not anymore."

Massey said Earl walked over to him and asked where was he staying. Massey wanted to know if he had asked the other people walking by the same question. Earl said no. Massey asked why.

"They are not loitering."

"How am I loitering? I am in an area that is public."

"You're sitting here."

"So, this area is off limits after a certain time?"

"Only if you are a guest," Earl shot back.

"I am a guest."

"You didn't tell me that," Earl asserted.

"I said that I am a guest."

In a YouTube video Massey showed his card and said, "Here is my ticket, my ah, room. I just checked in, my American Express." Massey's camera focused on the card with a handwritten 539 above a 12/23.

"We're trying to get to the bottom of this," a second security personnel said.

"There is nothing to get to the bottom of, sir. You want to check and see if I am a guest?"

The two security persons did not check to see if Massey was a guest at the hotel because when you are Black, the assumption is you are always out of place and you fit the description.

The cop came and of course Massey, a paying guest, was escorted off the property. The police did not even do an investigation to see if Jermaine Massey was a paying guest at the DoubleTree. Why would they? Massey was Black and according to the security personnel, he was "loitering" and he was "a risk to the safety and security of hotel guests."[19]

Black customers are always asked to justify their presence in hotels and other business places. This is a common assault on the dignity and personhood of Black people who are paying customers or guests.

Albert Law, a software executive, checked into a Hilton Richmond hotel in Virginia. He was waiting in the lobby near several White people when a security guard approached him, asked if he belonged there, and demanded to see his room key and identification.[20]

Richard Willock of Madison, Mississippi, checked into a Hampton Inn in Nashville, Tennessee, with his son, in October 2018.

Willock was watching two games in the lobby on his iPad and the television when the front office manager approached him and asked if he was a guest, and demanded his name and room number.

Willock asked why he was singled out in a lobby filled with other people, some of whom "appeared to be drunken Halloween revellers." Willock gave the manager his room number, but she continued to press him and threatened to call the police. The manager left and returned with a security guard.

Arnold Kemp is dean of graduate studies at the School of the Art Institute of Chicago. He went to the Palmer House, a Hilton hotel across the street from his School to meet a staff member. Almost as soon as Kemp sat down with his friend at the bar, a plainclothes hotel security officer asked the woman if she knew Kemp. "Yes, he's my boss," the woman said.

"Well, he looks like someone we don't want here," replied the security officer.

Attorney Ben Crump who represented a Black woman (and many other Black Americans) who had to show her room key to justify her and her children's presence in a hotel pool once tweeted: "For a hotel employee to DEMAND to see proof of being a guest only from the Black person and not from White people using the pool is BLATANT DISCRIMINATION. Calling the police is harassment."[21]

The problem, Attorney Crump, is the genetic and attitudinal descendants of the Founding Fathers still do not believe the descendants of the slaves their ancestors exploited, whipped, raped and murdered are "men," created by the same God they worship.

It Doesn't Matter If You're a Police Officer

On March 11, 2021, two Kansas City Police Department officers pulled over Herb Robinson, a 30-year veteran on the force. Herb Robinson was driving an unmarked car.[22]

White officer Cole Modeer and Hispanic Marco Olivas, approached Robinson, who had stepped out of his car in full uniform. That, however, did not modulate the officer's attitude towards Robinson. Robinson claimed in a lawsuit that the two officers racially profiled him and falsely accused him of misconduct.[23] In the dashcam video, one officer said, "Your plates don't come back to anything." Then he asked, "Where are you headed bro?"

This question showed the officer's contempt for Black people because Robinson was in uniform and had identified himself as a member of the force. Gerald Gray, the attorney representing Robinson, said, "If they treat one of their own this way, I'm afraid to see how they are treating minorities who are not cops."

"Bro? I'm Detective Robinson." His response was laced with authority. Still, this assertion failed to temper the officers' attitude towards Robinson. One of the officers told him to "Chill the fuck out." Remember, whenever police officers tell a Black person to calm down, stop resisting, what's the big deal? or chill the fuck out, they are setting up a situation where they can justify hurting you. These officers were mad they could not hurt Detective Robinson because after he drove away, they ranted, "Holy shit," "Fucking dumb ass," and "Fucking retard."

The Manhattan district attorney's office, led by Alvin Bragg, indicted Donald Trump in connection with his alleged role in a hush money payment scheme and cover-up involving adult film star Stormy Daniels.

Immediately following this indictment, Bragg came under ferocious and savage attacks. Rep. Marjorie Taylor Greene (R-GA) wanted him jailed and accused him of "hiding hundreds of pages of exculpatory evidence" and "trying to incite civil unrest."[24] (Once again, the pot calling the kettle black).

Trump bashed Bragg online, calling him a "Soros-backed animal who just doesn't care about right or wrong no matter how many people are hurt,"[25] even as he warned of the potential for "death and destruction" and reposted a violent picture of him cowardly creeping up on Bragg with an elevated baseball bat,[26] another case of a pot cursing the kettle black!

On two consecutive days, Fox hosts on "Fox and Friends" intimated Alvin Bragg was nothing more than a slave because he was a "Black prosecutor who has to pay his master back,"[27] and "he is listening to his master, George Soros."[28] Of course, the Fox onslaught was what it was because they were incensed that they were not Bragg's masters.

Prominent politicians like Ron DeSantis, a wanna-be US President (God help America!), denigrated the Manhattan DA as a "Soros-backed" lackey. If you are Black, it doesn't matter that you are a top law enforcement officer or that the indicted person has alleged mile-long criminal activities, they will attack you, if not with a tangible bat, a volley of hateful words.

"They treated me like a common criminal. A white person can call and say a Black man did something and leave," Pagedale Police Chief Eddie Simmons said in frustration. [29]

On his off day, Simmons was driving to his Barbershop when he pulled up behind a green Jeep in the fast lane. Simmons said he did not want to pass in the right lane like everybody was doing, so he tooted for the jeep to pull into a slower lane. The driver (a White man) did not vacate the fast lane, so Simmons went around the guy eventually. What do you think happened next?

The unidentified driver followed him for ten miles to his barbershop, and according to witnesses, was "belligerent with Simmons." The man called 911, reported Simmons for speeding and driving recklessly and left before the police arrived.

It is a safe bet this White man did not know Simmons was the police chief of Pagedale. Still, even if he knew, it would not have modified his attitude and behaviour toward Simmons because he knew he could weaponize the police against Black people who are assumed not to be "men" by America's Founding Fathers and their early Supreme Court.

Well, Alton police arrived and questioned whether Simmons was a police officer even after showing his badge and ID! Simmons complained that he felt he was racially profiled, even with proof that he was an officer. Alton police said Simmons wanted special treatment! Consider this: Police can tase you or beat an innocent citizen half to death and claim qualified immunity.[30] But if you are a Black police chief, you ain't getting no "special" treatment.

You should know by now about the scourge of White people calling the police on Black people. Do you remember the Karen who called the police to report that an African American man was threatening her life?[31] Do you remember what led Sureshbhai Patel from India to be slammed into the hard ground with his hands handcuffed behind his back? Do you remember how John Crawford lost his life? Do you remember how nine-year-old Bobbi Wilson had the cops called on her? White people call the cops on Black people all the time. And here again, we see a Black police chief falling victim to the same betrayal.

But wait, Simmons is not the only Black police officer who can testify of that. In August 2020, Waller County Constable Herschel Smith was pulled over on a felony stop. Deputies had their guns drawn on him, placed him in handcuffs.

A White motorist called the police and accused Herschel of pulling him over and pointing his gun at him before driving off.

Smith said the White driver was given more credibility than him. Smith added that he was wearing his constable's uniform and identified himself accordingly. "They ignored my badge, they ignored my uniform, they ignored my name, said the Constable. Every deputy that works for a constable knows what this means. That means that I am the constable, the elect official, they ignored that!"[32]

Herschel Smith, do you think you fall into the category of "men" because you are a Constable in uniform with a badge?

It Doesn't Matter If You're Innocent

The Central Park Five, Antron McCray, Kevin Richardson, Raymond Santana, Korey Wise and Salaam Yusef, a group of five Black and Latino teenagers from Harlem, were convicted of raping a White woman, Trisha Meili, while she was jogging in New York City's Central Park in 1989.

The boys' accounts of the rape contained discrepancies as to "when, where and how it happened." None of the five said that he had raped the jogger, but each confessed to having been an accomplice by touching or helping to restrain Trisha Meili while one or more others had raped her. Their confessions varied as to who they identified as having participated in the rape, including naming several youths who were *never* questioned.

The police had to stop questioning Salaam after his mother arrived at the station and insisted she wanted a lawyer for her son. *He neither made a videotape nor signed the earlier written statement, but the court ruled to accept it as evidence before his trial.*

Detective Tom McKenna *falsely* told Salaam that his fingerprints had been found on the victim's clothing, and according to McKenna, Salaam subsequently confessed to being present at the scene of the rape. Years later, Salaam said, "I would hear them beating up Korey Wise in the next room", and "they would come and look at me and say: 'You realize you're next.' The fear made me feel really like I was not going to be able to make it out."

Each of the five retracted their confessions within two weeks. They said that police coerced their statements and that their rights to counsel and Miranda warnings had been violated.[33]

Despite inconsistencies in their stories, no eyewitnesses and no DNA evidence linking them to the crime, the five were convicted in two trials in 1990. McCray, Salaam and Santana were found guilty of rape, assault, robbery and riot. Richardson was found guilty of attempted murder, rape, assault and robbery. Korey was found guilty of sexual abuse, assault and riot. They spent between six and 13 years behind bars.[34]

In 2002 a convicted serial rapist and murderer already serving time, confessed to the Meili attack. *Matias Reyes was a positive DNA match to evidence found at the crime scene.* On December 19, 2002, a New York Supreme Court justice vacated the convictions of the five previously accused men. It was just as Salaam told Judge Galligan at his sentencing hearing, "sooner or later the truth will come out."

If you ignore the million times America's legal system often brutalizes Black Americans, I hope you will sit up and note that even though the five were found to be innocent, in the mind of some, they were still guilty. "If the gloves do not fit, you must acquit," but even so, to this day, O. J. Simpson is still guilty despite the highfalutin assertion that every citizen is innocent until found guilty in a court of law.

After convicted serial rapist and murderer, Matias Reyes confessed to attacking and raping Meili, and his DNA was a positive match to evidence found at the crime scene, New York City Police Commissioner Raymond Kelly commissioned a panel to review the case. The panel was "To determine whether the new evidence indicated that police supervisors or officers acted improperly or incorrectly, and to determine whether police policy or procedures needed to be changed as a result of the Central Park jogger case."[35]

The panel delivered its report in January 2003. The panel did not "dispute the legal necessity of setting aside the convictions of the five defendants based on the new DNA evidence that Mr. Reyes had raped the jogger." However, the panel:

1. Disputed acceptance of Reyes' claim that he alone had raped the jogger. It said there was "nothing but his uncorroborated word" that he acted alone. The panel believed "the word of a serial rapist killer is not something to be heavily relied upon."
2. Concluded that the five men whose convictions had been vacated had

"most likely" participated in the beating and rape of the jogger and that the "most likely scenario" was that "both the defendants and Reyes assaulted her, perhaps successively."

3. Said Reyes had most likely "either joined in the attack as it was ending or waited until the defendants had moved on to their next victims before descending upon her himself, raping her and inflicting upon her the brutal injuries that almost caused her death."

4. Asserted the "inconsistencies contained in the various statements" did not "destroy their reliability."[36]

Shortly after the terrible and brutal attack upon Trisha Meili, Donald Trump, in May of the same year, called for the return of the death penalty for murder in full-page advertisements published in all four of the city's major newspapers. Trump said he wanted the "criminals of every age [who were accused of beating and raping the jogger in Central Park twelve days earlier] to be afraid".

Trump's ad said, in part, he did not think "hate and rancor should be removed from our hearts. I want to hate these muggers and murderers. . .. I want to hate these murderers, and I always will. ... How can our great society tolerate the continued brutalization of its citizens by crazed misfits? Criminals must be told that their Civil Liberties End When an Attack On Our Safety Begins!"[37]

Trump was being honest about "always" hating the convicted boys because he demonstrated that even after the Central Five were exonerated.

In 2013, Trump criticized an award-winning documentary on the Central Park jogger case. The documentary suggested the authorities could have connected Reyes to Meili's rape at the time of the attack. What was Trump's response to that? "The Central Park Five documentary was a one-sided piece of garbage that didn't explain the horrific crimes of these young men while in the park," Trump tweeted on April 24, 2013. [38]

In successive tweets, Trump called the Central Park Five "muggers," questioned their innocence and asked, "how many people did they mugg?"

After the city awarded the five men $41 million in a settlement, Trump maintained that the men — who were young teenagers when convicted — were still guilty.

Trump insisted in an op-ed published in the *New York Daily News* that "settling doesn't mean innocence" and that the settlement of the Central Park Jogger case was "a disgrace" and "the heist of the century."

Just before the 2016 election, Trump maintained his belief that the five exonerated men charged for Meili's attack, were still guilty. "They admitted they were guilty," Trump said in a statement to CNN in October 2016. "The police doing the original investigation say they were guilty. The fact that the case was settled with so much evidence against them is outrageous. And the woman, so badly injured, will never be the same."[39]

We can do nothing but agree with Mr. Trump. Meili was so severely injured that she was never the same. She continued to manifest some after-effects of the assault, including memory loss.[40]

However, in respect of his insistence on the guilt of the men in the face of evidence that proves otherwise, once again, we have a situation of the pot calling the kettle black.

At least 26 women have accused Donald Trump of sexual misconduct.[41]

In March of 2023, a New York grand jury indicted Donald Trump (former President) over his "alleged" role in a scheme to pay $130,000 payment to an adult film actress, Stormy Daniels, (during the 2016 presidential campaign) who claimed she had an affair with Trump.[42] (Alleged placed in open and closed quotes by author).

A Jury awarded E. Jean Carroll about $5 million in compensatory and punitive damages because they found that Donald Trump sexually abused the magazine writer in the 1990s and then defamed her by branding her a liar.[43] In the same trial, Jessica Leeds, 81, of Asheville, N.C., testified that Donald Trump silently molested her on an airplane during a flight in the late 1970s. She said Trump accosted her with what seemed like "40 zillion hands." Leeds was among the other witnesses who supported the testimony of Carroll.[44]

In January of 2024, a second jury awarded E. Jean Carroll $83.3 million in damages because of Donald Trump's continual defamation and denying her rape allegations.[45]

Donald Trump fastidiously proclaims his innocence (a virtue he refuses the exonerated five) relating to the sexual misconduct charges. But we have him on tape boasting about his sexual indiscretions and adulterous inclinations, to put it mildly.

> *You know I moved on her actually. She was down on Palm Beach. I moved on her and I failed. I'll admit it. I did try and fuck her. She was married. …And I moved on her very heavily. In fact, I took her out furniture shopping. She wanted to get some furniture and I said, 'I'll show you where to get some nice furniture.*
>
> *…' I moved on her like a bitch. But I couldn't get there, and she was married. … I better use some tic tacs (here you can hear what sounds like tic tacs being shaken in their container) just in case I start kissing her. You know I'm automatically attracted to beautiful - I just start kissing them. It's like a*

magnet. Just kiss. I don't even wait. And when you are a star, they let you do it. You can do anything. Grab them by the pussy. You can do anything.[46]

Donald Trump is a loud, dissonant, vocal advocate for the death penalty, not only for innocent Black and Brown people but for whistle blowers who report on his clandestine attempt to force Ukrainian President Volodymyr Zelensky to work with Rudy Giuliani and Attorney General William Barr to investigate former Vice President Joe Biden and to discredit the Russia probe. He told the Ukrainian President that the US does "a lot for Ukraine" and asked Zelensky to do him "a favor" and investigate Biden and the origins of the Russia probe. He also ordered the withholding of a nearly $400 million military-aid package to Ukraine,[47] you know, as a means to incentivize Zelensky to do him "a favor."

Trump wanted to know, "who's the person who gave the whistleblower the information? Because that's close to a spy." He added, "You know what we used to do in the old days when we were smart? Right? The spies and treason, we used to handle it a little differently than we do now."[48]

Trump wanted the death penalty for terrorists, killers, cop killers, spies, treason, people with psychological problems, drug dealers, pushers and abusers, hate crimes, mass murders[49] and as we have already seen, exonerated Black and Hispanic people.

I wonder, does Trump still ardently believe in the death penalty? He instigated an insurrection on January 6, 2021, when his followers attacked the Capitol, beat and murdered or caused the death of police officers, built a gallows, chanted "Hang Mike Pence," revelled in anticipation of harming or killing Nancy Pelosi and other Democratic or RINO politicians, wrecked and smeared shit on the hallowed wall of the Capitol building.

Far-right Oath Keepers founder, Stewart Rhodes, was sentenced to 18 years in prison after being convicted of seditious conspiracy for his role in helping to orchestrate the pro-Trump attack on the Capitol. Does Trump still believe in the death penalty for treason?[50]

A federal indictment unsealed on Friday, June 9, 2023, charged former President Donald Trump with 37 felony counts. Trump removed to his private residence when he left the White House in January 2021 a "massive collection of highly sensitive classified material" much of which consists of intelligence about the 'defense and weapons capabilities' of the United States and foreign countries."[51] The charging document also says that on at least two occasions, Trump showed classified records to visitors without security clearances at his golf club in Bedminster, New Jersey. The sensitive documents carelessly shown to visitors without security clearances included the map of a military operation to a representative of his political committee.[52]

Trump also had his aide, Walt Nauta, move boxes with classified records to hide them from investigators and his attorney who was preparing to search Trump's property to comply with court-authorized subpoenas to recover the records.[53]

Trump was hit with 31 counts of violating the Espionage Act through "willful retention of classified records" plus six counts which included obstruction of justice and false statements, "stemming from his alleged efforts to impede the investigation."[54]

Tell me, doesn't all this sound and feel like treason? Does Trump still believes in the death penalty for treason?

When should he be executed? "This capital punishment should be delivered quickly, decisively and without years of needless delay. Immediately . . . quickly. The trial should go fast, rapidly as possible. Not 15 years later, 20 years later."[55]

How does he want his execution to be administered? By lethal injection or the electric chair? "They give the death penalty where they give a slight injection so that they don't have pain when the needle goes in to slowly put them to sleep. I mean these people have to be treated very, very severely."[56]

But I digress.

If you are Black and putting out the garbage, you fit the description, because the police "don't know who (they) looking for yet." If the shoplifter is White and is in the act of committing the crime, a random Black man fits the description. If an armed White aggressor is nearby, a Black unarmed worker is a threat. If the witness says the clothes of a Black Veteran with a valid ID do not fit the description, and the picture from the video surveillance shows it was not him, he still fits the description - LITERALLY! Three Black females chilling in their car after a long and tiresome car ride fit the description, although the suspected criminals are males! If you deposit or withdraw your money from your bank account and are Black, you fit the description. If you are a Black nine-year-old girl collecting invasive insects harmful to over 70 different plant species, or a Black twelve-year-old boy playing alone in a park with a toy gun, you fit the description.

And if you are Black, and DNA evidence exonerates you, guess what? You still fit the description. Let's give you the death sentence. Quickly! "Bing, bang!"[57]

It Doesn't Matter If You're the President

As Barack Hussein Obama II sailed on to the presidency of the United States of America, he was *smeared* as a Muslim and a foreigner.

There is nothing nasty about being a Muslim or a foreigner, but if a cultured, intelligent, competent Black man, (even if his mother is White) sets his sights on the U. S. presidency, he fits the description.

The charge that Obama was steeped in Islamist ideology from a young age was first made by Andy Martin in 2004[58] and gained momentum after he announced his presidential ambition.[59] (Martin denied he ever questioned Obama's birthplace. He said he only accused him of embellishing his life story in his memoir, Dreams from My Father.)[60]

Hillary Clinton's supporters first propagated the assertion that Obama was not born in the United States in an email chain in 2008. One such chain email surfaced on the urban legend site Snopes.com in April 2008. It claimed Barack Obama's mother lived in Kenya with his Arab-African father late in her pregnancy. She was not allowed to travel by plane then, so Barack Obama was born there, and his mother then took him to Hawaii to register his birth.[61]

This conspiracy theory took root and grew into a monster. Many lawsuits were filed to prevent Obama from becoming president.[62] Seventy-two percent of registered Republican voters doubted President Obama's citizenship, according to a NBC News and SurveyMonkey poll conducted in June and July of 2016.[63]

In June of 2008, Obama's campaign posted his certificate of live birth on their "Fight the Smears" website and gave a copy to the liberal website Daily Kos. It was greeted with immediate cries that it was a fake.[64] But which Black person does not have to prove, verify, substantiate, demonstrate and validate their existence?

You could be sitting in front of your domicile or picking up trash, and a police officer will ask you for ID because the sign says no trespassing and they just want to be sure you have a right to be physically standing where you are. And if you object to such a disrespectful intrusion, they will call for other armed cops to surround you. The cops will believe you physically belong where you are after a White man who was never asked to show his ID says you are legitimate.[65]

You may be a worker in a parking garage, wearing your company's uniform, with knee pads on and a work ID hanging from your neck, and they will ask you, "What are you doing here?" You will say, "I am working." And they will say, "No, you don't work here; you don't belong here." They will ask for ID, attack you and call the police.[66]

You may be sitting in your backyard, when a neighbour accuses you of being a criminal and demands to see your lease to prove you live in your home. And then you get the cops called on you, and you have to show your ID.[67]

But there is no guarantee that people will be satisfied after you produce your papers. They will say it is fake, as Obama discovered.

Even as President, many Americans believed Barak Obama was trespassing and did not actually belong where he was. Donald Trump hopped onto the bandwagon of birtherism in 2011 and used his emblematic, skillful, deceptive wiles to feed the beast.

Why doesn't he show his birth certificate? There's something on that birth certificate that he doesn't like.

He's spent millions of dollars trying to get away from this issue. Millions of dollars in legal fees trying to get away from this issue. And I'll tell you what, I brought it up, just routinely, and all of a sudden, a lot facts are emerging and I'm starting to wonder myself whether or not he was born in this country.

He doesn't have a birth certificate, or if he does, there's something on that certificate that is very bad for him.

After President Obama released his long form birth certificate to the public, Trump continued to bulldoze the president's authenticity.

A lot of people do not think it was an authentic certificate. ... Many people do not think it was authentic. His mother was not in the hospital. There are many other things that came out. And frankly if you would report it accurately, I think you'd probably get better ratings than you're getting.

An 'extremely credible source' has called my office and told me that @ BarackObama's birth certificate is a fraud.

How amazing, the State Health Director who verified copies of Obama's 'birth certificate' died in plane crash today. All others lived.[68]

Even the immigrant, Melania Trump, cast doubt on the authenticity of the first Black president's birth certificate![69]

Barack Hussein Obama is an amazing individual, part descendant of people the Founding Fathers of America did not regard as falling in the category of "men" and, by implication, not created by the God they worshipped and acknowledged.

1. Obama spent two years at Occidental College in Los Angeles before transferring to Columbia University in New York City. He graduated in 1983 with a degree in political science.
2. He graduated magna cum laude from Harvard Law School in 1991. While at Harvard, he became the first Black editor of the prestigious Harvard Law Review.
3. He worked in corporate research and at the New York Public Interest

Research Group (NYPIRG)

4. Obama moved to Chicago, where he worked as a community organizer with a church-based group, the Developing Communities Project. He worked with low-income residents in Chicago's Roseland community and the Altgeld Gardens public housing development on the city's largely Black South Side.

5. Obama met and married Michelle LaVaughn Robinson, a fellow Harvard Law School graduate.

6. Obama taught at the University of Chicago Law School from 1992 to 2003.

7. In 1996, Obama won the Illinois State Senate election as a Democrat from the South Side neighbourhood of Hyde Park.

8. As a senator, Obama built support among Democrats and Republicans in drafting legislation on ethics and health care reform. He helped create a state earned-income tax credit that benefited the working poor, promoted subsidies for early childhood education programs and worked with law enforcement officials to require the videotaping of interrogations and confessions in all capital cases.

9. Barack Obama was sworn in as the first Black president of the United States on January 20, 2009. Obama's inauguration set an attendance record, with 1.8 million people gathering in the cold to witness it.

10. He won the 2009 Nobel Peace Prize.

11. Obama's presidency was marked by the landmark passage of the:

   • Lilly Ledbetter Fair Pay Act of 2009, which gave legal protection in the fight for equal pay for women.

   • Affordable Care Act, which was meant to give every American access to affordable healthcare by requiring everyone to have health insurance. It provided coverage for people with pre-existing conditions (a group that was previously often denied coverage) and required health insurance companies to spend at least 80 percent of premiums on providing actual medical services.

   • Killing of Osama bin Laden by Seal Team Six

   • Iran Nuclear Deal

   • Legalization of gay marriage by the Supreme Court.

Obama is a Christian. He is an exemplary family man - loving father, faithful husband, married to one woman (for 31 years up to the time of writing which means he has never been divorced and remarried once, twice or thrice) with two admirable, well-educated daughters. He and his wife are highly educated, refined, intelligent, decent, honourable, upright and proper people.

However, because of Obama's skin color, he fits the description and that gives intellectually and morally inferior people the right to malign their character and motives.

You may remember that a McCain supporter said Obama was a Muslim, but not many recall the other sinister accusation: "We are scared of an Obama presidency, and I'll tell you why. I'm concerned about someone who cohorts with domestic terrorists...."[70] (How many times will the pot curse the kettle black?). Trump heralded at one of his rallies that Obama was the founder of ISIS,[71] a militant Islamic fundamentalist group that emerged as an offshoot of al Qaeda in 2014 and said to be guilty of murder, ethnic cleansing, enslavement and rape.[72]

Understand this one fact: If you are Black, you fit the description. The late Dick Gregory, comedian, actor, writer, activist and social critic, once said: "Let Obama be your example. He did everything White folks told him to do. He had a White mother there to enforce him. He when to their best schools, studied under their powerful professors. And they treat that boy like he a third-grade dropout on death row." Need I say more?

You may be a retired Judge on a leisurely stroll, but you will fit the description of a younger man wildly running around, screaming and threatening people.

You may be a teenage girl riding home on your bicycle, but you will fit the description of a machete-wielding 25 to 30-year-old bald male.

You may be putting out your garbage, shopping, or standing at a door at your place of employment, and you will fit the description of a White suspect.

You may be a mother sitting in your car with your two daughters in a public place, but you will match the description of car thieves who happen to be males.

You may be sitting quietly in your car by the road, but you will fit the description of a burglar and be shackled like your forefathers were on the slave ships.

You may be a Veteran with proper ID, jogging to keep fit, but you will "literally" fit the description even if the witness and video evidence say you do not match the suspect.

It does not matter if you are a cop in uniform, you fit the description. A White citizen can level a bogus charge against you, and you will get pulled over, guns drawn on you, your ID ignored, and handcuffed.

If you are a Black child, you fit the description and will get the police called on you just for being, and if you are unlucky that day, murdered by cops who will falsely report that you, a 12-year-old boy, was an armed 20-year-old male!

And if you are the President of the United States, but you are Black, you still fit the description. You will be proclaimed a fraud, a cheat, illegitimate, and an accomplice with domestic and foreign terrorists. And they will dream of incarcerating you like they do many other innocent Black people by calling for your impeachment.[73]

Eventually, it will take the same White man who maligned you for years (and said water is wet and recommended an injection of disinfectant to cure the COVID-19 virus) to settle the issue of your birthplace and legitimacy.[74]

It does not matter who you are. If you are Black, you fit the description.

Chapter 12

Some People Never Fit the Description

ABlack and a White teen get into a scrap in the mall. They throw punches at each other, but the White teen is bigger and gets the better of the younger Black boy.

Two White police officers, a male and a female, rushed to the scene while the Black youth was on the floor, and the White one was still throwing punches.

The two officers drag the White teen off the Black, but the female officer gently places the White kid on a sofa while the male officer slams the Black teen to the ground, jams his knee in his back and starts to handcuff him. The female officer then rushes over to help her partner, places her knee on the Black teen's shoulder and helps with handcuffing the boy pressed into the hard mall floor.

The White teen stands up. He looks down at the officers still in the act of subduing his Black rival. He looks away, looks back down on the scene on the mall floor, looks away and looks back at his one-time challenger under the weight of two adult police officers.

He looks awkward and a

little confused.

"Oh, no!" A teenage female voice says off camera. "Yo. It's just because he is Black. Racially motivated."

The officers pull the Black teen to his feet. The female officer approaches the White teen, who immediately places his wrists together as if he expects to be handcuffed too, but the female officer gently pushes him back into a sitting position.[1]

Some people, offenders, criminal defendants and criminals never fit the description.

In this instance, the Black youth said he was defending a younger friend the bigger White Teen was fussing with.[2] The police officers could not have known that or that it was the White teen who first pushed the Black teen, but if they as adults and law officers were committed to a fair application of the law, they would have sat the two boys down and speak to them. But in their minds, some people never fit the description.

The Black youth's mother questioned the responding officers' handling of the incident. "If it wasn't for race, then what is it? What made them tackle my son, not the other kid? What made them be so aggressive with my son, not the other kid? Why is the other kid sitting down, looking at my son be humiliated and put into cuffs?"[3]

Mom, why? Some people never fit the description.

Attack Law Enforcement, Not the Offender

The former president, Donald Trump, is a classic example of how some people never fit the description.

1. As president-elect in 2016, he had to pay $25 million to settle fraud lawsuits over his Trump University real estate seminars.[4]

2. He also had to shell out $2 million in a court-ordered judgment for misusing his charity.[5] In one of his animated rants captioned "Trump and Our Two-Tiered Justice System," Jon Stewart marvelled at how Trump used his charity. "He used his own charitable foundation like a piggy bank or, as it's sometimes known, embezzlement." Stewart then cited other people who got jail time for the same crime. Diana Roman was imprisoned for two years for creating a phony charity to avoid paying taxes. Ex-Rep. Corrie Brown was sentenced to five years for stealing from a bogus charity, and Steve Stockman, Ex-Congressman, got ten years in prison for stealing charitable donations.[6]

3. A jury in Manhattan found Donald Trump's company guilty of a long-running criminal tax fraud scheme that lasted into his presidency.[7]

4. Trump's CFO went to prison.[8]
5. He froze aid to Ukraine to pressure President Volodymyr Zelensky to investigate his political rival, Democrat Joe Biden and was impeached for that corruption.[9]
6. After he lost the 2020 general election, he instigated an insurrection and is now being investigated by the DC Attorney General, a Federal Special Counsel, and sued by several groups. He was also impeached for this offence.[10]
7. Trump was charged with 34 felony counts in a Manhattan court stemming from a hush money payment to a porn star, Stormy Daniels, who says they had an adulterous affair. The prosecution says Mr. Trump falsified business records and broke election laws as he tried to cover up the payments. [11]
8. In August 2023, the Georgia prosecutor, Fani Willis, indicted the former President and 18 of his allies on racketeering conspiracy relating to their 2020 election interference.[12]
9. He was found liable of sexual misconduct in the Eugene Carroll defamation suit.[13]
10. Then there are the 37 federal criminal charges that he unlawfully kept national-security documents when he left office and lied to officials who sought to recover them.[14]

Donald Trump had a reputation for not paying his bills, according to an investigation by *USA Today*. There have been hundreds of liens, judgments and at least 60 lawsuits against Trump and his businesses because he has not fully paid workers for their work and, in some instances, refused to pay commissions for his lawyers and real estate brokers. His businesses have racked up multiple Fair Labor Standards Act violations for not paying employees minimum or overtime wage.[15]

However, Americans made him the 45th president of the United States and many are still defending him despite the slew of alleged criminal violations and the fact that he is now a two-time criminal defendant.

After a Manhattan grand jury voted to make Ex-President Donald Trump face criminal charges on the hush-money case, Republicans, the "law and order" party, began their "collaboration with Trump to vilify and denigrate the integrity of elected state prosecutors and trial judges."[16]

The former V. P., Mike Pence, called the indictment "unprecedented," an "outrage," a "political prosecution" on "a campaign finance issue."[17]

Florida Gov. Ron DeSantis denigrated Alvin Bragg as a "Soros-funded prosecutor" who "weaponized (his) office to impose a political agenda on society at the expense of the rule of law and public safety,"[18] the same crime DeSantis' -if not genetic - attitudinal ancestors committed against Black Americans for centuries.

Kevin McCarthy, then Speaker of the House, said it was an "outrageous abuse of power" by a "radical DA who lets violent criminals walk as he pursues political vengeance against President Trump," and vowed to "direct relevant committees to immediately investigate if federal funds are being used to subvert our democracy by interfering in elections with politically motivated prosecutions." Note that McCarthy's response was after Trump falsely claimed he would be indicted one week before the actual indictment.[19]

After Trump was eventually indicted, McCarthy told Andrea Mitchell in an interview that he was "sad and concerned." He belittled the work of the Grand Jury and of D. A. Bragg by claiming the indictment came not from "an Attorney General of the State, not even from a D. A. of New York City" but from a Borough and the "small political mind (of) this DA." He wanted to know what would prevent some small D. A. in a small county in a red state from going after a Democratic president.

When asked if he was worried they could lose the general election because their front-runner had been indicted and could face potentially more serious indictments, McCarthy revelled in the fact that the charge helped Trump to campaign better and had made his numbers stronger.[20]

Do you doubt my assertion that some people, offenders, criminal defendants and criminals never fit the description?

After Trump's indictment in the special counsel's classified documents probe (not by a "small political mind DA from a Borough"), McCarthy said it was "indeed a dark day" for America and deceitfully accused President Joe Biden of indicting "the leading candidate opposing him." "I, and every American who believes in the rule of law," McCarthy said, "stand with President Trump against this grave injustice. House Republicans will hold this brazen weaponization of power accountable."[21]

On June 21, 2023, McCarthy and the Republicans (acting like a D. A. in a small county in a red state) kept their promise to hold accountable the "brazen weaponization of power" by censuring Democratic Rep. Adam Schiff over his criticisms of then-President Donald Trump and for leading the first impeachment inquiry into him. They also voted on a resolution for the House Ethics Committee to launch an investigation into Schiff. Before this "shame! shame!"[22] act, they attempted to levy a $16 million fine against Schiff.[23]

Freshman Rep. Anna Paulina Luna, R-Fla. accused Schiff of being, "The perpetrator of . . . a web of deceit . . . on cable news, waking up every morning with

65

one goal: to lie, lie, lie to the American people that there was direct evidence of Russia collusion."[24] But you know who Luna and her Republican cohorts never censored? One of their own who said he was Jew-ish.

On May 10, 2023, Rep. George Santos (R-N.Y.) was criminally charged on 13 federal charges, including wire fraud, money laundering, theft of public funds, and lying to Congress. Santos's lies were many: He lied to collect unemployment benefits. He lied to donors and used their money to buy designer clothing. Prosecutors say that his financial disclosure forms in May 2020 and September 2022 were riddled with inaccuracies. Santos lied about where he went to school and college. He never worked on Wall Street. He lied about founding an animal charity.[25]

Santos' list of lies and suspected criminal activities are longer, but I will not tabulate all of them. The point I am making is that unlike Adam Schiff, or the two Black Democratic lawmakers, Justin Jones and Justin Pearson who were expelled from Tennessee's GOP-dominated house of representatives for their role in a gun control demonstration after the murders at a Nashville elementary school,[26] George Santos remained in good and regular standing in the GOP until December 1, 2023.[27] Democrats attempted to force the House to consider an expulsion resolution in May of 2023, after the first set of charges were made against Santos, but the Republicans skirted the matter by referring it to the House Ethics Committee. An attempt to oust him in November of the same year failed.[28] Why? **Some people, offenders, criminal defendants and criminals never fit the description.**

Many people dismissed the hush-money charges against Donald Trump as weak and unnecessary. It was said that even some Democrats were reluctant to defend the indictment. The media and pundits warned that Bragg's weak case was possibly undermining other efforts to indict Trump. However, the assaults on law enforcement and the rule of law heightened after Trump was indicted for more grievous offences: thirty-seven felony counts related to his mishandling of classified documents. Trump was charged with:

1. Felony violations of national security laws
2. Participating in a conspiracy to obstruct justice.
3. Sharing a classified map related to an ongoing military operation.
4. Improperly storing boxes containing classified documents at his Florida home, Mar-a-Lago, including in a ballroom, bathroom and shower.
5. Defying requests from the Justice Department to hand over classified documents.
6. Making false statements to the FBI.
7. Tapping his aides to help hide boxes of records.

At the announcement of the indictment, Special Counsel Jack Smith said, "Laws that protected national defense information were critical to the safety and security of the United States," and that violations of those laws "put our country at risk." [29]

Mike Pence did not know the details of the indictment before he dismissed it as lightly as he did the hush-money charges, but he surely must have been able to appreciate the seriousness of his country's security. Despite the former president's possible treachery, Pence said the indictment was a "sad day for America" and, like McCarthy (but with more deceptive finesse), accused Joe Biden of using his Justice Department to indict Trump.

Pence had hoped the Department of Justice would resolve these issues with the former president without charging him, although other people who kept classified material at their homes but were never accused of sharing it with anyone or aiding a foreign country, including during Trump's presidency, were convicted and sentenced to years in prison under the same Espionage Act provision Trump is now charged with breaking.[30] (Because, you know, some people never fit the description).

The former Vice President went on to say everyone is innocent until proven guilty. However, he framed the FBI decision not to charge Hillary Clinton as politicization. He implied the FBI was corrupt (not that Clinton was innocent) for this failure and vowed if he became president he would "clean house at the highest levels of the Department of Justice" and "install men and women of integrity."[31]

A Pat on the Back

The violent January 6 attackers do not fit the description.

Marjorie Taylor Greene, far-right Republican members of the House oversight committee and Colorado congresswoman Lauren Boebert visited the jailed defendants charged in deadly January 6, 2021 insurrection at the US Capitol. Greene and her Republican colleagues championed them as "political prisoners," high-fived them, shook their hands, and according to Democratic members of the oversight committee who went on the tour to "hold their Republican peers to account," treated them "like celebrities and patted them on the back."

Greene aims to "reframe the incarcerated January 6 rioters from alleged violent insurrectionists into martyrs of the far-right cause."[32] Some people, offenders, criminal defendants and criminals never fit the description.

Donald Trump began his first official 2024 campaign rally on March 25, 2023 in Waco, Texas, with a rendition of "The Star-Spangled Banner" sung by a group of inmates incarcerated for their role in the January 6 Capitol Hill attack. The defendants who called themselves the "J6 Choir," sang "Justice for All," and a version of the national anthem. Trump recited the Pledge of Allegiance over the track, stood with his hand over his heart as the song played and images from the Capitol riot, in which Trump supporters stormed the complex to overturn the 2020 election, played on a screen![33]

At the rally, Trump railed against his political adversaries and law enforcement who he declared more dangerous than Russia and China, a sentiment former Vice President Pence agrees with since he thinks it is absolutely necessary to clean house at the highest levels of the Department of Justice and install men and women of integrity! It is against this background that Republican politicians have defended Trump for possessing hundreds of sensitive classified documents and McCarthy's assertion that the classified documents Trump stole and locked in his bathroom were safe.[34]

Soon after Mike Johnson became the speaker of the house, he unashamedly boasted of his diligent process to "blur some of the faces of persons who participated in the events of that day because we don't want them to be retaliated against and be charged by the DOJ." Note that he also called the violent, savage attack on the Capital "the event." In the next breath, he called the January 6 Committee a partisan exercise. He charged that the two Republican members (quote unquote because here he made air quotes with his fingers) on that committee had "another agenda". He accused the J6 Committee of hiding important evidence.[35]

Why is Christian Mike Johnson, who played a vital role in the efforts to overturn the 2020 election results,[36] being so deceptive? Because some people, offenders, criminal defendants, and criminals never fit the description.

Republican presidential hopeful played with the notion of pardoning Trump and launched defamatory attacks on the Justice Department.

Vivek Ramaswamy said he would pardon Trump promptly on January 20, 2025 and "restore the rule of law in our country."

Nikki Haley would be "inclined in favor of a pardon," because "the issue is less about guilt and more about what's good for the country." She said this before she even knew the details of the indictment. After it was unsealed, she said Trump had been "incredibly reckless" even as she insisted that the Justice department had lost credibility!

Miami Mayor Francis Suarez would pardon Trump. Larry Elder is "very likely" to pardon Trump.

Vice President Mike Pence expressed concern about how the classified material Trump had could have fallen into the wrong hands and said the indictment contained serious charges he could not defend. While he did not commit to a Trump pardon, he still insisted he would "clean house" at the Justice Department and said he "can't believe that politics didn't play some role here!" Do you think

Pence would not pardon Trump?

Florida Governor Ron DeSantis also accused the Justice Department of being hypocritical and politically motivated. He tweeted that "The DeSantis administration will bring accountability to the DOJ, excise political bias and end weaponization once and for all." He did not commit to pardon Trump, nor has he ruled it out.

South Carolina Senator Tim Scott thinks the indictment is a "serious case with serious allegations" but accused the justice system of "targeting and hunting Republicans!"[37]

In addition to this drive to defend Trump, pardon him and attack law and order in America, Republicans intend to absolve Trump of his two impeachments. McCarthy favoured this expungement because he thought the proceedings against Trump were invalid: The first "was not based on true facts" and the second "on the basis of no due process." [38]

So, you see, in the first instance there were no "true facts" but in reality, if there were true facts it would not have mattered because McCarthy is still eager to absolve Trump in the second instance where there are "true facts." Trump was acquitted in the Senate in both impeachments cases because as I told you, some people, offenders, criminal defendants and criminals do not fit the description.

Seven of the eight Republican presidential candidates would support the criminal defendant, former President Donald Trump as the 2024 GOP nominee, even if he was convicted in a court of law for his crimes.[39] **You ought to know by now that if Trump were a Black man, everyone in America would know he was guilty of numerous harmful and shameful crimes.** And you ought to know that not one of those seven people would support former President Obama for wearing a tan-colored suit or to give the American people health care.

Jamie Raskin described Trump as the "twice impeached inciter of insurrection, sexual abuser, defamer of women and indicted pilferer of National Security secrets, war plans and top secret classified documents."

He reminded the house that Trump was "indicted by a Florida grand jury on 37 federal charges relating to obstruction, unlawful retention of defence information, storing dozens of classified secrets and top-secret documents at his Florida resort in his bathroom, his bedroom and beyond, and then refusing repeatedly for more than a year to return any of these official documents to the archives in the FBI."[40]

Yet the Christians at the Faith and Freedom Coalition's conference in Washington, D.C., on June 23, 2023, booed Chris Christie when he told them "He (Trump) has let us down."[41] And the "Christian" Mike Pence, who confessed he was concerned the classified material Trump had could have fallen into the wrong hands and admitted the indictment against his former boss contained serious charges he could not defend, still thinks the DOJ is corrupt enough for him to "clean house!" Do you know why this moral contradiction exists? **Some people, offenders, criminal defendants and criminals never fit the description.**

Let's Pardon the Murderer

In July 2020, Daniel Perry honked at and drove his car into a crowd of Black Lives Matter demonstrators in downtown Austin. Garrett Foster was in the crowd. He was openly carrying an AK-47 rifle. Eyewitness reports conflict about which man raised their firearm first, but Perry, who was also legally armed shot and killed Foster, and then fled the scene. He later called police and told them he had shot Foster but had done so in self-defense.

In April of 2023, a jury found Perry guilty of the murder of Foster. Immediately after this verdict, Texas Governor Greg Abbott began the process to pardon Perry.[42] Abbott referenced the state's "Stand Your Ground" laws of self-defense, which do not allow Black people to stand their ground. Remember Trayvon Martin? He was walking home, minding his business when a White man, George Zimmerman, attacked him and then murdered him because he was allowed to "stand his ground" but not unarmed Martin who was attacked!

Zimmerman contacted the nonemergency line of the Sanford Police Department, told them there had been burglaries in the neighbourhood, that he observed "a real suspicious guy" who was "walking around, looking about." Essentially, that was what was reported about a visiting Indian grandfather taking a morning stroll. Do you remember what happened to him?

Zimmerman described Martin as "up to no good, or he's on drugs or something." Do you see how Black people always fit the description? The dispatcher told Zimmerman not to follow Martin, but Zimmerman approached Martin. A violent confrontation ensued, and Zimmerman shot Martin at close range and killed him.[43]

When police arrived, Zimmerman argued that he had been assaulted by Martin and fired in self-defense. **Martin was unarmed.** The police released Zimmerman because no evidence contradicted his version of the event (**and because the unarmed Martin was dead**) and the state law permitted the use of deadly force in self-defense or "stand your ground."

The stand your ground law allows for deadly force if someone believes themselves in danger but prohibits someone from claiming self-defense if *they* incited or provoked violence in any way. Zimmerman was the one who provoked Martin and Perry drove into the crowd. Zimmerman was found not guilty and Perry who was convicted of murder is about to receive a pardon. **Some people, offenders,**

criminal defendants and criminals never fit the description.

Abbott wrote that the stand your ground law cannot be nullified by a jury or "progressive District Attorney." "I have made that request and instructed the Board to expedite its review," the governor wrote, concluding that he has already "prioritized" reigning in "rogue district attorneys."[44]

Some people, offenders, criminal defendants and criminals never fit the description.

Go Easy on Actual Election Fraudsters

Harvis Rogers, a Black Texan, was arrested and jailed in 2021 on the charge of two counts of illegal voting from ballots he cast in 2020 and 2018. Rogers was facing a 40-year prison sentence. A judge set Hervis' bail at $100,000![45]

On the other hand, Donald Kirk Hartle, who was featured in a GOP ad as an example of voter fraud, later pled guilty to one count of Voting More Than Once in the Same Election (he cast a ballot using his deceased wife's name in the 2020 general election) a category D felony. Under his plea agreement, Hartle got to serve a one-year term of informal probation and pay a $2,000 fine. If he stays out of trouble for that year, he will be allowed to withdraw his felony plea and enter a plea of guilty to the charge of Conspiracy to Commit Voting More Than Once at Same Election, a gross misdemeanor.[46]

Edward Snodgrass, a Republican official and a Porter Township trustee in Delaware County, Ohio, signed his dead father's name on an absentee ballot and then voted again as himself in the 2020 presidential election. He claimed he made "an honest error" and was trying to fulfill his father's dying wish. He was expected to plead guilty to a reduced charge of falsification and receive a sentence of three days in jail and a $500 fine.[47]

Barry Morphew, charged with the murder of his wife, Suzanne Morphew, who has been missing since May 2020, was also charged with forgery and offences relating to mail ballots for voting for Donald Trump in the 2020 presidential election using his wife's mail-in ballot. He allegedly told the FBI agents that he did it because he wanted Trump to win, and he thought his wife would have voted for him anyway. He pleaded guilty to the voter fraud charge in July 2022 and was fined $600. His bail for this charge was set at $1,000, according to a court document from Colorado's Eleventh Judicial District.

Black Harvis Rogers fits the description of a voter fraudster to a "T" but not those who willfully and deliberately committed the crime. The Black man was on parole for 16 years for a crime committed in 1995! He held down two jobs - one in the morning and the other late at night, but his industry did not matter. More than a year after Hervis' arrest, a district court judge dismissed the charges against him. If The Bail Project had not posted the $100,000 bail, he would have likely been locked up in pretrial detention that entire time.

The Black sister of Song of Solomon always fits the description but not the other offenders, criminal defendants and criminals.

Chapter 13

What is the Value of a Black Life?

Like George Floyd, Jordan Neely was in a fatal chokehold. George was able to call out to his dead mother, but Neely couldn't cry out to any deceased relatives because the former U.S. White marine under him had him in a vice-like death grip. Neely's arms thrashed about uncontrollably, and one foot swung from left to right as his body screamed out in vain for air.

A moment before, Neely complained loudly about being hungry and said he was ready to die. May 1, 2023, was his lucky day because Penny came up behind him, grabbed him around the neck and restrained him on the floor of the subway car.[1]

Two passengers helped to restrain the helpless Neely by holding his thrashing arms.[2] Apparently, they did not know that Neely's thrashing arms were his body's natural reflex responses to having its natural air supply deliberately cut off.

Daniel Penny's lawyers said Daniel never intended to harm Mr. Neely and "could not have foreseen his untimely death."[3] However, the viral videos of the deadly chokehold showed it lasted more than three minutes.[4]

Juan Alberto Vazquez who video recorded the incident, said Penny held Neely in a chokehold position for about 15 minutes. Penny denied he had Neely in his death grip for so long since the incident occurred between stops, which, in Penny's estimation, is less than five minutes.[5] Dr. Richey said on his "Indisputable with Dr. Rashad Richey" that the chokehold lasted 15 minutes,[6] but we can give Penny the benefit of the doubt on the duration of his death grip. However, Dr. Richey showed a screenshot of Neely's glossed-over eyes while Penny had him in his stranglehold.

The question then is, was the hungry, starving Neely still a threat two or three minutes into Penny's death clutch? If Neely's "somewhat aggressive speech" about being "hungry, . . . thirsty," and "didn't care about anything, . . . going to jail" for "a big life sentence,"[7] was threatening to the commuters, were his aggressive speech still a threat to the other passengers one minute into the chokehold? What about one and a half minutes? Two minutes? What about after he stopped struggling?

Neely was hungry, thirsty, and just sick and tired of life, but no one offered him a dollar. Instead, one man and two accomplices killed him.

What is the value of a Black life?

The Price for a Slave

According to the website, Statista, between 1638 and 1775, you could buy a slave in the Thirteen Colonies for 16.5 to 44.08 pounds sterling if they were from Britain's colonies in the Americas or between 1.87 and 17.43 pounds for slaves transported from West Africa.[8]

The National Archives currency calculator estimates that in 1750, seventeen pounds had a value of almost two thousand pounds and would have bought you two horses, or three cows, or 36 stones of wool, or ten quarters of wheat or paid a skilled tradesman for 170 days of his labour.[9]

In 1845, after the death of Joseph Maddox, who happened to be the great-great-great-grandfather of South Carolina Senator, Republican Lindsey Graham, someone wrote a receipt for the sale of eight of the deceased Maddox's slaves. The "Negro man Sam" was sold for $155.25. The names of the slaves appeared alongside items such as a sorrel horse for $10.50 and a folding table valued at $9.87. In an 1829 appraisal of the estate of Henry Coe, Senator Tammy Duckworth's great-great-great-great-great-grandfather, the names of Coe's slaves and their assessed dollar values were "bookended by seven sheep and a lamb, and a bull calf."[10]

In reality, enslaved Africans had no more value than livestock, and it is highly doubtful that some modern-day people believe Black and non-white people value more than a few horses, cows, sheep, bags of wheat, a $10 folding table or a few days of cheap labour.

In the Introduction, I quoted a young French Black man who said that in his country, everyone is equal in theory, but in reality, "if you're a young Black or an Arab man, we are not all treated equally."

Once again, France is rocked by violent protests. Towards the end of June 2023, a police officer shot and killed a teenager, Nahel, who was of Algerian heritage, during a traffic stop in the Paris suburb of Nanterre.

Footage of the incident captured by a passerby showed two officers standing on the driver's side of the car. One discharged his weapon at the driver despite not appearing to face any immediate threat, although, in immaculate police tradition, the officer claimed he fired his gun because he was scared the boy would run someone over with the car.

People of color in France say they are more likely to be victims of police brutality than White people. A 2017 study by the Rights Defenders, an independent human rights watchdog in France, found that young men perceived as Black or Arab were 20 times more likely to be stopped by police than their peers.[11]

Did that police officer think the life of teenager Nahel was worth more than a cow or horse or a few bales of cotton? And what do some modern Americans think about the value of Black lives? Let's peek into the mind of a Trump supporter whose interview was posted on YouTube.

"What do you think about woke culture," an interviewer asked one such supporter.

"I think it's a bunch of crap," the elderly man blurted. "They're trying to change what our children think in the schools."

"What would you like to see happen?"

"I'd like get back like it was in the Sixties."

"Before the civil rights stuff?"

"Before all the civil rights stuff," the man affirmed with not the slightest sign of embarrassment.

"So, you would like to see things go back to before the civil rights movement?"

"Oh, yes. Oh, yes. Where people have their freedom in this country."

"Well certain groups didn't have as much at the time, right?"

"Right. They didn't have as much at the time. But we still got to get back where this country stands up for this country,"[12] the senior Trumper and descendant of the Founding Fathers insisted.

The host of the video rightly observed that this man wanted to take the country back to when the government was "weaponized against the poor, the Queer, Black and Brown people, Asians, immigrants, Jews, Muslims, women, the ill or disabled."

Yes, this man and the people who think like him want to take America back to the terror days of the Ku Klux Klan, to the brutal lynchings and sitting at the back of the bus. He wants to resurrect the dark, foreboding days when Black Americans were subjected to segregation, discrimination and stereotyping from his kind of people.[13] He longs for the days when Black Americans were discriminated against based on race, color and origin and excluded from many lucrative opportunities. He had no concern for the people who had no freedom back in the 1960s, whose lives were so impossibly oppressive that their lifespan was seven years less compared to the Whites and, the children of African Blacks had half the chance of completing school successfully.[14]

Do you know what accounts for this mentality? A subconscious, if not conscious, belief that the value of a Black life has not inflated by much since the Founding Fathers declared, "All men are created equal," while they bought and sold Black people for between two- and 18-pounds sterling.

Black People for Target Practice

As I write this chapter, we have news of the Villa Rica Police Department, Georgia, posting images and videos on social media of a Black man being used on a poster as a target during a firearms safety class for civilians.[15]

The police department issued a statement that said the images of a Black man as a target were part of a package which included target images of people from various ethnic groups. But as Dr. Rashad Richey pointed out, those black target images were at other shooting ranges.[16] If you are melaninated, you should take the police department's statement with a few grains of salt because America has never subconsciously accepted that Black Americans are "men" or innocent beyond a shadow of a doubt until proven guilty.

Trayvon Martin was walking home, but Zimmerman saw a Black man who was a "real suspicious guy," "walking around, looking about," and was "up to no good, or he's on drugs or something." A Black mother sitting in her car with her seat reclined, and, no doubt, chatting with her daughters, appeared to a police officer as the people stealing cars in the area. A lone child playing with a toy gun in a park scared the hell out of an adult who called the police, who murdered the child seconds after they arrived on the scene. A Bed, Bath and Beyond store called the police to report that Black people were shoplifting while they were in the process of shopping.[17] Why did they accuse the Black shoppers of shoplifting? They had big purchase items. For big purchase items, "there's usually a question," one of the clerks said. Another clerk said she called the police because they had a "potential shoplifter." So, do you believe this store calls the police every time a shopper picks up a big purchase item? Black fits the description if all you are doing is shopping.

So, Black people should take the same attitude the Carroll County NAACP took to the Villa Rica Police's apology: It "lacked sincerity and sensitivity towards minority residents. This target is extremely offensive to many Villa Rica and Carroll County residents. These types of targets have been used by other police departments within the U. S. and have been deemed racially inappropriate and unacceptable."[18]

What is the value of a Black life?

Dismissed with Prejudice

"I had everything a child could need," Viola Ford Fletcher, 107, told the House Judiciary Subcommittee on the Constitution, Civil Rights, and Civil Liberties. "The night of the massacre, I was awakened by my family. My parents and five siblings were there. I was told we had to leave, and that was it. I will never forget the violence of the hate mob when we left our home. I still see Black men being shot, Black bodies lying in the street. I still smell smoke and see fog. I still see Black businesses being burned. I still hear airplanes flying overhead. I hear the screams."[19]

The centenarian recalled the painful memory of the night her Greenwood District in Tulsa, Oklahoma, was aerial bombed, looted, burned to the ground, and 300 Black people massacred.

The evening before, the Black men intervened in a White mob's attempt to lynch Black 19-year-old Dick Rowland, who was accused of sexually assaulting a White female. The end result of that was the utter destruction of a prosperous community.

The Black citizens of Greenwood received no compensation in 1921 and now, in 2023, a judge dismissed with prejudice[20] the case Lessie Benningfield Randle, 108, Viola Fletcher, 109, and Hughes Van Ellis, 102, brought to secure compensation for a lifetime of loss and hardship that resulted from the total destruction of their community.

The lawyers for the City of Tulsa argued that the city's connection to the event should not allow plaintiffs to "seek compensation," a cringe-worthy similarity to the sentiment of Tulsa City Commission's report issued two weeks after the destruction of Greenwood's homes, businesses, churches, a school, a hospital and a public library.[21]

> *Let*
> *the blame*
> *for this negro uprising*
> *lie right where it belongs — on those armed*
> *negros and their followers who started this*
> *trouble and who instigated it, and*
> *any persons who seek to put half*
> *the blame on the white people are*
> *wrong,"*

Remember, America was founded upon the assumption that Black people are not "men," and traditionally cannot hope to receive any redress for atrocities done to them.

Native Americans have received some form of reparations, even if inadequate. Japanese Americans were a little more fortunate in the reparations they received for their internment during WWII. In 1988, Congress voted to extend an apology and pay $20,000 to each Japanese-American survivor of the detention. More than $1.6 billion was paid to 82,219 eligible claimants.

Congress confessed their sin: The internment was "carried out without adequate security reasons and was motivated largely by racial prejudice, wartime hysteria, and a failure of political leadership." The Japanese were pleased: Representative Robert T. Matsui, a California Democrat who was interned with his parents as a child, said the bill produced "a wonderful feeling" among Japanese-Americans and lifted the specter of disloyalty that hung over us for 42 years because we were incarcerated. We were made whole again as American citizens."

Yes, some Black people in America have received some compensation, but they were never as happy as Japanese-Americans who were "made whole again as American citizens."

North Carolina set $10 million aside to compensate surviving victims who were sterilized under a decades-long eugenics program. However, conflicts arose over who was eligible. A state commission and state courts denied claims from relatives of victims who had died, and others were deemed ineligible because they had been sterilized by county welfare offices and not the state eugenics program.[22]

Chicago compensated 57 victims, nearly all African American, who police beat, shocked, suffocated and psychologically tortured to obtain confessions. A $5.5 million reparations fund was reserved for that atrocity, along with finance for a Torture Justice Center to provide counselling to scores of victims and other survivors of police brutality.[23]

In 1994, Florida reserved $2 million for those who survived the 1923 massacre that government officials failed to stop. The payments were "modest," and some survivors used the relatively tiny amounts to re-roof their house, do some remodelling and, in the case of one family, used it to pay the taxes on the property where her aunt had grown up[24].

Black people, as a whole, will never be appropriately compensated for the centuries of exploitation and violence done to them. Understand, their lives value no more than a horse, a cow, a bale of cotton or an old folding chair. If the Tulsa massacre survivors appeal to the higher courts, the result will be the same.

People bark at reparations for Black people, but the slave masters received compensation as an incentive to end the devilish practice of slavery, relocating slaves by force, breaking up their families, and murderously whipping and raping them. Compensated emancipation was enacted in the colonies of Britain, France, Denmark, and the Netherlands. The practice was also initiated in most South American and Caribbean nations, Brazil and Cuba. Slavery was prohibited in the District of Columbia, where over 900 slaveholders were paid by the federal government an average of about $300 for each slave they had to emancipate.[25]

Even the Haitians, who ended slavery with a violent revolution, agreed in 1824 to pay a large indemnity to former slaveholders in exchange for French recognition of its independence![26] Ah! But the French are experts at garnering compensated emancipation. To this day, 14 African nations pay France 500 billion in colonial taxes. [27]

Do you think these enslavers were satisfied with being paid to gradually free their slaves? They complained that their compensation was small compared with their loss and what they could have sold an enslaved person for on the open market![28] Well, guess who until this day got no compensation. The slaves and their descendants.

It is just as Ike Howard, grandson of Viola Fletcher, said about the ruling that denied the three centenarian reparations for the destruction of their neighbourhood in 1921: "They were blighted and once again not made whole,"[29] a far cry from the Japanese-American experience of being "made whole again as American citizens."

But in the meantime, White women are still accusing Black men. "He's an African-American male, and I don't know what his deal is, but it's making me not feel very comfortable." And White men, in this case, police officers, are still looking to "lynch" them.[30]

Devon Myers parked his car to get some food, but he did not know that a White woman had just made a 911 call to report him for looking at her suspiciously.

Do you remember the accusations against Dick Rowland in 1921 and Emmett Till in 1955? Well, in August 2019, Myers found himself surrounded, first by two police officers before others pulled up on him. While the woman who accused Myers of looking at her suspiciously sat undisturbed across the street, police demanded Myers' identification and harassed him.

Luckily for this 20-year-old Black man, another White woman was there to film the entire incident. What would have happened to the videographer if she was also Black? Thank your lucky stars, Mr. Myers.

The police department did apologize[31] to Devon Myers - a rare and infrequent **reparation** a Black person can have.

What is the value of a Black life?

Black Genocide - Ahhh!

Adolf Hitler is known as the most detestable human for approving the gassing, starving, torturing, brutal medical experiments, and machine-gunning of six million Jews. However, Leopold II, who ruled Belgium from 1865-1909, slaughtered 10 million Africans. Yet no one ever talks about this guy as evil and despicable for his mass African genocide.

Leopold II brutally exploited the Congolese people by forcing them into cheap labour to extract rubber for export to Europe and North America. This criminal King declared all vacant land in the interior, including uncultivated land and all forests, "uninhabited" and thus belonged to Belgium. The rest of the land was personal private property for Leopold, who never set foot in the Congo.[32]

Leopold used the Force Publique – a colonial military force with its vicious and brutal methods to ensure the unending and uninterrupted supply of rubber. When the local people failed to meet the quotas, they were punished by violence and death: The Force Publique burned villages to the ground, raped women, took them and children, hostages, tortured and extorted the people, mutilated and or killed men who did not reach their quotas.

Since ammunition was expensive to import from Europe, soldiers had to account for the bullets used in killing people by bringing a hand for every bullet they used. Basket of hands became a gruesome nightmare of Leopold's Red Rubber Terror in the Congo and proof of the killings done. They sometimes paid soldiers for severed hands because it was proof that they were carrying out the system of terror in the colony.

Since the rubber quotas were unrealistic to fill, small wars broke out between villages in which they fought for hands. Hands were a way to buy the loyalty of the White officers to show that the system of terror to force rubber extraction was being implemented. Each hand proved a killing, but sometimes the soldiers would cut off the hands of victims to save ammunition – leaving the victim to either die or survive.

King Leopold's Nazi-like brutality in the Congo resulted in an unprecedented reduction in the population of the local people - or genocide if you wish to call a spade by its correct name. Since the rubber took center stage, little production of food took place. The result was famine and starvation, which killed many more people. Some men who refused to comply with colonial orders were taken to prisons where the conditions were deplorable, resulting in mass death. To add to this African cataclysm, the White people imported diseases such as smallpox, venereal diseases (syphilis and gonorrhea), and amoebic dysentery and sleeping sickness, all of which added to the deadly decimation of the local people.

But who laments the genocide of the Congolese people? Who recounts the chopping off of hands of men and women? Who has ever depicted King Leopold as the demonic monster that he was? Have you ever heard of the ten million Congolese genocide this White colonialist caused? Nope! Because Black lives have no value.

The Nazis and their collaborators killed millions of people they perceived as inferior—including Jehovah's Witnesses, gay men, people with disabilities, Slavic and Roma people, and Communists. However, the term "Holocaust" applies strictly to *European Jews*.[33] Did you know the Nazis murdered millions of other people? Bet you didn't.

If someone kills five million Europeans, everybody hears about it, but if Europeans kill ten million Black people - ahhh! What's the big deal? Leopold's statues stood proudly in Belgium until 2020 when police officer Derek Chauvin murdered George Floyd in broad daylight. The statues of Leopold II inside the "palatial walls of Belgium's Africa Museum" is still "protected by heritage law."[34]

Some people disagreed with removing Leopold's statues from public places because "they're part of history,"[35] the same argument some White Americans use to defend their brash and intimidating display of the Confederate flag.

One descendant of Leopold, Prince Laurent, defended his ancestor, saying Leopold II was not responsible for atrocities in the colony "because he never went to Congo".[36] Well, was Hitler at the crematoria and mass graves he engineered?

In 2010, former Belgian foreign minister Louis Michel called Leopold "a hero with ambitions for a small country like Belgium". A former president of the Free University of Brussels, Hervé Hasquin, argued there were "positive aspects" to colonization, listing the health system, infrastructure, and primary education Belgium brought to Central Africa. Isn't that the same sad argument the descendants of the people who ravaged Africa and enslaved its population by the hundreds of millions use to rationalize their forefather's criminal behaviour?

In the not-too-distant past, after the disinterment of the native children who mysteriously went missing from the Canadian Indian Residential School, financed by the Canadian government and ran by Christian Churches, one Roman Catholic clergy, Msgr. Owen Keenan, resigned after he asserted the Residential Schools did a lot of good for indigenous children.[37] That was a mild censor compared to his Church's crimes against the Indigenous population. Regrettably, there is no such censor for the Belgians (and other Europeans) who benefited from the brutal exploitation of Africans and now use the same arguments as the Catholic Monsignor.

What is the value of a Black life?

Black People Must Answer the Question, Too

"Mr. Francis, you are a poor excuse for a teacher. You possess none of the skills a qualified teacher should have." The irate and disparaging mother at the end of the line spoke perfect English with a cultured accent, making her aggression feel like it was wrapped in folds and folds of silk and satin.

I sunk deep into the inadequately cushioned school-supplied chair. I had called this mother, expecting she would be an ally in her daughter's education. The girl was unfocused, undisciplined, impolite and discourteous, and she had failed all the subjects I taught but showed no concern.

"You cannot control your class. You have not effectively communicated with your students or built a relationship with them."

I was dumb-struck. A sense of helplessness washed over me. This was not what I expected from a Black parent. My uneasiness transmuted into despair as the mother continued to berate my teaching skills. Many of the Black students in the classes I taught were not doing well in their studies. They were raucous, ill-mannered and disruptive. This mother's child was at the top of this failing list, but I was not going to have her cooperation to sculpt a grand future for her daughter.

In my brief teaching career, I never needed to call the parents of my Filipino, Indian or White students. Sure, some very dull White and average Indian students were outshone by one or two brilliant Black students, but the number of malfunctioning Black students alarmed me.

I do not remember how the abusive phone call with this mother, who happened to be the wife of one of the pastors in the Greater Toronto Area, ended.

However, the following day her daughter breezed into my class like a conqueror and loudly heralded to everyone: "Mr. Francis, you thought you could turn my mother against me!"

This student's abrasiveness and insubordination worsened, and her grades plummeted further.

I have always wondered what became of that girl and a few boys who never responded to my earnest and patient teacherly admonitions.

Black people, including Black parents, must also answer the question: What is the value of a Black life?

While we can justifiably mourn about Europe's rape and ravage of African treasures and people, we cannot deny that Black African political leaders have done the same to their own people. Many oil and diamond-rich African nations have their citizens living in abject poverty. Maternal deaths are high, life expectancy is low, unemployment is through the roof, and sometimes millions of Africans perish at the hands of murderous dictators. While the masses suffer, the ruling class lives lavish, affluent, opulent, sumptuous and luxurious lives.[38]

Some Black leaders treat their own people worse than they would their horses, cows, dogs and pigs and old folding chairs!

In January of 2023, Black Memphis, Tennessee, police officers beat a Black man, Tyre Nichols, to a pulp. A camera caught these Black officers repeatedly delivering sledgehammer-like blows to his head and body while they wedged his hands behind him. One officer slammed his right foot into Tyre's head as he would a football while his partners in crime forcibly held him down. They pepper sprayed him and repeatedly punched and kicked the helpless Nichols for good measure. The unfortunate man died three days later.[39]

Do not be naive. Some Black people do not value the lives of their own Black brothers and sisters either. Some of the Black police officers in uniform who had guns drawn on them and placed in handcuff were subjected to such humiliation by other Black police officers! Remember that in the Congo, during the genocidal terroristic reign of Leopold, small wars broke out between African villages where they fought for hands to buy the loyalty of their White oppressors. That would suggest that Black Congolese, like Leopold's Force Publique, also chopped off the hands of their brothers and sisters.

Some Black people (politicians, social influencers, pastors, judges, Black people who bleach their skin) do not think Black is beautiful and like others, may also think black fits the description.

"You are going to move to Canada with all those racist people?" The young man regarded me with deep incredulity. I felt Canada was a safe place to immigrate to based on my research. Twenty-seven years later, I am happy to say I was right. White Canadians have been good to me but unfortunately, the insults, deception, betrayal and the desertification on my life have all been done by Black people. To be brutally frank, I must admit that Black people treat every other race more favourably than their own. I am no exception to this rule.

In 2003, in a desperate attempt to recover from a divorce that stripped my life to the bones and left me homeless and hungry, I bought and sold merchandise to stay afloat. A Black neighbour who sometimes purchased some of my inventory one day casually remarked that I was stricter on my prices with Black customers than I was with the Indians and the Whites. His remark threw me for a loop, but a quick mental reflection on all the haggling I had done with my prospective customers confirmed this man's observation.

Perhaps I should not have made such a sweeping generalization about Black people's favourable regard for people of other races. I do not have an exhaustive knowledge of the psychology of Black people from other parts of the world. However, I believe Black people from the Caribbean, particularly Jamaicans, are favourably biased toward people of different ethnic groups.

I told you about my mother's hypnotic love for White beauty. That rubbed off on me. I think other Jamaicans were affected in the same way. The psychological damage of slavery and colonization takes centuries to dilute. One fair skin Jamaican young woman told me she once worked in a grocery store with a bar attached. Her boss observed that the men spent more money on liquor when she served in the bar. Her employer, therefore, spared her all the tedious and non-glamorous work needed to make the business function efficiently. He used her exclusively to serve in the bar or man the cash register in the grocery store.

The Black patrons subconsciously favoured a Jamaican with a lighter skin tone than their own. Perhaps, they, too, grew up hearing, "Anything black no good."

Do not get me wrong, now. It is a beautiful thing that Black people love other races, and perhaps, another reason Black people have a high regard for other races is because Black people, at heart, are good souls. When they are abused, burnt out, lynched, and shot down like dogs, the first thing they talk about is forgiveness!

But Black people need to love themselves more. They need to love the color of their skin more. They need to love their noses more. They need to love their lips more. They need to love their hair more.

Black people need to foster as sacred a regard for themselves as they have for others.

Chapter 14

Black Beauty Unveiled In a Colorless World

M r. Chairman, that was unbelievably inspiring," Freshman Eli Crane, Representative Republican of Arizona, hunched over the podium, but that may have been because the microphone was not tall enough.

The fingers on his left hand, which supported his weight, opened and closed around the edge of the podium a few times. "My amendment," he continued, his eyes peered upward to compensate for his hunched over frame, "has nothing to do with whether or not colored people or black people, or anybody can serve. OK, that has nothing to do with...."

"Mr. Speaker!" A firm, indignant female voice interjected, but Freshman Eli Crane continued with his response.

"... any of that Stuff. What we want to preserve and maintain is the fact that our military does not become a social experiment. We want the best of the best. We want to have standards that guide who's in what unit, what they do. And I'm gonna tell you guys right, now, the Russians, the Chinese, the Iranians, the North Koreans, they are not, they are not doing this because they want the strongest military possible. I hope my colleagues on the other side can understand what we're doing. Thank you so much."[1]

The term "colored people" harks back to when Freshman Eli Crane's parents, grandparents, great-grandparents, great, great-grandparents treated Black Americans worse than their dogs. Amelia Butterly, in a 2015 article, "Warning: Why using the term 'colored' is offensive," said the term is a "highly offensive racial slur" because it "recalls a time when casual racism was a part of everyday life." The "Jim Crow laws" from the 1870s to the 1960s imposed segregation on Black Americans, keeping them separate from White people – relegating Blacks to "colored-only" facilities such as public transport, drinking fountains, and waiting rooms.[2]

The uncivilized monstrosity of the "colored people" era is shamefully laid out in painful details in an online *History* article, "Jim Crow Laws."

Crane's ancestors imposed "Black codes" – local and state laws upon the newly emancipated people. These laws determined where and how formerly enslaved people could work and for how much compensation. They were a legal way to put Black citizens into indentured servitude, swindle them of their voting rights, control where they lived, how they travelled, and seize their children for labour purposes.

Former Confederate soldiers became the police and judges, making it difficult for African Americans to win court cases. That system of unjust laws worked in conjunction with labour camps to ensure the incarcerated were treated like slaves. Black offenders typically received longer sentences than their White equals and often died in prison because of the gruelling work.

The local and national governments collaborated to thwart the progress of Black people. Then there was the Ku Klux Klan, a private club for Confederate veterans. Their violence endangered the existence of the people who once worked centuries to enrich them. They vandalized and destroyed Black schools while bands of violent White people attacked, tortured and lynched Black citizens at night. Families were attacked and forced off their land across the South.

For one hundred years, perhaps longer, the KKK harbored not only the "lowest echelons of criminal back alleys" but people at the highest levels of government who terrorized Black communities.[3]

And in 2023, a member of government reached way back into the dark, evil days of Jim Crow when he called Black people in America "colored people." The GOP lawmaker said he "misspoke" when he referred to 'colored people' on the House floor.[4] But mark my word, even though Crane is only 43 years old and was born some 20 years after the "end" of Jim Crow, he has inherited the subconscious belief that Black people are not "men" created by his God, and therefore, he "misspoke" from the "abundance of his heart."

Do you doubt the above assertion? What, then, was Crane's burden on the House floor? A refutation of DIVERSITY in the military because that would **lower military standards**. He argued that "The military was never intended to be, you know, inclusive." "Diversity, equity and inclusion" is a game, Crane said. And he automatically equates such noble states with weakness – with "messing around and we keep lowering our standards."

Understand this. Crane and his GOP compatriots do not think any differently than their Jim Crow progenitors. If the military is not "white," it cannot be strong. If it has one drop of Black blood, it is Black, although it is visibly White!

Crane was on the same track as Republican Sen. Tommy Tuberville, who accused Black Americans of criminality because they wanted reparation and who wanted White nationalists to comprise the military because "they are Americans." Like Tuberville, Crane does not want diversity, equity and inclusion because that **degrades**, not strengthens the military. Ahh! But then he realized that he, like his forefathers, still wanted "colored people" to die on the battlefield for his White military and White America, so he had to inject the statement: "It has nothing to do with whether or not "colored people or black people, or anybody can serve."

It is true, as Crane said, that a military should have high recruiting standards. But understand, Crane denies the US military currently has any high standards and has been degraded simply because of diversity, equity and inclusion. In his mind, the US military can only be strong if it has only White combatants.

Crane is so steeped in and blinded by his Jim Crow heritage that he went on to make the silly remark that Russia, China, Iran and North Korea had no diversity, equity and inclusion in their armed forces. To begin with, all four countries Crane mentioned are oppressive, abusive, murderous totalitarian states, a few notches below the exalted belt of a free democracy, but the devalued state to which Crane and the Republicans wish to bring modern America. Secondly, those countries are not diversified in the same way America is. They are not populated by the descendants of Africans their ancestors stole from Africa and abused for four hundred years. Therefore, their armies would primarily comprise the native people who populate their countries.

Colorless in a World of Color

It is fascinating that the people who claim God and freedom for themselves also claim to be colorless even as they exist in a universe ablaze with color.

"Colored" is generally used for people who are not "White." I place the word

White in open and closed quotes because White people are not white. They are pale or, at best, beige in color. However, I digress. When White people refer to non-whites as colored, they imply firstly that being White is "normal" or a "default" state, as was observed in the online article, "Warning: Why using the term 'colored' is offensive." Remember, one drop of black blood makes a visibly White person Black,[5] meaning, they are assigned to the subordinate group[6] and could possibly be subjected to "Jim Crow" treatment. Ask Meghan Markle to tell you about that.

An inadvertent result of the term "colored people" is that the ones who consider themselves superior, dominant, natural, and normal disparage and besmirch color, the one element that stamps beauty on *their* God's creation! Whenever they contemptuously use the "colored people" nomenclature, they automatically exclude themselves from all that is *radiant, dazzling, luminous, beautiful, sublime, glorious, lovely, goodly and godly* and retreat into a dull, lifeless, dead, zombie-like zone. But they had already done that to themselves by brutally enslaving, beating, raping, breeding, murdering and experimenting on Africans for centuries. So, perhaps, they subconsciously know they can never, in reality, partake of all that is lively, dazzling, beautiful, festive and colorful.

Imposed Obscurity

The lover of the Black Beauty of Song of Solomon delighted in her intoxicating love in his private chambers but was reluctant to appear with her in public.

> *Tell me, you whom I love, ... Why should I be like a veiled woman beside the flocks of your friends? (1:7).*

Sarah "Sally" Hemings was the daughter of Betty Hemings, who was the daughter of an enslaved African woman and English Captain, John Hemings.[7]

John Wayles, an American colonial planter, slave trader, and lawyer in colonial Virginia, fathered six children, including Sally, with Betty Hemings.

Thomas Jefferson, the third president of the United States, married Martha, Wayles' daughter, and inherited his father-in-law's slave girl, Sally.[8]

After Martha died, Jefferson impregnated Sally Hemings multiple times and had six children with her over the span of many years.[9]

Now, despite "multiple lines of evidence, including modern DNA analyses," there is a debate over whether Jefferson had children with his slave. The Thomas Jefferson Foundation hired a commission of scholars and scientists who worked with a 1998–1999 genealogical DNA test and published in 2000 that they found a match between the Jefferson male line and a descendant of Hemings' youngest son, Eston Hemings. The Foundation asserted that Jefferson fathered Eston and likely Sally's other five children. However, the Thomas Jefferson Heritage Society commissioned a panel of Scholars of History in 2001, and they unanimously agreed that it had not been proven that Thomas Jefferson fathered Sally Hemings' children.[10]

George Washington Parke Custis, whom George Washington formally adopted, fathered several children with Washington's slaves. (Look! A Founding Father who valued freedom and fought a war for it, was an enslaver). However, "history books have downplayed this for centuries," says an article on the Smithsonian website.[11]

The people and their descendants who drank their fill of the Black Woman's love or raped and pillaged her in private are still determined not to acknowledge her in public. So she still cries: "Tell me, you whom I love, ... Why should I be like a veiled woman beside the flocks of your friends?"

The Black Beauty must unveil herself, assert herself, and flaunt her blackness and beauty. She must lay a firm and vigorous hold upon "the great principles of political freedom and natural justice," upon "equality," and her "unalienable Rights, Life, Liberty and the pursuit of Happiness." The Black damsel of Song of Solomon must herself discard her imposed obscurity and break forth into the light of civilized day, her beauty, as radiant as the sun, unveiled and dazzling. Because those who hate her, exploit her, imprison her, demean her, abuse her - those who say she fits the description, will never admit that she is human and their equal.

No Other Race Is Obligated to Treat Black People Well

No other race is obligated to love or treat Black people with respect. In this life, some are first to the finish line and some stagger in last. There are those who are highly esteemed and those who are despised - the Brahmins and the untouchables. If you are last, lowly venerated or an Untouchable, most times, you cannot expect other humans to rescue or promote you, and that is because, by default, humans are evil.

Darkness is the default situation in this endless universe. Light is the exception. Light is an interdiction of darkness - the default reality. According to Genesis 1:2, darkness predated creation: ". . . darkness was over the surface of the deep." God did not need to create darkness, but he was compelled to create light. "And God said, 'Let there be light,' and there was light" (Verse 3). Darkness is the rule. Light is the exception.

Just as darkness is the default condition in the physical universe and light is the exception, human nature is evil by default. His acts of virtue are exceptions.

Humans are selfish. They have always enslaved each other, sometimes for absolutely no remuneration, and at other times, for a minimum wage. Humans will steal your food, land, treasures, and people. They will wage war on you even if you did not provoke them. They will invade your country for weapons of mass destruction, which you never had, or accuse you of being a Nazi and lob massive missiles into your cities, hospitals, nurseries and apartment buildings while you and your children sleep. And other humans will applaud them for their crimes. They will invade your village and town, gun you down while you are celebrating, sleeping, or having a meal. They will chop off your head, rape your wife and daughter in your presence, murder your baby and take hostages.

They will rain down a thousand bombs upon your city and flatten it, kill tens of thousands of civilians, make refugees out of millions and starve hundreds of thousands.

The very best things about humans are evil - their Gods and religions. Humans will sacrifice you to their Gods, set off bombs in your marketplaces in the names of their Gods, stone you for your "sins," murder you for violating slight and inconsequential religious mores, hang you in their public square for challenging their religious oppression and wage holy wars in the name of their divines.

They will decimate your culture and way of life as missionaries and rape your little boys who stand at their altars. They will burn you alive because of your religious beliefs, gas you for your spiritual heritage, invade your land and expel you on the say-so of their Gods and make you a perpetual refugee.

Humans will hate you for your ethnicity and skin color, pass laws of suppression and discrimination against you and exclude you from the social and economic richness you created while they were sucking you dry of a viable future.

In a 2021 interview, Jon Meacham (a renowned presidential historian, contributing writer for *The New York Times Book Review*, contributing editor at *TIME*, a Pulitzer Prize-winning author, a member of the Council on Foreign Relations and of the Society of American Historians, a distinguished visiting professor at Vanderbilt University), said in a thoughtful, erudite manner that "The American story is full of violence and oppression." He also said that his country's history was "full of peace and liberation." This, indeed, is factual, and what Meacham said about his country applies to all other countries and cultures.

However, Meacham emphasized that "All history comes out of conflict, whether it's racial or class or economic or political, tribal." Meacham then thoughtfully added, "That's inevitable." Why is that inevitability rooted in human reality? Humans are evil by nature.

Of course, Jon Meacham was not as crass as I am in my analysis of human nature. He used more graceful, refined, and elegant colors to portray human vileness. "We live in a fallen world. We don't live in a perfect world. We don't live in a place where people come together and say, how can we make things better because that's the right thing to do. We live in a world where there are clashes of interests. There are winners, and they're losers."

Ah! Winners and losers. That is a fact of life. Someone will always be at the back of the line, bringing up the rear or being crushed at the bottom of the barrel. It's just life.

Meacham continued in his careful, measured manner. "The moments that speak to us most are not the ones that feel Olympian and distant, but which feel messy, complicated, contingent, close run. . ... We live in a world that is sinful and disappointing. . . in which tragedy is far more often the state of things than a kind of comic conclusion. There's a reason Shakespeare's tragedies are performed more often really than his comedies because I think they speak to us more."[12]

Meacham articulated in a circuitous and gentle way what I make in a direct and aggressive manner: Humans are evil by nature. They are the darkness that predates creation. The good humans are the exceptions – like the light that had to be created.

If you are among the oppressed, suppressed, abused, and downtrodden, you cannot expect that those who mistreat you will volunteer to amend their ways. If you are among the invaded, it is useless to appeal to the invader to turn back to his homeland in peace. If you are among the financially disadvantaged, do not think the excessively wealthy will give you manageable interest rates and pay more taxes to help offset your society's financial burdens. If you are among the hunted, the political prisoners and persecuted, do not think that the murderous authoritarian will suddenly conduct free and fair elections or give you a fair trial before judges they bought and intimidated.

If human darkness is to be interdicted, someone has to create light. In the same vein, if the Black, beautiful woman of Song of Solomon is to be respected and honoured, not loved, for that would be asking for too much from evil humans, she has to MAKE the people of other races respect and honour her.

If you are in last place in a race, would you expect the athlete in first place to wait for you to catch up? Would you appeal to the first-place champion to let you pass him? If you stumble, would you expect the runners behind you to stop and help or for the ones ahead to turn back to offer you a hand? Yes, stricken athletes have received help from others who sacrificed the opportunity to finish before the fallen, but like light and goodness, those instances are exceptions to the rule.

In his July 5, 1852, speech, the ex-slave, Frederick Douglass lamented: "O! had I the ability, and could I reach the nation's ear, I would, to-day, pour out a fiery stream of biting ridicule, blasting reproach, withering sarcasm, and stern rebuke."

Save your breath, Douglass!

What would you need to do to beat the first-place runner next time? Practice. Exercise. Exert and apply yourself to the task of running. If a country invades your homeland, what would your citizens need to do to live another day? Fight like hell! Similarly, Black people must make other races respect and honour them; not by making appeals to their oppressors and citing their noble ideals of "all men are created equal," and claim of color blindness. Rather, Black people must assert themselves "not (by) light ... but fire; ... not (by) the gentle shower, but thunder." Black people "need the storm, the whirlwind, and the earthquake," because even after such an assertive stance, "the feeling of the nation (may not) be quickened; the conscience of the nation (may not) be roused; the propriety of the nation (may not) be startled; but "hypocrisy of the nation (must) be exposed; and its crimes (if not against the God they worship) against man be proclaimed and denounced."

How Black People Can Advance from Last Place

If you ask Black people how they can advance from the last place in this life rigged against them, most will tell you to pray and trust in God. I wish to here and now raise a dissenting voice to this impractical approach to the numerous challenges melaninated people face.

If praying to God worked, slavery and Jim Crow would not have lasted as long as they did. Neither would there be the current attack on Blackness underway in the United States with redistricting, fake wokeness and the Supreme Court's dissolution of some provisions that helped to even out the racist playing field upon which that nation was founded.

On July 30, 2023, Rep. Steven Horsford, the chair of the Congressional Black Caucus, pointedly called out the attack on Black people in his country. He denounced the Republicans and white supremacists for their efforts to undermine voting rights, civil rights, and racial justice.[13] Trust me when I insist that no amount of praying will save America from the threatening monster of re-energized racism and the current creeping authoritarianism.

Whatever rights and protection Black Americans gained came through effort and sacrifice, blood and cracked skulls, imprisonment and assassinations, cross burning and lynching, firehoses and gunfire, church burning and bombings, sit-ins and long marches. No improved status came to Black Americans on a silver (or prayer) platter. It came always through the blood, sweat, and tears of the oppressed and the support of conscientious White Americas and people of other races.

If Black people in America sit back and pray, the sundial will reverse on them. Why do I belittle praying? Because God has no hands but ours.

Teresa of Avila (1515-1582) said it poetically:[14]

> *Christ*
> *has no*
> *body but yours,*
> *No hands, no feet on earth*
> *but yours,*
> *Yours are the eyes with which he looks*
> *Compassion on this world,*
> *Yours are the feet with which he walks to do good, Yours are*
> *the hands, with which he blesses all the world.*

Dylann Roof killed nine Black Christians during a Bible study at the Emanuel African Methodist Episcopal Church on June 17, 2015. No Angels came to rescue the faithful who were studying the sacred words of their God. However, if one of them had a chance to jump Roof or had a gun, they could have saved a few lives, if not all nine. God has no hands but ours.

Audrey Hale invaded a *Christian* school on March 27, 2023, fired 152 rounds and killed three children and three adults.[15] The adult Christian educators dialled 911 and "pleaded for help in hushed voices."[16]

One caller told a dispatcher she could hear gunshots while hiding in an art classroom closet. "It sounds like somebody is shooting guns," the caller said. There was a pause in the shooting, and then it resumed. "I'm hearing more shots," she said. "Please hurry!"

On that fateful day, at least three people called the police, but none of them made a telephone call to Glory! Who took out the murderer of defenceless children? An angel? Did God strike the heartless murderer with lightning from above? NO! It took humans - police officers who themselves were shot at and could have been killed - to take out this crazy, heartless gun touting woman. God has no trigger finger but ours.

Can someone say Uvalde? An 18-year-old massacred 19 students and two teachers in a school in Uvalde on May 24, 2022. According to a 77-page report, 376 law enforcement officers (a force larger than the garrison that defended the Alamo) descended upon the school, stood around and did nothing for more than an hour![17] Did God do anything to save those 19 children? No! Because God has no body but the bodies of law enforcement officers.

The divine is powerless without human effort, involvement, and sometimes

93

lifetime sacrifices such as imprisonment (remember Nelson Mandela?) or surrendering their life (Martin Luther King Jr.) to improve the lot of their fellowmen.

Whenever humans settle into an absent-minded lull, the forces of evil creep back into society and force people to double their efforts to move humanity to a greater evolutionary height of goodness, decency, fairness, equity, and all that is good and noble.

In such times of danger, if humans sit back, disinterested, distracted, too self-absorbed to care or just scared, evil overwhelms and dominates them. They must then suffer for a long time, perhaps even a century, since evil people live long lives (and God has no hands, feet or eyes but ours) before they can hope for deliverance.

All-night prayer meetings will not rescue Black people (or the poor) who are disadvantaged, oppressed, bullied, imprisoned, murdered, dehumanized, enslaved, or falsely imprisoned. Only their engagement, activity, stress, strain, and exhausting battles can deliver them. They must also forearm themselves - think ahead and design long-term plans. If Black people fail to engage life in this manner, (by fire. . . and thunder. . . and storm, the whirlwind, and the earthquake), they will be like the unforearmed (okay, I just coined a word) Ukraine, wide open to savage bombardment.

The sooner the Black and beautiful woman understands this, the better life will be for her.

So, what can Black people, the world over, do to improve their lot on this physical plane?

Money Is Power

Two and a half million dollars. That is how much Daniel Penny raised for his legal defense as of May 19, 2023, after he strangled to death a Black man, Jordan Neely, who expressed his frustration with life and said he was hungry.[18]

On the other hand, Tennessee state Representatives Justin Pearson and Justin Jones raised just a little over $2 million **combined** (less than 2.5 million) after the Republicans kicked them out of office, but not their White colleague, Rep. Gloria Johnson, who joined them in protest, calling for the GOP to pass gun control measures after the March 27, 2023, deadly shooting of little children at a Nashville school.[19]

Hey, Black, beautiful daughter, the people of no color do not march, pray, go to church or call upon God when they perceive they are in trouble. They fund their way out of trouble.

Former President Donald Trump raised over $4 million within twenty-four hours after news of his indictment in Manhattan became public.[20] He raised another

$7 million after he was indicted for illegally retaining classified government documents after he left the White House and then conspired to obstruct a federal probe of the matter.[21] On August 4, 2023, Trump's Alabama fundraiser had 2,700 attendees, each paying $250 per ticket.[22] His campaign claimed they raised $9.4 million after he released his mug shot. [23]

Money is power; a valuable lesson Black people need to take to heart.

$2.00 vs $25.6 Million

Shannon Phillips, a former Starbucks regional manager, was awarded $25.6 million US after she alleged that the company unfairly punished her and other White employees after the high-profile arrests of two Black men at a Philadelphia location in 2018.[24]

"Get out, you have to leave. You're not buying anything, so you shouldn't be here," one of the police officers who had surrounded their Starbucks table said.

Rashon Nelson and Donte Robinson could not have known that the Starbucks manager had called the police two minutes after they settled at their table. "Hi, I have two gentlemen at my café that are refusing to make a purchase or leave."[25]

Rashon Nelson and Donte Robinson were waiting to meet a potential business partner at the Starbucks in Philadelphia's Rittenhouse Square neighbourhood on April 12, 2018. The Starbucks manager approached them and asked if they wanted to order anything. They declined and told her they were just there for "a quick meeting." They had meetings at Starbucks all the time.

When Robinson saw the cops walk in, he thought, "They can't be here for us." Such a stray thought running through the mind of a young, budding real estate entrepreneur may seem peculiar and out of place since there were other (White) people in the store, but in a country where Black fits the description, it was not. And now, Robinson was looking up in the faces of several police officers who had come to boot them out of the Starbucks store.

The two young men told the officers they were waiting for a business partner. They even called the business partner as proof, but the officers would hear nothing they had to say. By the time the business partner arrived, the officers had arrested and were handcuffing Nelson and Robinson.

"What did they do! What did they do," the business partner asked in obvious befuddlement.

"They weren't doing anything, you know, like violent or angry," a White female eyewitness said, incredulity twisting her facial lines. Ahh, eyewitness lady. But they were Black and descendants of Black people who were once quartered in "Negro Only" spaces. They were arrested for "defiant trespassing" and locked up for eight hours!

Nelson and Robinson, who were racially profiled and denigrated precisely like their parents, grandparents, and great-grandparents were treated, settled with the city for $1.00 each and a measly $200,000 grant that would go toward a pilot program for high school students who aspire to be entrepreneurs.[26]

On the other hand, Shannon Phillips, the former Starbucks regional manager who said she was unfairly punished for the incident with Nelson and Robinson, sued Starbucks and got $25.6 million. Phillips' lawyer also indicated that she may seek $3 million from Starbucks for lost pay and roughly $1 million for lawyer fees.

It appears that Phillips had a strong and reasonable case and should be reasonably compensated. **However, note that she did not dabble in one-dollar bills.** Okay. Nelson and Robinson had an undisclosed settlement with Starbucks, but I doubt it was within the vicinity of $26 million.

The Black, abused beauty of Songs of Solomon does not fully understand the power of money. Robinson was quoted as saying the best way to see change is not to reach for "a right-now thing that's good for right now" but to work for "true change over time." He is absolutely right - but what long-lasting change can anyone do with a $200,000 grant?

A Better Long-lasting Change

Century Foundation, a liberal think tank, showed that 68 years after the U.S. Supreme Court issued the Brown vs. Board of Education ruling, schools segregated by race were inherently unequal. The area comprising Philadelphia and Delaware County is the most segregated in the country for Latino students and ranks ninth for Black-White segregation.

"This segregation results in the inequity of funding for schools due to a heavy reliance on property taxes," said Zahava Stadler of the national think tank Education Trust which studies desegregation. "Wealthier communities are always incentivized to keep the walls up around districts to keep local dollars in and high needs students out," Stadler said. "This is especially true in a state like Pennsylvania, which has very little policy governing those local dollars." Philadelphia spends less per student than most of the surrounding districts, she noted, even though its students — most low-income students of color — generally have more needs. [27]

If Nelson and Robinson had sued the city for $26 million (instead of a Mickey Mouse $200,000) they could have funded the schools where "low-income students of color" with unmet greater needs attend.

Strangle Oppressive Systems

As important as it is for Black people to have money for their protection, it is equally vital to withhold it for the same. Oppressive systems will treat you fairly, if not with love, when you withhold your resources because, like I said, money is power. The '55 - '56 Montgomery bus boycott by African Americans convincingly illustrates this point.

The Montgomery bus boycott began when Rosa Parks, sitting in the "colored" section of the bus, was ordered to give her seat to a White passenger. She refused and was arrested, fined $10 and another $4 for court costs.[28]

The Black leaders and commuters of Montgomery began a boycott of Montgomery City Lines in December 1955. Since over 70% of the city's bus patrons were African American, a one-day boycott of 90% success was a sledgehammer blow to the bus company.

The Montgomery Improvement Association (MIA) challenged the constitutionality of the city busing laws. On June 5, 1956, a three-judge U.S. District Court ruled 2-1 that segregation on public buses was unconstitutional. However, the city of Montgomery appealed the U.S. District Court decision to the U.S. Supreme Court and continued to practice segregation on city busing.

For nearly a year, the "separate but equal" (1896 US Supreme Court ruling) Black commuters walked and carpooled to work and wherever they had to go. The Montgomery buses were virtually empty, although some African Americans had to walk as many as eight miles daily.

Montgomery City Lines lost 30,000 to 40,000 bus fares each day during the seven-month boycott but still would not reverse their contemptuous disregard for Black people. Instead, the local police harassed Martin Luther King, Jr., other MIA leaders and carpool drivers, whom they arrested for petty traffic violations.[29] Montgomery's White population was not to be outdone by the police because they vented their anger against peaceful Black people walking for the right to be treated as "men" and bombed the homes of Edgar Nixon and Dr. King.[30]

Don't forget that in White American's consciousness, Black people were not "men" "created equal" "by *their* Creator with certain unalienable Rights," such as "Life, Liberty and the pursuit of Happiness." Why would they have any regard for the U.S. District Court ruling that segregation on public transportation was unconstitutional?

Despite the harassment, threats and violence, the boycott remained over 90% successful. The company reluctantly desegregated its buses only after November 13, 1956, when the Supreme Court ruled Alabama's bus segregation laws unconstitutional.

Do you think the 1956 U.S. Supreme Court ruling ending segregation on public transport in Montgomery signalled a sudden blossoming of love and sacred regard in the heart of the White Power Structure for the Black citizens?

The U.S. Supreme Court based its decision on the 14th Amendment. But consider this: The 14th Amendment, which guarantees "citizenship to all persons born or naturalized in the United States, including formerly enslaved people, and guaranteed all citizens "equal protection of the laws," was passed by Congress on June 13, 1866 and ratified on July 9, 1868. This means that for almost 90 years, no one in law enforcement, the legal system or the judiciary was bothered about a large percentage of their citizens who were not equally protected under the law!

Twenty-eight years after the ratification of the 14th Amendment, Homer Plessy, a Black man (actually, he was half White) who boarded a whites-only car in Louisiana and was detained, challenged the state law that required separate facilities for Whites and Blacks. The U.S. Supreme Court upheld the legality of segregation in 1896 under the "separate but equal" doctrine.[31]

In March 1955, nine months before Rosa Parks' act of defiance, 15-year-old Claudette Colvin refused to give up her seat to a White passenger on a Montgomery, Alabama bus. The White female passenger could have sat beside Colvin, but she would not sit beside a creature that was not classified among "men."

At the next stop, there was a police squad car waiting. Two policemen boarded the bus and confronted Colvin, but she still would not cave.

"They knocked my books out of my lap, and one of them grabbed my arm. I don't know how I got off that bus, but the other students said they manhandled me off the bus and put me in the squad car."

The cops took the 15-year-old to an adult jail instead of a juvenile detention centre. The jail cell was small, with nothing but a broken sink and a cot without a mattress. "I was scared, and it was really, really frightening," Colvin recounted. "It was like those Western movies where they put the bandit in the jail cell, and you could hear the keys. I can still vividly hear the click of those keys."[32]

Years before the bus boycott, Dexter Avenue minister, Vernon Johns, challenged the segregated bus system. Then there were Susie McDonald, Mary Louise Smith and other women who were also arrested for resisting the same injustice. [33]

And yet, there was always the 14th Amendment.

So, do you think the 1956 U.S. Supreme Court ruling signalled America's newfound love for Black people? No! Segregation continued in other spaces such as schools and restaurants. In Montgomery, while the buses were integrated the city maintained segregated bus stops. Integration was met with violent resistance such as snipers firing into buses.[34] Schools were segregated up until the 1970s! Whatever progress was made in the desegregation of schools has been steadily eroded throughout the 1990s and into the 2000s.[35]

The 1956 U.S. Supreme Court ruling had nothing to do with principle, love or the milk of human kindness but was a result of the Black citizens of Alabama withholding their substance, their power, their money. If the Montgomery bus system was not on the verge of financial collapse, the demise of segregation would have taken another decade, if not longer.

It is just like I said. No other race is obligated to treat Black people fairly, respectfully, or as equals. The athlete in last place must exert himself to beat the one leading the pack. It would be futile for him to bemoan his competitor's lead, or the foul committed against him in the first lap of the race. When the athlete in last place overtakes his competitors who tried to trip him up, he will still be disliked, but that won't matter when he stands elevated and triumphant on the dial in first place.

Black people must follow the example of the Montgomery bus boycott and strangle people, organizations, politicians and systems that refuse to treat them as "men," "equal under the law," and made by *their* Creator's hand.

Following Governor DeSantis' latest assault on Black Floridians, Alpha Phi Alpha Fraternity, Inc. announced it would not hold its 2025 general convention in Orlando. Willis L. Lonzer III, the fraternity's general president, said the move will cost the greater Orlando area $4.6 million in revenue.[36] However, in an interview with Roland Martin at the Alpha Phi Alpha National Convention in Dallas, Texas, he speculated that the loss could be closer to $10 million.[37]

"We will not spend our money where Black people and other marginalized communities are continuously harmed by policies at the highest level of government," Lonzer told The Hill.

The Alpha Phi Alpha Fraternity, Inc. is also spearheading an "Inter-organizational Coalition" to respond to Florida's "slew of damaging and discriminatory laws regarding demonstrations, voting rights, public schools and diversity, equity and inclusion."

In the interview with Martin, Lonzer said, "In the new Jim Crow, we have to use . . . economic tactics and be willing to sometimes go into the fire and stand close to lift up the community. . .."

Martin reminded his viewers that Dr. Martin Luther King, Jr. called upon Black Americans to "redistribute the pain" – not to spend their dollars at places that do not reciprocate. "America understands the money," Martin said. "Our best way to send a message is to speak with our dollar. Either we are giving it or withdrawing it."

If America did not "understand the money," do you think the US Supreme Court would have ruled to end busing segregation in Montgomery in 1965? Recall that the same court, from its inception, made adverse rulings against their Black citizens when they were most powerless right after the so-called abolition of slavery. The modern US Supreme Court, which is bought and paid for by billionaires, is once again demonstrating an inclination to strip women and minorities of their rights and any initiative to level the discriminatory playing field established by the Founding Fathers, slave masters and the instigators of Jim Crow laws.

Black people, the poor, women and minority groups will all be thrown back to the dark days of oppression, suppression, injustice, and unmitigated violence if they do not financially strangle their oppressors.

Have a Warrior Mindset

In 2022, when images of swastika, the N-word, antisemitic and anti-LGBTQ graffiti were found on lockers, bathroom stalls, and interior doors at public schools in Newmarket and Toronto schools, the response of the authorities and the people affected was weak and emotional.

Michael Levitt, president and CEO of The Friends of Simon Wiesenthal Center (FSWC), a non-profit human rights organization committed to countering racism and antisemitism, said of those racist events, "We are saddened."

Cecil Roach, associate director of education for the York Region District School Board, said, "We are disappointed that these incidents have occurred in our schools, and we recognize and apologize for the hurt and harm that such incidents can cause."[38]

Students at the Etobicoke School for the Arts mourned out expressions such as "deeply disturbing," "I was so hurt," "feel hurt and not accepted," and "made me feel scared and terrified." [39]

In 2019, CNN anchor Victor Blackwell broke down on camera and shed tears, or came very close to it, after he gave a stalwart response to then President Trump's characterization of his hometown district as "a disgusting, rat and rodent-infested mess."[40]

I liked that Blackwell illustrated the many times racist Trump used the word "infested" to describe Black countries and Black people but disapproved of his weak, emotional, tearful disintegration in the middle of his otherwise assertive disapproval of Trump's assault on Blackness.

People like Trump and those who left racist scrawls on walls want to hurt, harm, frighten, break down and make Black people feel excluded from society. Why give them that satisfaction by responding weakly and pitifully? Black people must respond to racism with a warrior mindset.

In *The 33 Strategies of War*, Robert Greene maintains that we are always in a state of war because the world has become "increasingly competitive and nasty." We face opponents who will do almost anything to gain an edge.[41] How should we react when people go to war with us?

Greene says it is counterproductive to deny or repress your "aggressive responses." Neither should you melt into emotional states like fear, anger, impatience, overconfidence and love and affection.

You must see your emotional responses to events as a kind of disease that must be remedied. Fear will make you overestimate the enemy and act too defensively. Anger and impatience will draw you into rash actions that will cut off your options. Overconfidence ... will make you go too far. Love and affection will blind you to the treacherous manoeuvres of those apparently on your side. Even the subtlest gradations of these emotions can color the way you look at events. The only remedy is to be aware that the pull of emotion is inevitable, to notice it when it is happening and to compensate for it.

Like Victor Blackwell on CNN, the students and the authorities in Toronto, Black people often become emotional whenever they are unfairly treated. There are many instances of Black people shouting at or physically resisting corrupt police officers who try to detain and arrest them, although they committed no crime. Some people flee in fear and get shot in the back, often with no retribution to such law enforcement officers.

Then there are those Black people, like my mother, who said anything black no good but regarded white skin and a straight nose as beauty, who express more love and affection for the very people and systems that oppress them. They love their own less.

As noble as the ideals of peace and cooperation are, what is more practical is the knowledge of how to deal with conflict and the daily battles you face, Greene writes. "If there is an ideal to aim for, it should be that of a strategic warrior. The man or woman who manages difficult situations and people through deft and intelligent Maneuvers. . ... All successes and failures in life can be traced to how well or how badly we deal with inevitable conflicts that confront us in Society."

So, Black people, to stand before a TV camera and say you are terrified, fearful and hurt or break down because some subhuman scrawled anti-Black nonsense on the walls of your school or use demeaning verbiage to describe you is to wallow in defeat. You are not a warrior, and only warriors can survive the onslaught of the aggressors.

One of the students who expressed hurt and fear over the racist graffiti was assertive for a few seconds when she said the person who did that was a "terrible person." That motif, with no trace of fear or hurt, should have been her assertive rant the entire time she stood before the camera. When the authorities respond to racism, they should belittle the uncivilized behaviour of the offenders, not wallow in pitiful, regretful tones.

I submit that if no one was caught scrawling those racist epithets, they should have been taken down without a word said about them. That would have deflated the racists and frustrated their aims. But publicly mourning them in the media energized and affirmed the culprits. However, if someone was caught in their disparaging acts, they should be dealt with severely, including a ferocious social media publication of their faces and crimes.

It is just as *The 33 Strategies of War* says: Rather than getting emotional, see things exactly as they are and deal with them thus.

Black people, you need a warrior mindset if the Black Beauty is to be unveiled in this colorless world.

All for One and One for All

The Black damsel of Song of Solomon often stands alone, defenceless, exposed and unprotected like a straggler prey.

One day, I went on a stroll through my neighbourhood, which comprises people of Indian extraction. It slowly dawned on me that all real estate agents (depicted on signs), construction workers, technicians, or service providers I saw were Indians.

Perhaps you've eaten at restaurants and shopped at supermarkets where every last employee is Asian. Chinese, Indians and Filipinos are tight-knit communities. They live, work, play together and circulate their wealth within their community. When I was a boy, hitchhiking to and from school when I had no bus fare, a Black Jamaican or a White tourist would give me a ride, but never a Jamaican Chinese. Yet our motto is "Out of Many, One People."

On the other hand, Black people embrace every other race more than their own. Black people are comfortable with a White real estate agent, spend their hard-earned dollars at the Asian supermarket and hire an Indian service provider to fix their furnaces. They often bypass the Black entrepreneur to collaborate with someone outside their immediate community or racial group.

I should hasten to say that I can only speak from my observations and experience. I do not possess comprehensive first-hand knowledge of the attitude of Black people from other countries and contexts beyond the one that nurtured me. But I think I can say that generally, Black people are more splintered than any other group of humans.

If Black people are to run to the head of the herd or rise from the bottom of the barrel to the top, they must stand in solidarity and support each other within a united group. The group must support the one, and the one has to be loyal to the group.

This is not a call for Black people to hate other people. Although much of the disunity and self-hate that exist among Black people can be traced back to enslavement, colonization, and centuries of conditioned disparagement, it is also true that their love and sacred regard for other races come from their humanity, love and dignity, virtues the people who hate Blackness while claiming a superior and more civilized perch, do not have.

Black people are like the straggler baby calf, which the beast of prey devours.

"I am a little upset right now," Bishop Tony Caldwell said into the camera. "The reason I'm upset is because we got four young ladies that have been murdered within the last week here off 85th and Prospect. We got a serial killer again. And ain't nobody saying nothing. The media is not covering it. We got three young ladies that are missing. Ain't nobody saying a word. What is the problem? Why? Why can't we get some cooperation? Where's our community leaders? Where's our activists? Where's our public officials? Where's our police department? Where is those folks at in President Gardens? Come on, now. We need to start knocking doors. We need to start making sure that this is brought to the light. We cannot continue to let this happen."[42]

After Caldwell's video went viral in September of 2022, the Kansas City Police Department said there was "no basis to support this rumor"[43] and "to date, we have had no reports of missing black females from that area."[44]

But on October 7, Lisa Johnson heard a faint knock on her door and a desperate cry, "Help me!" A 22-year-old Black woman, garbed in a short S&M dress made from black plastic, with duct tape and a homemade shock collar around her neck, stood cowering at her door. She told Johnson she had escaped from a White man who held her captive in his basement for nearly a month. He had whipped, tortured and raped her repeatedly.[45]

Timothy Marrion Haslett, Jr. was arrested on October 7 and charged with first-degree rape, first-degree kidnapping and second-degree assault. The escaped Black woman alleged Haslett killed two of her friends, but no bodies were found.

This unfortunate incident in Kansas City, Missouri, illustrates the necessity of Black people rolling as one coherent unit to defeat the predatory systems that gobble up their individual comrades.

In a case like this, a large group of people acting as one should have reported the mysterious disappearance of their citizens. The said group should have used a massive social media club to smash through the police's disinterest in the community's concern. There should have been billboards along the highways displaying the faces of suspected victims and law enforcement's response that it was all a rumor. There should have been publicized appeals to the leaders of the different strata of government - Councilor, Mayor, Governor, Senator and President.

Of course, the group would need professional guidance. Hopefully, there would be lawyers, social workers, counsellors, educators, and professionals of every stripe already members of the all-for-one group. If not, they would need to reach out to similar groups in adjourning towns and cities and to already established civil rights organizations like the NAACP.

Money is crucial in the fight against this predatory system, but we live in the age of GoFundMe. Every Black person or people of any race who value social justice, equality and love for their neighbour would give generously to such an appeal. Remember, Black peope, all night prayer meetings are pointless if you have no money. A fundraising page collected more than £44,000 for two Metropolitan Police officers sacked over the stop and search of two black Olympic athletes, Dos Santos and Bianca Williams[46] (see pp. XXVI - XXVII).

Whenever the authorities fail the citizens, as they did in Kansas City, Missouri, they should go after them with a massive class action suit where possible and, quickly vote them out of office or have them fired.

If the Black damsel continues to walk alone, she will always be set upon, denied, decried, detested, dehumanized and destroyed. Jordan Neely hungry and frustrated, was a straggler. He fell, a helpless prey to a predator. Where was his family? Where was the Black community?

The Black Beauty of Song of Solomon can only thrive and prosper if she runs with her pack.

Vote! Vote! Vote!

"Vote. Vote. Vote," said President Biden in his usual lackluster, lack of enthusiastic, fire-in-the-belly mannerism. He never says for whom the American people should vote, which makes no sense to me, at least. But perhaps he would transgress the Hatch Act if he said, "Vote for Democrats."

"Voting is a waste of time," one of my friends told me. "It doesn't matter which party is in power; my life is still a struggle."

I largely agree with my friend. Citizens mainly elevate the worst among them as leaders while they demonize or assassinate the few good ones they have had. The people generally end up with leaders who are religious or political dictators who crush and abuse the populace. Leaders often enrich themselves, their friends and the wealthy. At the same time, they deny the working class a living wage, undercut their medical care, postpone their retirement funds, and shut down the government, which leaves the citizens without income and vital services. At the same time, the political leaders who cripple the government still draw down their salaries. They also start wars and local conflicts that leave tens of thousands, if not millions, of their citizens dead, deformed, crippled and poverty stricken.

However, unlike my friend, who never votes, I do. I live in a fantastic country, Canada. In my 27 years as a Canadian citizen, I have never waited more than twenty minutes to vote, unlike Hervis Rogers, who waited six or more hours to vote and nearly got two 20-year life sentences![47]

I know no government is perfect, but I cast my vote for what I perceive to be the lesser of two (or more) evils.

If no one else votes, the Black sister of Song of Solomon must vote. That was not a privilege willingly granted to her, and she has always suffered from rigged voting systems. It was a broken voting system that gave South Africa its "racist system of oppression that lasted for over 40 years," Owen Winter, Co-founder of Make Votes Matter, student and activist, wrote for HuffPost UK.

Most White South Africans did not vote for the National Party in 1948. Only 37% voted for a divided South African society, and although the National Party received fewer votes than the United Party, the National Party won most of the seats because of the "distorting effect of the First Past the Post (FPTP) voting system."

In ten general elections, the pro-apartheid National Party won a majority every single time, sometimes with "upwards of 80% of the seats, despite receiving less than 50% three times and never getting more than 65% of the vote."[48] The consequence of this rigged voting system was a brutal and merciless beat down of the Black but beautiful woman for decades.

The Struggle for Voting Rights

The Opelousas, massacre of September 1868 lasted for two weeks, during which time African-American families were killed in their homes, shot in public, and chased down by vigilante groups. By the end of the two weeks, an estimated 250 people, the vast majority of them African-Americans, were killed.[49]

What precipitated the Opelousas murderous rage? The Louisiana Constitution of 1868 established a bill of rights which gave Black men the right to vote, established an integrated public education system throughout the state, and gave Blacks guaranteed access to public accommodations.[50] That's it. It was not because a Black man raped a White woman. From that time in America, it was hell to pay for Black citizens who dared to vote or claimed the equality the Founding Fathers declared was given to "men."

The Colfax, Louisiana massacre took place in April 1873. A mob of more than 150 White men, mainly comprised of former Confederate soldiers, members of the Ku Klux Klan and the White League, surrounded a courthouse filled with an all-Black militia that was attempting to prevent the local Democrats from seizing control of the Grant Parish regional government, which was almost evenly split between Black and White citizens.

On April 13, the two forces fired at each other until the Black defenders were forced to surrender. But the White mob murdered many of the Black men, shooting some and hanging others. Records show that the massacre resulted in the deaths of three White men and an estimated 60 to 150 African-Americans.[51]

The Wilmington insurrection of November 10, 1898 (or a coup d'état) resulted in a massacre carried out by a mob of 2,000 white supremacists in Wilmington, North Carolina. The white press in Wilmington originally described the event as a race riot caused by Black people, a DeSantis-like approach to later massacres committed against Black people who were making economic progress.[52]

The insurrectionists overthrew the legitimately elected local Fusionist biracial government in Wilmington. They expelled opposition Black and White political leaders from the city, destroyed the property and businesses of Black citizens built up since the American Civil War, including the only black newspaper in the city, and killed an estimated 60 to more than 300 people.[53]

On May 31, 1921, and into the next day, a White mob destroyed the Black Greenwood District (Black Wall Street) in the single-most horrific incident of racial terrorism since slavery. An estimated 300 people were killed within the district's 35 square blocks. The marauding mob burned to the ground more than 1,200 homes, at least 60 businesses, dozens of churches, a school, a hospital and a public library.[54]

Rev. George Lee of Belzoni in Humphreys County, Mississippi, was one of the first Black people registered to vote. He used his pulpit and his printing press to urge other Black people to vote. Of course, he was threatened and White officials offered him protection on the condition he end his voter registration efforts. Lee refused and was murdered on May 7, 1955.

On August 23, 1955, in Brookhaven, Mississippi, Lamar Smith who had organized Black citizens to vote in a recent election, was fatally shot on the courthouse lawn by a White man in broad daylight while dozens of people watched. The killer was never indicted because no one would admit they saw a White man shoot a Black man.

Herbert Lee of Liberty, Mississippi worked with civil rights leader Bob Moses to help register Black voters. On September 25, 1961, he was killed by a state legislator who claimed self-defence (you know, like stand your ground) and was never arrested. Louis Allen, a Black man who witnessed the murder, was later also killed.[55]

About 600 activists set out in Alabama to march from Selma to Montgomery, on March 7, 1965, to protest for Black voting rights. When the marchers reached the Edmund Pettus Bridge in Selma, they were attacked by White state troopers, who tear gassed and bludgeoned them with billy clubs.[56]

On June 25, 2013, the Supreme Court, the judicial body with a long, sordid history of dehumanizing Black Americans and prohibiting their rights, weakened the Voting Rights Act (VRA) of 1965 by freeing jurisdictions with histories of racial discrimination in voting from having to gain federal approval, called "preclearance," before changing their election laws. An avalanche of voting rights restriction laws immediately followed the court's ruling[57] from then till the present.

As of October 2023, at least 14 states have enacted laws making it harder to vote. Some of these laws are described as "restrictive" and others have set the stage for "election interference schemes" in 2024. A restrictive legislation contains one or more provisions that would make it harder for eligible Americans to register, stay on the voter rolls, or vote as compared to existing state law. A legislation is categorized as election interference if it either threatens the people and processes that make elections work or increases opportunities for partisan interference in election results or administration.[58]

On January 6, 2021, a Trump loving and worshipping, Confederate flag-waving mob laid siege to the US Capitol. They, like their 1898 Wilmington insurrectionist murderous forefathers sought to overturn Biden's victory in the November election. Their foreparents expelled opposition Black and White political leaders, destroyed the property and businesses of Black citizens, and killed an estimated 60 or more people. But fortunately, although they erected a gallows and chanted "Hang Mike Pence," threatened to drag politicians through the streets[59] and bludgeoned police officers, they failed where their forefathers succeeded, to overthrow the democratically elected government. This violent assault was nothing more than a White backlash to racial equality, given the decisive role that Black voters played in the 2020 election.[60]

Black Beauty Losing Interest in Voting

On September 6, 2023, ordained Baptist minister and former Arkansas Republican governor Mike Huckabee said on his Trinity Broadcasting Network (TBN) that the current president of the United States, Joe Biden, was using police agencies to arrest his opponents for "made-up crimes" in an attempt to discredit them. He prophesied that if Biden used this tactic to prevent Trump from running or winning in 2024, "it is going to be the last American election that will be decided by ballots rather than bullets."[61]

It is against contexts like the Huckabee promise of violence that we hear many reports of Black Americans cooling on Biden and the Democratic party. A November 28, 2023, Politico article carried an exhaustive article on why Black voters are less than enthusiastic about supporting the party they have backed for decades. Below, I have itemized them.

1. A gulf between what Biden has accomplished in his first term and what voters give him credit for.
2. Several polls in six battleground states found support for Trump among the Black electorate had bumped up from 22 to 26 percent.
3. Some Black people saw Trump's name on stimulus checks in 2020 and think that means something was done for the Black community.
4. The Black population is no longer homogeneous. Individuals have different needs. Black businesspeople, for example, have concerns that go beyond racial issues.
5. Some Black voters feel that the Democratic Party has failed them. The polls demonstrate that.
6. Turnout among Black voters is falling.
7. Black voters complain that they have been voting for Democrats for 50 to 60 years; they don't have much to show for it.
8. Younger Black voters, Black men and non-college-educated Black voters have lost interest, which has been exacerbated by COVID-19, inflationary pressures, and the unemployment shocks felt in communities of color more than in other communities.
9. Biden administration's focus on the wars in Ukraine and Israel means

those countries get billions of dollars in aid while they get nothing and are suffering and struggling to keep a roof over their heads, to have food on the table for their kids, to buy a house.

10. People are very disappointed because Democrats have not done as much as they wanted concerning voting rights and police reform.[62]

The concerns expressed above are legitimate. Historically, Black people have been used, abused, dismissed, discounted, cheated, red lined and disenfranchised.

But the truth is Black, beautiful woman, the struggle never ends because evil is the default reality. You will never advance from the last place by surrendering. You will never climb from the bottom of the barrel by disengaging. Your disinterest will not build on the successes and battles won by your ancestors, who frequently gave up their lives for the right to vote and to secure a better future for you.

There has never been a time when you did not suffer and struggle, and there can never be a time when you do not have to fight for your and your children's advancement and well-being.

If you think Biden and the Democrats have not served you well, just wait till you fall into the clutches of the likes of Huckabee, who wants bullets, not ballots to decide subsequent elections, DeSantis, who intends to scrub Black history from the classrooms, Trump, who wants to steal your votes and declare you a terrorist if you dare assert that Black lives matter, and Nikki Haley who refuses to say the civil war was instigated by people who wanted to keep your great, great, great grandparents as slaves.

The struggle will never end because even if your standard of living, civil rights, equal protection under the law, and economic situation improve one hundred percent, you will still have to struggle to keep it.

Disengage from the political process or vote for a third party, and then I will ask you like Trump did, "What do you have to lose?"

It's been reported that Black Americans, particularly the younger generation, are upset with Joe Biden for his unwavering support of Israel as they level Gaza and kill thousands of civilians. Black people's sympathy for suffering and helpless groups is reflective because they know what it means to suffer, and they, unlike their mother's children, (Song of Solomon 1:6) love every race. But I want Black Americans to remember White apartheid South Africa, which divided the population into Blacks, Colored, Whites, and Asians. Which group was at the bottom of the barrel? Black people.

When the rubber hits the road, the world will treat Palestinians, whom they

hate and refuse to grant statehood, better than you if they are forced to choose between you two.

Do you remember how Africans were treated at the border of Ukraine and Poland after Russia invaded Ukraine? There was a hierarchy of refugees: Ukrainians first, Indians second, Africans last. (see the Introduction, Being Black Ukrainian Refugees).

Black people are not treated any better in that part of the world now under Israeli bombardment. Isra El-Beshir, an Arab-American of African descent, said the first time she came "face-to-face" with the word 'abeed' was from the "mouths of Arabs and Muslims."[63]

"Abeed" is an Arabic word which means "servant" or "slave," and dates back to the Arab slave trade. It is often used as an ethnic slur for Black people.[64]

"Here they say, 'We aren't racist,' that we are all Arabs and Muslims until they see my skin," says a Sudanese refugee in Amman, Jordan. "Then they call me 'slave.'"[65]

The African Quarter in Old Jerusalem is called "habs Al-abeed," a derogatory Arabic term meaning "slaves' prison."[66]

Amir Al-Azrak wrote in an article, "Uncovering anti-Blackness in the Arab world," that Black Arabs are underrepresented and largely invisible in "white" Arab-dominated countries and "excluded from political, academic, artistic and religious institutions." The negative image of Black people in Arab cultures emerged from three streams:

1. The controversial anthropological conception that culture — including religion, language, laws and values — defines what it means to be human.
2. The Biblical narrative of Noah cursing his son Ham's descendants — considered darker-skinned — with servitude.
3. The Greek philosopher Ptolemy's theory of the seven climes posits that a person's geographical location determined their race, as the proximity to the sun "prepared" humans in ways ranging from raw and undercooked to burnt and overcooked.[67]

Black Iraqis (an estimated 1.5 to 2 million) are the descendants of immigrants and enslaved people from Sub-Saharan and East Africa. Their presence in Iraq dates back to the Abbasid empire (566–653 CE).[68]

Slavery was officially abolished in the nineteenth century and is supported by Article 14 of the 2005 Iraqi Constitution, which stipulates "equality without racial-based discrimination." Yet Black Iraqis still endure systematic discrimination, marginalization, and structural racism "embedded in historical stigmas and xenophobia against black people in the Arab world," activists report.

The variety of ethnic, religious, and cultural communities can easily fade in the crowd due to similar physical features but not so Black Iraqis who are the "visible others who cannot be unseen or concealed. Hundreds of invisible cultural and social lines segregate, ostracize Black Iraqis, and reaffirm their otherness in urban design, tribal allegiances, and marriage arrangements."[69]

"Palestinians are racist to Black people," said a Palestinian young lady who went viral on the Internet. "And if you look around, it's Black people that are out there advocating for the rights of Palestinians. This should be a lesson for Palestinians and the Arab community in general. So, stop being racist towards Black people. Because when shit hits the fan, it's Black people that come out, and they fight for the oppressed. . ..

"Look within yourself. You as an Arab, you as a Palestinian, you in your own family, how many of you are racist to people that are black Palestinians? Even broader Muslim communities, from Pakistani communities to Bangladeshi communities, Moroccan, Libyan communities, and Gulf communities. How many people say we are Muslims, and in the same breath, they mistreat other Muslims because of their skin color or their country of origin?"[70]

I stumbled upon two YouTube videos on countries Black people never want to visit. The list includes Spain, Italy, Morocco, Cuba, Brazil, Mexico, Colombia, Switzerland,[71] Greece, Germany, Russia, and India.[72] I excluded the USA, France, Ukraine and China since I already detailed or mentioned Black people's experiences in those countries.

In these countries, Black people are subjected to unwarranted I. D. checks and followed around stores. Racist citizens bellow racial chants and slurs such as monkeys, cannibals, and pigs at Black people. People clutch their handbags when a Black person walks by.

Black people are subjected to verbal and physical abuse. They are questioned about their origin even when they live in African countries.

People report them to the police for entering their own apartments, swimming in a public pool, sitting in a hotel lobby, or arriving to work early.

Police shoot unarmed Black people in the back for unjustifiable reasons, and often, routine stops end up being fatal for Black motorists.

Governments fail to provide access to education, health care, and employment for their Black citizens, and they disproportionately have lower representation in government.

Upward mobility and housing are restricted to Black citizens, and they are ignored by service providers. In some cases, their educational achievements are downgraded.

So, Black, beautiful woman, feel the pain for Palestinians and other suffering people as much as you like because that is your nature. But if you disengage from your political context, you will fall into the clutches of insurrectionists, dictators, and people who want to execute Judges and police officers who uphold the law. You will have to consume a lifetime extracting yourself and your children from under a gerrymandered political and legal system, which will inflict upon you the same wrath that makes you cry for the suffering and helpless.

Do you think the people who subject you to extreme Karennicity, call the police on you when you are just being a Black person, arrest and shoot your little boys and girls and your unarmed men in the back, dehumanize you, falsely arrest and jail you for decades for crimes you did not commit, pass restrictive voting laws that also outlaws giving water to people waiting for eight hours to vote and gerrymander voting districts are any less lethal than their ancestors who massacred your forefathers, burned down their towns, shot them down and hanged them, overthrew a legitimately elected bi-racial government, and attacked marchers on the Edmund Pettus Bridge in Selma? Well then, stay home and don't vote.

Support Law Enforcement

Rev. Al Sharpton has been the "leading eulogist for Black victims of police violence."[73] So says Eliza Fawcett of *The New York Times*. He has eulogized or delivered remarks at the funeral of:

1. Tyre Nichols who died three days after a January 7, 2023, traffic stop that turned into a brutal and eventually fatal assault by five officers.
2. George Floyd, whose 2020 death in Minneapolis sparked national protests.
3. Daunte Wright, who was shot by a police officer during a traffic stop outside Minneapolis in 2021.
4. Eric Garner, whose dying words on a New York City Street were, "I can't breathe."
5. Alton Sterling, who was shot by the police in Baton Rouge, La., in 2016.
6. And much older cases, including the 1997 death of William J. Whitfield, an unarmed man shot on Christmas Day in Brooklyn.

I do not know if the Reverend attended or participated in the memorial service of a police officer killed in the line of duty. If he has not done so yet, he should at least express a desire to do so in the future.

However, the crux at issue here is not that Rev. Sharpton specifically should attend funerals of slain police officers but that the Black community, starting with the leaders, should express sympathy for slain officers and lend support to their grieving families.

The Ontario Police Memorial Foundation website lists fifteen Constables killed in the line of duty between 2010 and 2023.[74] Did local Black Lives Matter representatives attend any of those services, express public sympathy and support for law officers, and affirm their desire to keep law and order in their communities?

I can fully understand if Black people bark at the suggestion to support slain police officers. I would not expect them to show any kind of support or express sympathy for corrupt cops slain on the job. However, the support I am advocating in this context is also part of the struggle to improve the lot of the Black damsel.

The International Association of Chiefs of Police (IACP) has an excellent article on how citizens can engage with law enforcement. A nine-item summary follows.

1. Serve on a Citizen Advisory Board
2. Participate in a Citizens Police Academy
3. Compliment or Complain
4. Participate in Neighborhood Watch
5. Participate in Police Initiatives, Projects, and Programs
6. Attend Community Meetings
7. Participate in Law Enforcement Surveys
8. Get Your Kids Involved
9. Follow Your Police Department on social media[75]

Show Police Officers Respect

When someone shows you respect and courteously interacts with you, doesn't it feel like they contributed to your sense of well-being? The person who treats you respectfully may not love you, but you may feel admired and valued, and at the least, you can appreciate being treated with esteem and honour.

Thoughtfulness and gracefulness improve interaction between two or more people. Such graces lend to better communication and collaboration, reduce stress, problems, and conflicts, and positively energize the atmosphere. People will trust you, respect you in turn, and be eager to go the extra mile for you.[76]

Maya Angelou is reputed to have said, "People will forget what you said, people will forget what you did, but people will never forget how you made them feel." We always leave a lasting impression, positive or negative, on the people we meet.

I saw a YouTube video of a police officer responding to a citizen's call about a neighbour causing some trouble. When the officer arrived, he saw a random Black man standing at his gate. He emerged from his squad car and addressed this man as if he were the suspect. The man responded to the police officer rudely and condescendingly. The officer escalated the interaction, although the citizen who had made the 911 call shouted to the officer that the random man standing at his gate was not the guilty party!

As is the standard practice in the United States, a White police officer treated the first Black person he saw as a criminal. The offending officer eventually tased, arrested, and handcuffed the innocent man with the citizen who had called for help standing nearby. He also lied and said he heard the man say the innocent Black man was the offender.

However, on this occasion, the barbarity, ignorance, lies and injustice this corrupt cop inflicted on a blameless Black man is not my focus. I wish to highlight the demeaning and disrespectful reply the citizen gave the officer when he first addressed him.

Indeed, the honourable and chaste citizen, who was just chilling at his gate, had the right to the First Amendment and cannot be justly criticized for insulting the officer who no doubt only saw the color of his skin, which he immediately assumed fit the description of the perpetrator. However, this citizen, like thousands of others, was disrespectful to the officer simply because he was in the right.

What if this man had responded with a sunny, "Good evening, officer. Welcome to our neighbourhood. How may I be of help?" The officer may have softened immediately, but if he did not and continued to press his accusatory assault on the man, he could have politely said, "Oh no, officer. I think it's my neighbour across the road who called you," or "I am sorry officer, but I don't know what you are talking about."

Now, it's possible the corrupt officer would have still treated the man as a criminal and demanded to see his ID. When you're Black, there is no guarantee. Ask Micah Washington. A female cop demanded to see his ID when all he was doing was changing a punctured tire by the side of the road. Even after he produced his ID, he was handcuffed and tased several times.[77] If you are Black, showing your ID is no guarantee that you will be treated fairly and justly. President Obama produced his birth certificate, and they said it was fake!

However, respect and politeness may lower the temperature. You could argue convincingly that the police do not deserve respect because respect is earned, not demanded or acquired through force or doled out to public servants who are grossly and overtly corrupt and criminal. But respect can go a long way to smooth over challenging and uncomfortable encounters.

If a society does not respect law enforcement, there can be no order, safety, security, direction, peace and guidance. Disrespect for law enforcement results in criminal and social chaos. Danger lurks in every corner where law officers can get no respect. And where there is disorder and danger, the Black damsel will be blamed for it (like they blamed her for the January 6 insurrection) and is primarily at risk.

Generally speaking, people in modern society are crude, rough, aggressive, raw, forceful, pushy, bossy and domineering. If the Black, beautiful woman were always kind, considerate, warm, caring, gracious, thoughtful, polite, considerate and courteous, she could swing the society's coarse and jagged state back to a positive and effervescent atmosphere. Of course, some of her brothers and sisters would still look askance at her because of her black skin, but they would have to work so much harder to abuse her.

Remember the random Black man out for his evening run in chapter 6? He was a veteran who produced his ID, and still, he was handcuffed because he "fit the description." Often, the Police and Karens ask the Black damsel for her ID as if that will absolve her of any criminal suspicion. However, this Black man smiled and acted respectfully and politely in this case. He did not cower or show fear but remained calm and assured. A few other officers pulled up in their cars, and they would have swarmed this innocent man and beat him to death if he had asserted his right not to give his ID, be searched and handcuffed since they did not see him commit a crime. His calm, respectful attitude protected him.

If the Black damsel's brothers and sisters still abused her when she was being respectful, if they attacked her when she was being polite, if they tased her or smashed her face into the windshield or the ground after they handcuffed her, she could, like Micah Washington and the Black mother in chapter 7, sue for hundreds of millions of dollars and use the money to improve her community.

Being respectful and polite to cops, even when they intend to harm you, is not an act of surrender. It is one strategy beautiful Black people must use to fight and defeat a system designed by the Founding Fathers to oppress and abuse them and deny they are "men" created by the "God" they worshipped.

Don't Resist

Officers approached a Black woman and a man sitting at a bus stop by a highway with vehicular traffic roaring back and forth. The afternoon was soft with radiant sunshine, and a blue sky with expansive cotton-candy white clouds lazily hanging just overhead. But the clement weather would soon turn into a dark, foreboding, thunder and lightning experience for the young couple.

"What's up guys? Just hanging out?" one officer said walking up to the couple.

"Just got off a work." Tension laced the young Black man's voice. If you are Black and sitting peacefully at a bus stop by a busy highway and two police officers approach you, it is natural to feel tense.

"Eh?"

"Just got off a work," the young man repeated as he and the woman appeared in one officer's body camera with a second cop creeping up behind them.

"What did we do wrong?" the female asked. Black people know if the police approach them and ask if they are just hanging out they are not there to make friends.

"Well, it smells like you smoking weed." Aaha!

The Black male said something about coming from the store and it sounded like he named the particular store (THCA) they had just come from. The second officer who made his approach from behind eventually sided up to the right of the pair.

"You smoking weed, got more weed?"

"Just coming from the store," the man indicated once more, his lit cannabis product still in his hand.

"I can smell it coming from that," one officer pointed toward the couple.

"We got it from the smoke shop," the woman emphasized with a confident tone as she gesticulated with her right hand which held her lit product.

At this juncture, the police officer who had approached the two from behind reached for the hand of the male and said, "Do me a favor, put your hands behind your back."

"Whooo-whooo! What are you doing," the young woman exclaimed and sprang to her feet, pushing away the officer from her companion. Instantly the other officer grabbed her arm and ordered her to put her hands behind her back. The woman screamed, "Why are you touching me? Stop!" Police body camera showed the woman struggling with and striking the officer.[78]

"Marijuana in that jurisdiction is typically not an arrestable offence," Dr. Richie said on his show, Indisputable.[79] Ah! But if you are Black!

Marijuana is illegal in North Carolina, but sales of certain types of related products are not.[80] The couple got their joint from a smoke shop, so I am assuming they had the legal kind. My research showed that in a cannabis dispensary, consumers can often find "flowers, concentrates, prefilled vape cartridges, edibles, hemp oil, CBD, and more cannabis products."[81] The question that naturally arises, then, is why the two officers treated the Black couple as criminals even after the young woman said they got their products from a smoke shop.

You can get yourself into trouble if you consume, possess, grow or sell illegal Marijuana in that state. Consequences and legal punishments for possessing illegal Marijuana in North Carolina vary on the amount possessed and whether there was intent to distribute the substance. Selling or delivering any amount of Marijuana in the state is considered a felony, as is cultivating it.[82]

Even if the couple apprehended by the two police officers had illegal Marijuana, they were not growing, selling and distributing it. Remember that the consequences and legal punishments vary on the amount possessed and whether there was intent to distribute the substance. It looks like Dr. Richie made a valuable point when he said Marijuana in that jurisdiction is *typically* not an arrestable offence. But the couple was Black, and Black people are easy pickings.

However, having said all of the above, resisting arrest - saying to a police officer, "Why are you touching me? Stop!" or "Don't put your hand on me!" is a brain-dead strategy to employ in your fight against agents of an oppressive system. To begin with, a police officer is invested with credible authority to enforce the law. We all need law enforcement to protect us from criminal elements in the society.

Secondly, you do not have the power, resources, or skills to resist or flee from the police successfully.

Thirdly, many police officers who apprehend Black people are themselves psycho-criminals with a badge and unlimited authority and that includes Black officers like the ones who beat Tyre Nichols to a pulp. Remember, they have qualified immunity, which means they can tase you to death and walk free.

If a police officer orders you to put your hands behind your back or roll over, just do it. There is no guarantee they will not strangle, tase, or fatally shoot you while you are complying, but it is foolish to resist or run.

The Black man was charged with carrying a concealed weapon, and the woman with assaulting a government official. Both were also charged with resisting officers and marijuana possession. However, all of the charges were later dropped.[83] Why were the charges dropped? It was reasonable for the Police to drop the Marijuana charge because that was a minor infraction for which citizens are not typically arrested. If they had kept the charge of assault of a government official, you could understand that, too. If these two Black people, sitting at the bus stop at the end of a back-breaking day of work, smoking legal Marijuana, were as dangerous to society as the two officers who approached them with the predetermined intention to arrest them thought, why drop those charges?

Assumptions make an ass out of you and me, the saying goes, but it is a reasonable assumption that after they had ganged up on the woman and beat her like savage wild dogs, it would have been too tedious to press those charges.

But what if the two Black people had stood up, put their hands behind their Backs with no resistance? The young woman would not have been brutalized, we hope, because there are no guarantees for Black people in police custody. They could snap their spines[84] before they reach the police station. But the Black community could have passionately highlighted the usual bias of the police officers who arrested the couple for an offence for which they do not usually arrest people. All for one and one for all. And if this particular arrest was illegal, they could easily have sued for tens of millions of dollars.

You may disagree with me on this issue, but I hope you see that resisting arrest and telling the Police not to touch you or to let go of you is an ineffective strategy to defeat your oppressors and assert your rights and humanity.

An effective strategy for Black people to use to advance from last place is to unreservedly support law enforcement even as they expose, shame, and sue them for their racist, criminal and abusive behaviour.

Skin Folks and Kinfolks: Know the Difference

In November 1799, Vesey Denmark won the "East-Bay Lottery" and netted a small fortune of $1,500, an amount for which an enslaved person would have to work ten years to accumulate. He bought his freedom with $600 of his jackpot winnings and began to think about emigrating to the English colony of Sierra Leone. But Denmark had married an enslaved woman, and their children remained slaves. Vesey Denmark decided to orchestrate a rebellion, get his children and leave the country.

Denmark planned his escape for nearly four years. He and his followers planned to make their assault at midnight on Sunday, July 14, slay their masters, and sail for Haiti and freedom. But the plot unravelled in June 1822 when two slaves revealed the plan to their owners. Vesey Denmark was captured on June 21 and hanged on July 2, together with five other rebels.[85]

Dr. Claud Anderson (president of PowerNomics Corporation of America, Inc. and The Harvest Institute, Inc, best-selling author, activist and business visionary) said the enslavers used the Meritorious Manumission Act to control the Black enslaved population. He referenced the law passed by Virginia in 1710, which rewarded Blacks for being "good." If any Black person saved a White person's life, protected their property, invented something that made money for a White person or squealed on his fellow enslaved Black neighbour planning a revolt, they would gain their freedom. Dr. Anderson said that from 1710 to the 1860s, there were about 207 possible slave revolts, but in every case, a Black person "squealed" on every one of them.[86] Vesey Denmark would confirm Dr. Anderson's assertion. Is that why Black people love other races more than they love their own?

It is painful to see some Black people disembowel their Black community on national TV and social media. It is just as Charles Barron, an American activist and politician who serves on the New York City Council, representing Brooklyn's 42nd district, once wrote, "We still have some 'meritorious manumission' Black leaders running around here today who prioritize their personal ambition and rugged individualism over the liberation of the masses of our people from colonial capitalism and its by-product called poverty."[87]

What damage do "meritorious manumission Black leaders" do to their community? Roland Martin energetically spotlighted the devastating destruction those people do to their kind on his show, #Roland Martin Unfiltered.

> When people like Candace Owens set out to be so destructive against African Americans, what they're actually doing is they're playing to white supremacy. They're White folks in America who love nothing more than to find a Black person who would say some of the most evil and vile things about other Black people. Because, see, then, they get to speak to Black people through that Black person. [88]

Playing to white supremacy. Isn't that what the two Black slaves did when they betrayed Vesey Denmark? Martin, like a heat-seeking missile, was on target when he asserted that White folks get to speak to Black people through Black people who disparage other African Americans. That was precisely what White folks (with the help of two Black people) on Fox News did, using Kanye West as their medium:

"I was blown away by Kanye West. I really was."

"It was fascinating. This was an unvarnished authentically. . . ."

"We've rarely heard a man speak so honestly and so movingly about what he believes."

"Kanye West is wise. He's unique, and certainly, he's fearless."

"He's a critical voice."

"There is such authenticity to that, it just makes me want to hear more."

"Speaking truth to power, calling things out. And Kanye West does that."

"He speaks truth to power."

"And he is one smart guy."

" Is Kanye trying to be a force for good? Absolutely."

"Very special intellectual renaissance. When you consider people like Tucker or a Kanye. . . ."

"Kanye's genius."

"I'm gonna make an analogy. Kunta Kinte in Roots. They got him out on the tree, and they're whipping him. "What's your name?" And they wanted him to say left wing liberal." (Said by, of all the people on Fox, a Black man!!!)

"Kanye West refuses to live in that box."

"You can't help but like him. Because he is not apologetic."

"I think he's dead-on, on this one."

"I know, for me, it just made me think, man, we could reach so many more people with this powerful movement that believes in freedom."

"I know that what I'm listening to is unique and interesting."

"Kanye West believes it. Imagine how many more people out there maybe aren't talking about it. But would like to."[89]

Has West behaved like a "meritorious manumission Black leader"? Charlamagne (Lenard McKelvey), an American radio host, television personality and comedian said of West: "... there aren't too many people in the world who openly seek white validation like Kanye West."[90] Isn't that what all the Black slave squealers between 1710 and 1860s wanted when they betrayed their Black brothers who sought to liberate them from their bitter bondage? Is Kayne West any different? Judge for yourself. In an interview with Tucker Carlson, West begged for Carlson's approval. "Have I reached Alex Jones territory yet?"[91]

Charlamagne further evaluated West with admirable accuracy.

> Whenever he's going through something, whenever he's beefing with a corporation, with his ex-wife, he becomes so pro-black. But when he's up, and things are fine, it's 'slavery was a choice', 'black people focus on race too much,' and when he's in these circles like the one he was in at that Paris fashion show, it's 'White Lives Matter.

Charlamagne's final verdict was that "Kanye West loves White validation—he longs for it."

In his interview with Carlson, West said some things I can relate to, if not wholly, partially. Like West, I believe that White lives do matter. But when in the history of the world has the sacredness of White lives been doubted and debated by Black people? Remember, Black people have a favourable leaning toward people of other races.

When did the Black Founding Fathers declare all men are created equal while they kept White people in brutal bondage? When did Black people enact a thirteenth and fourteenth Amendment to their Constitution but kept White people from voting and demanded that they sit in the back of the bus and compel them to surrender their seats to a standing Black commuter?

Are there any pictures of Black people smiling with the bodies of two white Euro-Americans they just lynched? And did they make any greeting cards with those pictures?

Did Black Americans relegate White citizens to inferior "Whites Only" accommodations? Did they invade a White town, burn it to the ground and kill over 300 White people who had to run and hide in terror? Did Black people stand on the sidelines with their faces twisted into ugly masks of hate, anger and contempt as Black soldiers protected defenceless White children who were to be integrated into an all-Black school?

Are there any Black Karens around demanding to see a White tenant's ID before they can enter their *own* apartments? Are there any Black people in America chasing after White Amazon or FedEx delivery drivers or White joggers, trying to murder them?

When, I pray thee, Christian Kanye West, called by God, was there any debate or doubt about the value of White lives?

It is galling to see Black people rooting for Donald Trump, who let loose law enforcement personnel to beat up peaceful Black Lives Matter protesters after Derek Chauvin heartlessly murdered George Floyd but instigated a murderous insurrection after he attempted to rob mostly Black people of their votes. It is disturbingly worrying to hear about "Blacks for Trump" when he thinks Black Lives Matter activists are terrorists, but criminal insurrectionists are hostages.

Dealing With Meritorious Manumission Black Leaders

So, what do we do about Black people who demonize, destroy, assault and jilt their own? To begin with, we must recognize as the Atlanta-based Black Voters Matter Action PAC ad boldly declared: "All skin folk ain't kinfolk."[92] It has never been about color; it has always been about content.

Kentucky Attorney General Daniel Cameron, a Black man, wanted Democratic Governor Andy Beshear's (a White man) job. But Cameron, one who could justifiably be called a "Meritorious Manumission Black Leader," had aligned himself with Donald Trump and the MAGA movement, which most African-American voters viewed as inherently racist – to quote a Black Professor, Brian Clardy.[93]

Cameron told ABC News Political Director Rick Klein and Chief White House Correspondent Jonathan Karl on the "Powerhouse Politics" podcast in 2020 that President Trump was "best" for America. "Whether it be economically, or whether

121

it is related to how he fights every day for the American worker . . .. I appreciate the values that this party upholds, and I think they've been consistent with the way that the president has conducted himself in the last four years."[94] This was his barefaced view despite Trump's inflammatory rhetoric on race.

In 2023, he boasted about Trump's endorsement for the Governor's race. In a TV ad he trumpeted (pun intended): "I'm the only candidate endorsed by President Trump and the only candidate who stood up to Joe Biden."[95]

In addition to Cameron's umbilicus connection to Trump and the MAGA insanity, The Black community held Cameron responsible for not pursuing serious charges against the police officers who killed Breonna Taylor in her own apartment in Louisville but rather charged a third officer for "endangering Taylor's neighbors."[96]

Against this "meritorious manumission" background, Cameron wanted to be Governor of his state. But Black people would not stand for that. Black Voters Matter PAC released a radio ad.

> What's up, Kentucky? It's election time, and all skin folks ain't kinfolks. Over the past few years, we've taken to the streets to demand racial justice, to demand healthcare and the right to make decisions about our bodies. And now Uncle Daniel Cameron is threatening to take us backwards. The same man refused to seek justice for Breonna Taylor now wants to run our whole state. We can't let that happen. We won't let that happen. On November 7, go Andy Beshear for governor.

Cliff Albright, co-founder and executive director of Black Voters Matter, appeared on #Roland Martin Unfiltered Daily Digital Show to throw lucent light on the compelling reasons Daniel Cameron's governorship would be disastrous to Black citizens.

1. He refused to charge the police officers who killed Breonna Taylor, although there were all types of violations that could have been filed just as the Department of Justice did against the cops who murdered Breonna. When Cameron said there was nothing he could do, he was repeating Judge Tany's line from the Dread Scott case that a Black man or woman sitting or sleeping in her own apartment has no rights, which a White man or White police officer is bound to respect. [97]
2. He peeled back Medicare expansion – a direct attack on the health of the Black community.

3. He made an unsolicited attack against affirmative action after the Supreme Court affirmative action case, which dealt only with education. Cameron sent letters to other General Attorneys warning companies they needed to end their affirmative action hiring policies. That was an attack against the jobs and wages of the Black community.

4. He has been a threat to the Black community as the staunchest White supremacist.

5. He's decided which team he wants to be on - the side of the police union and Mitch McConnell's, who regards him as a protege. He picked the side of anti-blackness – the side against Black people's safety, health, economic well-being, education, and maternal health.

6. On his Attorney General's website, one of his priorities is to stop wokeness.

7. He wants Donald Trump back in office in light of all he knows about what he has done.

8. Cameron's campaign website listed three major priorities: Better schools, strong economy, safe streets. Under those main headings were things like work requirements for welfare, bringing income tax to zero, fighting fentanyl and illegal drugs and tougher sentencing for criminals. Albright said zero income taxes meant reducing taxes for the wealthiest in the country, not for regular struggling people. Safe streets was meant to scare people about crime, which meant more police, more profiling and more Black people getting shot. Better schools was code for the privatization of the school systems all across the country.

Andy Beshear's website was a radical and refreshing contrast to Cameron's.

1. Early learning and childcare
2. Fiscal responsibility and transparency
3. Job and economic development
4. Boosting Kentucky's Signature Industries
5. Infrastructure
6. Expanding High-speed Internet
7. Expanding access and reliability of clean drinking water
8. Expanding healthcare access and affordability
9. Prioritizing public education
10. Investing in higher education and workforce development
11. Fighting inflation
12. Public safety - actions taken
13. Rebuilding Kentucky after disasters

14. Supporting our military
15. Revitalizing Appalachian Kentucky and leadership of the Appalachian Regional Commission (ARC)
16. Promoting Kentucky Values and the Golden Rule
17. Protecting Kentucky families
18. Supporting seniors and the most vulnerable
19. Protecting your rights.

Also appearing on Beshear's site was a list of important accomplishments.

1. Vetoed a bill cruelly designed to prevent access to potentially life-saving medical care for minors and strip away parents' rights to seek appropriate treatment for their children.
2. Vetoed a bill to strip away parental participation in making decisions on school personnel and curriculum.
3. Vetoed extreme legislation that would eliminate abortion options for victims of rape and incest.
4. Vetoed numerous bills, including those later proven to be an unconstitutional waste of time, attempting to weaken the executive branch and grab power for other branches of government and constitutional officers.
5. Vetoed bills creating additional unnecessary barriers to access essential health care services.
6. Vetoed legislation stripping the Governor's authority to take life-saving action in emergencies.
7. Vetoed bills to weaken transparency and accountability to the public and to weaken Kentucky's Open Records Act.

Roland Martin, commenting on Beshear's website, said it was an example of a White Democrat who was more aligned with Black voters than Republican Black Daniel Cameron.[98]

Like I said, it has never been about color; it has always been about content.

Beshear defeated Republican Daniel Cameron with 53% of the votes,[99] which brings us back to the question of what to do about Black people who demonize, destroy, assault and jilt their own. After recognizing that not all skin folks are kinfolks, the Black community should strangle such people as they did the segregated transportation system in the sixties. Those people should be isolated, voted out of positions of power and influence, and their businesses shunned by Black customers and clients.

The other thing to do about Meritorious Manumission Blacks is to expose and call them out as vigorously as Roland Martin does. Why is it critical that we call them out? Because somebody else might be listening to them, says Martin.[100] And you know people were listening to former U.S. Secretary of Housing and Urban Development Dr. Ben Carson, a Black man campaigning for Donald Trump, when he said slavery should not be a source of shame for America.

You look back to the beginnings of this country and our founders; a lot of people are trying to denigrate them now, saying that they were horrible people, maybe because some of them had slaves, and that America is a horrible place because we had slavery.

People who say stuff like that obviously don't have a good grasp of world history because every society has had to deal with slavery, and there are more slaves in the world today than there have ever been at any point in time.[101]

And, boy, weren't they listening when in 2014, Carson compared President Obama to Vladimir Putin![102]

Meritorious Manumission Black people are just as dangerous to the safety, progress and prosperity of their Black brothers and sisters as they were between the 1710s and the 1860s. Here is a Black leader who accused Barack Obama of "taking liberties with the system" and being "very much like Putin," campaigning for a man who demonized a Black athlete who took a knee to protest racial discrimination and police violence against Blacks,[103] let loose security forces on peaceful Black Lives Matter demonstrators,[104] expressed fawning love and admiration for violent insurrectionists[105] and dictators, like Putin,[106] wants to abolish the Constitution,[107] claims absolute immunity for crimes committed as president,[108] stole classified documents,[109] liable for sexual abuse and defamation of his victim,[110] guilty of business fraud,[111] instigated violence against the Judiciary, their staff and law enforcement,[112] just to name a few of the imperfections of Carson's champion. But of course, Carson thinks Trump is like King David, a man after God's own heart.[113]

Can you appreciate the duty to call out skin folks who denigrate their own? And we must call them out as vociferously and energetically as they denigrate their own people and promote the agenda of our adversaries.

Help Define the Struggle and Give Support

"Black Lives Matter is not about that. It's about homosexuality."

I was one of a small group discussing George Floyd's death and the global Black Lives Matter demonstrations. The statement above was made by a young Christian man who was a sucker for right-wing media disinformation.

"Look," I addressed the fellow, "If I say that my life matters and you respond by saying I don't mean what I say, I really mean something else, then *you do not have to address my concern that my life matters*." To his credit, he acknowledged my concern and apologized.

Donald Trump is a pro at recasting the concerns of the Black community. Colin Kaepernick took a knee to spotlight his concern for racial discrimination and police violence against Black people. But Donald Trump made it about disloyalty to the country and disrespect for the flag; Kaepernick's crusade was lost in the aggressive and deceptive verbiage of the then president.

When Fox News lambasted the violence done by a few people, some of them White, during Black Lives Matter demonstrations, they did not have to give assent to the assertion that Black lives, in fact, matter. If someone responds with "All Lives Matter," when you insist that Black lives matter, then they absolve themselves of any responsibility for the historical and current devaluation of Black lives.

Never let anyone reframe and morph the issues Black people, the marginalized, and the oppressed are concerned about. But how can you refocus the spotlight on the justifiable concerns if you are clueless about the struggle?

Debra Thompson, Associate Professor of Political Science and Canada Research Chair in Racial Inequality in Democratic Societies at McGill University, wrote an extensive, analytical, insightful and informative article on the Black Lives Matter organization in Canada. She accentuated the purpose and goals of Canadian BLM activism.

1. Highlight the violence faced by marginalized communities such as Indigenous people, sex workers, homeless populations and the trans community.
2. Lobbied to stop deportations of Black migrants.
3. Called out anti-Black racism in schools.
4. Allied with Indigenous peoples' Land Back movement.
5. Seek to change the circumstances for Black people in Canada – including undocumented Black people, homeless Black people, queer and trans Black people, disabled Black people and others on the margins of the margins.
6. Bring attention to police violence in Canada as well as other kinds of state surveillance of Black citizens.

126

7. Conduct an inclusive and intersectional struggle and work in solidarity with other communities that desire a better, more just world.

If Black Beauty is ignorant of the issues that define and constrict her existence, how can she unveil her effulgent glory? How can she rise to the top if she listens to her enemy's malicious reframing of the problems weighing her down at the bottom of the barrel?

Hey, Black people! It doesn't matter how often you go to church, pray, fast and give tithe and offerings; if you are divorced from the life and concerns of your community, you will always be poor and powerless.

One of the many things Black people can do to begin to command respect from people of other races is to be *aware*. They must educate themselves about the history of the Black community and the issues they face. Then, it will be impossible for other people to denigrate Black leaders, activities and organizations that are leading the charge to advance the life experiences of Black citizens.

Black people must buttress their community to move from the back of the pack to the front. Here are some examples of how they can do this.

Support Black-owned Businesses

By supporting Black-owned businesses, you can help create jobs and build wealth in the Black community. You can find Black-owned enterprises where you live by using the Black Owned Business Directory. A Canadian website is https://www. afrobiz.ca/.

Isheka N. Harrison, in a 2022 article, "The Lifespan Of A Dollar In Black Community Is Only 6 Hours: Fact Or Myth?" quoted experts who disputed the claim that the dollar only circulates for six hours in the Black community compared to dozens of times in others, like the Jewish and Asian communities. Apparently, there is no study undergirding such a claim.[114]

However, speaking from my observation, it is reasonable to conclude that the dollar circulates many more times in other ethnic communities than in the Black. I already observed that you will never see a White or Black technician or service provider working for my Indian neighbours. As a rule, only Asian people work in Asian businesses. However, Black people spend their money with any ethnic group and are open to embracing them socially, intimately, religiously and economically. Recently, I went to shop at a supermarket with Black ownership. I saw Indian and White employees, but perhaps the Black workers weren't on that shift.

Roland Martin, a herald for Black businesses, highlights how mega business enterprises want Black customers to spend their money with them, but they, in turn, do not support black-owned businesses.[115]

Fox News built its power on Black programming, which enabled it to offer a billion dollars for NFL rights. However, as soon as Fox News attained that milestone, they cancelled all Black programmes.

Now that we have come to the digital age, Black viewers and actors are again supporting Fox News through Tubi, which the Murdochs own. "Wherever Black viewers go, so do the advertising dollars," Martin said.[116] In essence, Black people are financially enriching their arch-enemy (Not Martin's verbiage, mine).

It may be true that there is no data to support the claim that the dollar stays only six hours in the Black community. Still, I doubt it stays much longer than that, and no one can gainsay Roland Martin's concerns about Black people financially supporting adversarial systems.

Volunteer

Volunteering is a great way to give back to your community. You can volunteer at local organizations that support the Black community. Here are some Canadian organizations.[117] Seek out the ones where you are.

1. Black Youth Helpline
2. Freedom School Toronto
3. Federation of Black Canadians
4. Zero Gun Violence Movement
5. Harriet Tubman Community Organization
6. Black Lives Matter
7. Black Legal Action Centre
8. Black Women in Motion
9. Black Business and Professional Association
10. The Most Nurtured

Donate

Donating to organizations that support the Black community is another way to make a difference.

Speak Out Against Racism

Speaking out against racism is crucial in elevating the station of the beautiful Black damsel. You can speak out against racism by attending protests, writing letters to your representatives, and sharing information on social media. And where possible, join class action suits. I think there should be less protests in the streets and more righteous reprisals in the courts.

Be a Mentor

Mentoring is a great way to help young people in the Black community. Black Ladders is a group of Canadian Black professionals who use their knowledge and experience to help other Black people reach their full potential and succeed in their careers.[118]

Mentor Canada was launched in 2019 by Big Brothers Big Sisters of Canada, the Alberta Mentoring Partnership and the Ontario Mentoring Coalition. Mentor Canada's goal is to have organizations from across Canada work to promote the mentoring movement and build sector capacity to empower every young person to fulfill their potential.[119]

Vote

Voting for candidates who support policies that benefit the Black community is an important way to make your voice heard. Fortunately for Canadian Black citizens, no one here is attempting to suppress or steal Black votes.

Support Black Artists

Supporting Black artists is a great way to promote Black culture and creativity. You can support Black artists by attending their shows, buying their art, and sharing their work on social media.

Black people should support every sector of their society and people of other ethnic extractions who are their allies, but they should never disregard their own. If they do, they risk a fate worse than complete extinction - an existence of degradation, counted as a mere three-fifths of a human who was never created by their oppressors' God.

Black people, never forget, no other race is obligated to regard you as a human or their equal. It is you who have to make them treat you with respect and dignity and you cannot accomplish this feat from a position of weakness, poverty and powerlessness. It is you who must unveil and assert yourself, flaunt your blackness and beauty. It is you who must take a firm and vigorous hold upon "the great principles of political freedom and natural justice," upon "equality," and your "unalienable Rights, to Life, Liberty and the pursuit of Happiness."

Chapter 15

Conclusion: Don't Blame the Stars

"As if this country's core institutions have not been degraded or diminished enough ... Joe Biden announced in January his plan to choose the next Supreme Court Justice on the basis of appearance."[1]

This was how Tucker Carlson opened one of his shows around March 2022 before Fox News axed him for obscure and nebulous reasons (possibly for misogyny, anti-Semitism, subjugating women based on "vile sexist stereotypes" and typecasting religious minorities and "belittling their traditions, among other reasons) without so much as "a goodbye tweet."[2]

Tucker was about to launch another of his pathetic, contemptible racist assaults on another Black American -Judge Ketanji Brown Jackson.

"The Supreme Court, unlike the Sociology department or a business, 'really matters,' so why was Joe Biden choosing a Justice based solely on appearance and genetics? What does appearance have to do with ability or fealty to the Constitution?" Of course, Carlson is a descendant of the people who once stereotyped Ketanji Brown Jackson's forbearers as Sambos – "lazy, ignorant fools who were subservient and linguistically challenged" and deserved nothing more than enslavement and segregation because of the size of their skull.[3] Therefore, he eloquently charged down the thorn and weed-overgrown pathway of racism again.

"How do genes determine your ability as a Supreme Court Justice, or a surgeon, an airline pilot, or anything else? We would love to hear Joe Biden explain that. But he didn't. Instead, he embarked on a predictably short nationwide search for such a candidate and located, in the end, a person called Ketanji Brown Jackson. Not surprisingly, given how she got this job, most of the talk in Washington was not about what she's done, how she thinks, what she's like as a person, but instead about how she looks."

In a previous broadcast, Carlson was distressed because he did not know what Jackson's LSAT score was. "It might be time for Joe Biden to let us know what Ketanji Brown Jackson's LSAT score was. Why wouldn't he tell us that? That would settle the question conclusively as to whether she's a once-in-a-generation legal talent at hand. It would seem like Americans in a democracy have a right to know that and much more before giving her a lifetime appointment."[4]

You must know by now that if Carlson had seen Jackson's LSAT scores, he would have declared it fake, as fake as Obama's birth certificate was or the ID of a Black tenant trying to get into his apartment building.

Carlson never fretted about the LSAT scores of Gorsuch, Kavanaugh, and Barrett because, you know, that bunch qualified for the Supreme Court on appearance and genetics alone. And did Carlson question Putin's intelligence when he went to interview him?

Tucker Carlson's racist attack on Justice Jackson's intellectual prowess fell flat and left him looking like a pitiful, small-minded, silly man.

"I regret to inform you that Tucker Carlson has said something incredibly stupid about the legal profession," LegalEagle said in response to his demand to see Justice Jackson's LSAT score. "Once you get into law school, no one will ever ask for your LSAT scores again. The LSAT score has nothing to do with the practice of law. Lots of really great lawyers and judges did terribly on the LSAT score and vice versa.

"It's impossible to claim that she's not qualified to sit on the Supreme Court," LegalEagle continued. "She went to Harvard Law. She served as an editor of the Harvard Law Review. She clerked for three judges at all federal levels, including on the Supreme Court. She has almost nine years of judicial experience, which is more than four current justices, Thomas, Roberts, Kagan, and Barrett, combined."[5]

Indeed, Carlson said something (and looked) "stupid" when he asked to see Jackson's LSAT scores. And Hilary Clinton placed him in the strata of "useful idiot"[6] for his interview and servile, subservient, docile, fawning over Putin.

The Russian President told the Russian TV anchor, Pavel Zarubin, that Carlson was a "dangerous man," and he expected a more aggressive interview. "Honestly, I thought he would behave aggressively and ask so-called sharp questions. I was not just prepared for this. I wanted it. Because it would give me the opportunity to respond in the same way."[7]

Hah! Do you know who Carlson can be aggressive with? Non-whites like Judge Ketanji Brown Jackson. He can ask aggressive questions like why Joe Biden chose a Justice based solely on appearance and genetics? What does appearance have to do with ability or fealty to the Constitution? How do genes determine your ability as a Supreme Court Justice or, a surgeon, an airline pilot, or anything else? And he can intimate that Judge Ketanji Brown was dumb because Biden found her in a "predictably short nationwide search" and "most of the talk in Washington was not about what she's done, how she thinks, what she's like as a person, but instead about how she looks."

Putin continued his presidential assault on Carlson. "He chose another tactic. He did try to interrupt me a couple of times, but he turned out to be surprisingly patient for a Western journalist. He listened to all my lengthy dialogues, especially the ones on history. And he did not give me excuses for me to do what I was prepared to do, so frankly, I did not get full satisfaction from this interview."

After the interview, Carlson said he thought Putin was not good at explaining himself, although "he's smart, no question about that."

Nightmare Terror

Now, having outlined Tucker Carlson's egregious and demeaning attack on an accomplished Black woman, you may think I am deeply disturbed by his behaviour. I am not. Okay, maybe a little, but my nightmarish terror comes from the Black woman's propensity to cannibalize herself.

Think back to Tim Scott's sickening and vomit-inducing subjugation to Donald Trump, and you will immediately feel the terror that haunts and sends chills down my figurative spine. "I just love you," Scott lovingly told Trump in the presence of thousands of people.[8]

Some descendants of the Black but beautiful woman who fought like hell to pull themselves up from the bottom of the subjugation barrel are now open to selling their freedom and dignity for a few silver coins.

Sexyy Red, an American rapper, declared her love for Donald Trump on a conservative-leaning podcast. She spoke on behalf of Black people in the hood who had grown to regard Trump with favour, because he got Black people out of jail and gave them free money. "Aww baby, we love Trump. We need him back in office. We need him back because, baby, them checks. Them stimulus checks. Trump, we miss you."[9]

Trump sent a letter with stimulus checks to 130 million Americans. He wanted to send a $2000 check instead of $600. Democrats jumped to fulfill the President's demand, but Republicans killed that plan.[10] Do Sexyy Red and the people in the hood know Democrats agreed to let them have a $2000 check?

After Joe Biden became the President, he signed a $1.9 trillion COVID Relief bill, which gave Americans another $1400 stimulus check, extended a $300.00 per week unemployment insurance supplement, expanded the Child Tax credit and put funds into vaccine distribution. Democrats passed this bill on their own because it was opposed by every last Republican.[11] Do Sexyy Red and the people in the hood know all this?

Ignorance and a few silver coins will keep the beautiful Black woman subjugated in perpetuity.

Curses On the Black Beauty

"I saw the curse pronounced by Noah upon Ham moving toward the latter like a black cloud and obscuring him. His skin lost its whiteness, he grew darker. His sin was the sin of sacrilege, the sin of one who would forcibly enter the Ark of the Covenant. I saw a most corrupt race descend from Ham and sink deeper and deeper in darkness. I see that the black, idolatrous, stupid nations are the descendants of Ham. Their color is due not to the rays of the sun but to the dark source whence those degraded races sprang."[12]

So said the Augustinian mystic, Marian visionary, ecstatic and stigmatist, Anne Catherine Emmerich, sometime between 1774 and 1824 when she died.[13]

Noah pronounced a curse of slavery upon Canaan, the son of Ham, who saw him sprawled out, naked in an intoxicated stupor, but failed to cover him as his brothers Shem and Japheth did. According to the Catholic mystic Emmerich, that curse gave rise to Black people who comprised a "most corrupt" and "degraded" race.

This "curse," unfortunately, was bequeathed to the Black damsel, and her entire existence has been marred by it. The people who retained their "whiteness" used the curse of Noah to justify her enslavement and abuse.

In the fifteenth century, Dominican friar Annius of Viterbo invoked the Curse of Ham to explain the differences between Europeans and Africans. He claimed that due to the curse imposed upon Black people, they would inevitably remain permanently subjugated by Arabs and other Muslims, and slavery was proof of their inferiority. Through these and other writings, European writers established a connection between Ham, Africa and slavery, which justified the transatlantic

133

slave trade.[14] Hence, the beautiful Black woman has always needed to tell her siblings, "Don't look at me like that. I am black but beautiful."

Without equivocation, I declare it is pure, unadulterated evil for the Gods and their favourite people (Muslims, Arabs, Jews, Whites, Europeans) to enslave, castrate, lynch, and demean Black people. However, in reality, no God or people can place an actual curse upon melaninated people. But Black people have often placed a curse upon themselves.

Black people enslaved each other before Europeans sought slaves in Africa. After Europeans came looking for slaves, Africans sold their people, driving them shackled over 485 km from the interior to the coast. They loaded and offloaded ships and supplied the foreigners with food and other provisions. They negotiated prices for slaves and collected royalties from sellers and buyers. The slave trade in south-eastern Nigeria lasted until the late 1940s and early 1950s![15]

A 2017 CNN report revealed there were over 40 million slaves globally, but this modern slavery was the most prevalent in Africa. Twenty percent of the continent's children were shackled in child labour, which was described as work that "directly endangered their health, safety and moral development."[16]

Sustained conflicts in Africa have forcibly displaced over 40 million people.[17]

Even if it can be argued that European powers are behind some of these conflicts, it is Black people who are butchering their own and committing the crimes of ethnic cleansing, sexual violence, and mass murders.[18]

These perpetual conflicts have ripped many African communities to shreds and left people without food, shelter, and primary health care, which in turn have exposed millions, including children, to starvation, diseases and death.[19] And guess what? There are no White men imposing the curse of Canaan on Africans. Yet, they are still, in the words of Anne Catherine Emmerich, a "corrupt race sinking deeper and deeper in darkness."

In many instances, it has been Black people who called down the curse on themselves. They rob and murder their own, bleach their skin, enslave their kin, and stand (and vote) shoulder to shoulder with the descendants of their slave masters who want to disenfranchise, devitalize and rob them of their resources, dignity and even their votes!

Black people affirm they are cursed when they prostitute themselves before Donald Trump, who heralded to the world that Black people love to wear his $19.00 mugshot T-shirts and that his indictments are why they like him so much.

Rev. Al Sharpton rightly classified the above statements as insults. Trump implied by his mugshot and indictment statements that all Black people are criminals. His supporter who claimed Black Americans would vote for Trump because he gave them sneakers was just as insulting. Rev. Sharpton pointed out that two of Trump's four indictments relate to his attempt to steal Black peoples' votes after they had fought and were beaten, bloodied and killed to get the right to vote.

"So let me get this right," Rev. Sharpton said in distressing incredulity," he didn't support George Floyd Justice in Policing Act, Biden did and signed an executive order. He didn't support the John Lewis Voting Rights Act, but we're supposed to go for sneakers and a mugshot! And those Blacks that are standing there with him, have you no shame?"[20]

Obviously, they have no shame, but they also invoke a curse upon themselves and their children, their children's children, on into perpetuity.

Own the Blame, Rewrite the Story

The fault, dear Brutus, is not in our stars,
But in ourselves, that we are underlings.[21]

In 2020, after that cop murdered George Floyd in broad daylight, it was heartening and refreshing to see the global White community (and people of every tribe, kindred and tongue) take to the streets with a resonant, clarion declaration that Black Lives Matter! The Black sister of Song of Solomon can use all the help she can get.

Indeed, she has always gotten help from good people who are the exception to the evil in the world and the light that interdicts human darkness.

James Reeb was a Kansas-native pastor who participated in the Selma to Montgomery civil rights marches. He died in 1965 after he was severely beaten by white segregationists.

Vilola Liuzzo was an activist who was murdered by members of the Ku Klux Klan in Selma.

Jonathan Daniels, a White seminarian from New Hampshire, lost his life while shielding a Black teenager from a fired shotgun in Hayneville, Alabama.[22]

Anne Braden was a journalist, organizer, and advocate who was deeply involved in the fight against segregation and racial injustice. She co-founded the Southern Conference Educational Fund (SCEF) and worked tirelessly to promote integration and civil rights in the American South.[23]

John Howard Griffin was an author and journalist best known for his book *Black Like Me.* In 1959, he darkened his skin and travelled through the segregated South to experience firsthand the challenges faced by Black Americans. His work exposed the harsh realities of racism and discrimination.[24]

Allard K. Lowenstein, a lawyer, politician, and activist, strongly advocated for civil rights. He was crucial in organizing the Freedom Summer campaign in 1964, which aimed to register African American voters in Mississippi.[25]

Mildred Loving, alongside her husband, Richard Loving, was part of the landmark Loving v. Virginia case that led to the Supreme Court's decision to strike down laws prohibiting interracial marriage.[26]

As in America, many White South Africans opposed the racist, oppressive apartheid system of government that systematically set out to dehumanize, enslave, imprison and murder native Black South Africans.

Many White women in South Africa supported the Black Sash organization, which actively opposed apartheid. They advocated for human rights, protested discriminatory laws, and provided support to victims of apartheid policies.

Molly Blackburn was a dedicated anti-apartheid activist. She stood up against racial segregation and injustice.

As a lawyer and political activist, Bram Fischer, a White Afrikaner, defied his own privileged background to fight against apartheid. He provided legal assistance to anti-apartheid activists, including Nelson Mandela, and faced persecution for his fight against the racists in his country.

Arthur Goldreich was an artist, architect, and anti-apartheid activist. He was involved in underground resistance activities. He played a critical role in sheltering Nelson Mandela and other activists at Liliesleaf Farm, a secret hideout, before their arrest.

Ruth First faced harassment and imprisonment and ultimately lost her life due to a letter bomb sent by the apartheid regime because of her political activism and righteous stance against the oppressive system that devoured the lives of Black South Africans.[27]

Indeed, as they say, not all skin folks or kinfolks. Many of these White people who stood up for oppressed Black people and the millions around the world who protested George Floyd's murder would, like Rev. Al Sharpton, ask Black individuals supporting Trump's regime, have you nor shame?

Black people, you should welcome the help of good people from every ethnic group, and you should celebrate and acknowledge those who lend a helping hand in your struggle for a dignified, safe, and prosperous space among humanity. However, you must realize you are primarily responsible for that struggle.

There is nothing to gain from mourning your inferior state. No progress can be made by appealing to pretend ideals (all men are created equal) when, in reality, and practice, the foundation of your oppressors' systems is dystopian. No advancement can be made from disengaging because of the dogged determination of evil people to keep you oppressed.

And let me tell you something else, Black people. No Gods or angels will traverse the billions and billions of light years (one light year equals 9.5 trillion km/5.88 trillion miles) separating Earth from heaven to rescue you from the fiery furnace. You are on your own!

Redeeming yourself is solely your responsibility because the Gods are quadriplegics. They stood by wordlessly and helplessly as your ancestors were enslaved, your great grandparents lynched, your grandparents redlined, and you denied justice and voting rights. They stood by helplessly as a sniper lined up Martin Luther King Jr. in his (or her) sights. No angels came to rescue James Reeb when he was being beaten to death by White segregationists. Neither did they stay the hand of Ruth First when she was about to open the letter bomb that blasted her to pieces.

I am not saying there are no Gods. Still, Jehovah and Allah and the rest of them never came down to speak to their worshippers, who were and are the staunchest racists and oppressors, plundering other people's bodies, resources and lands and denying the poor, disadvantaged and helpless dignity, human rights and protection from harm. Nothing on Earth improves if humans do not roll up their sleeves and put their lives on the line to make it so. You may find inspiration in the pages of your Holy Bible and Holy Qur'an, but it is YOU who must tread the fairy vale and walk through the valley of the shadow of death.

It is you who must stand up. It is you who must protest. It is you who must march. It is you who must file the lawsuits.

It is you who must regard yourself as noble and worthy. It is you who must educate yourself. It is you who must learn new skills. It is you who must build your community. It is you who must start and support black businesses. It is you who must protect and brace up your brothers and sisters.

It is you who must face the criminal cops. It is you who must be unfairly imprisoned. It is you who must jut your chest to your enemy's bullets. It is your head that must be smashed open by riot police. It is you who must be teargassed. You must be the one run down by a racist's Dodge Challenger.

Black, beautiful woman of Song of Solomon, pray all you want, but it is you who must face down the Dylann Roofs while you are on your knees. If you are economically, intellectually, politically and militarily powerless, no one will respect you or treat you like their equal, made in the image of *their* God and worthy of liberty, property and happiness, although you are holy and saintly.

So, WAKE UP, BLACK PEOPLE! You cannot wholly absolve your oppressors of the blame, but you must be solely responsible (with whatever little help you get from others) for rewriting the story. No one is obligated to treat you fairly, but you must make them.

The reason Black people are treated as underlings can justifiably be said to be rooted in other people's evil nature and their ignorance. But what is certain is that a perpetual recitation of that fact is futile, as futile as looking for deliverance from the stars. If people of African roots fail to advance to the place where they are automatically respected and treated as equals, then the "fault, dear Brutus, is in ourselves."

Until the day comes when humans are civilized enough to treat everyone, including Black people, as their equals, the ebonized sister of Song of Solomon must continue to assert, "I am black, but comely." She must do this not to convince herself of her worth, but to open the eyes of all men to her effulgent glory.

Also by Pricely D. Francis

LET THE UNIVERSE DELIVER REVISED
How to Have Your Wishes Magically
Delivered to Your Front Door Even if
You Have No Money, Means, Influence,
Power, or the Know-how

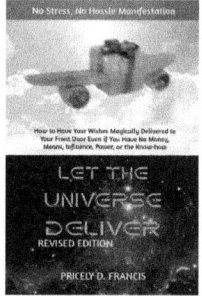

Customer Review

"There was no question this book was set in front of
me by my desire. Each chapter explains a principle,
gives the author's experience, and gives practical
guidance to do the the same yourself. The book is
inexpensive, but the information here is priceless.

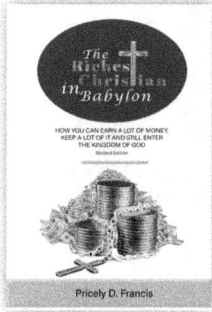

The Richest Christian in Babylon
HOW YOU CAN EARN A LOT OF MONEY, KEEP A LOT OF IT
AND STILL ENTER THE KINGDOM OF GOD

ONE NATION UNDER GOD!
NOOOOO!
How God, Religion and Religious
People Could Turn Your Cushy

21st-century Life Upside Down

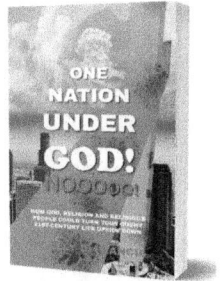

FRESH BREAD
The Best of My Bible for Soul
Nourishment and Inspiration

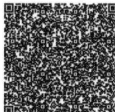

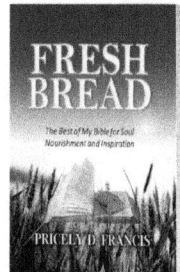

About the Author

PRICELY FRANCIS is a people person and has invested his entire professional life supporting, restoring and caring for those in need. He currently provides spiritual care for seniors in long term care and retirement. He is fully committed to the idea that everyone can live their best life in the here and now as well as in the hereafter. Pricely lives in Brampton, Ontario, Canada.

Endnotes

Introduction
Black Fits the Description

1   Selwyn Romilly. (2023, August 19). In *Wikipedia*. https://en.wikipedia.org/wiki/Selwyn_Romilly

2   BC Black History Awareness Society. *Selwyn Romilly*. https://bcblackhistory.ca/selwyn-romilly/

3   Chan, Cheryl. Ip, Stephanie (2021, May 16). *Vancouver police apologize after arresting retired judge based on suspect description*. Vancouver Sun. https://vancouversun.com/news/local-news/vancouver-police-apologize-after-arresting-retired-judge-matching-suspect-description

4   Keane, Isabel. (2022, November 22). *Former NJ councilman Gordon Lawshe calls cops on young black girl who was killing lanternflies.* New York Post. https://nypost.com/2022/11/22/nj-man-calls-cops-on-bobbi-wilson-black-girl-who-was-killing-lanternflies/

5   Little S. (2021, May 15). *Vancouver mayor apologizes to retired Black B.C. judge wrongly handcuffed by police.* Global News. https://globalnews.ca/news/7865656/mayor-apologizes-black-judge-handcuffed/

6   Chan, Cheryl. Ip, Stephanie (2021, May 16).

7   Bell, Debra. (2013, June 11) *George Wallace Stood in a Doorway at the University of Alabama 50 Years Ago Today.* USNnews. https:// www.usnews.com/news/blogs/press-past/2013/06/11/george-wallace-stood-in-a-doorway-at-the-university-of-alabama-50-years- ago-today

8   *Biography.com Editors. (2020, June 10). Civil rights leader Medgar Evers is assassinated.* History. https://www.history.com/this-day-in-history/medgar-evers-assassinated

9   Biography.com Editors. (2014, April 2). *Byron De La Beckwith.* The Biography.com website. https://www.biography.com/crime-figure/byron-de-la-beckwith

10   Birmingham Public Library. (n.d). *10 sticks of dynamite... four dead children.* Birmingham Public Library. Digital Collections. https://cdm16044.contentdm.oclc.org/digital/collection/p4017coll2/id/529   https://www.ferris.edu/HTMLS/news/jimcrow/witnesses/sixteenthstreetbaptist.htm

11   Murders of Chaney, Goodman, and Schwerner (2023, March 15). In *Wikipedia*. https://en.wikipedia.org/wiki/Murders_of_Chaney,_Goodman,_and_

Schwerner

12   History.com Editors. (2023, January 11). *Jim Crow Laws.* History. https://www.history.com/topics/early-20th-century-us/jim-crow-laws

13   Tulsa race massacre. (2023, March 30). In *Wikipedia.* https://en.wikipedia.org/wiki/Tulsa_race_massacre

14   Kuypers-Denlinger, C. (2021, December 17). *The Life and Legacy of Lucy Byard Honored at Recognition Event.* Adventist Review. https://www.adventistworld.org/the-life-and-legacy-of-lucy-byard-honored-at-recognition-event/#:~:text=It%20was%20determined%20that%20because%20of%20the%20color,University%20Hospital.%20She%20died%20some%2038%20days%20later

15   Baker, B. (n.d.). *March 2019 Feature: The Lucy Byard Story.* Columbia Union Conference. https://www.columbiaunion.org/content/march-2019-feature-lucy-byard-story

16   Baker, B. (n.d.). *March 2019 Feature: The Lucy Byard Story.* Columbia Union Conference

17   blacksdahistory. (2022, May 25). *Whites Only in Cafeteria at Church Headquarters.* [Video]. YouTube. https://www.youtube.com/watch?v=TXflQRnAFB4

18   Smithsonian, (2019, June 8). *Black is beautiful: The emergence of black culture and identity in the 60s and 70s.* National Museum of African American History and Culture. https://nmaahc.si.edu/explore/stories/black-beautiful-emergence-black-culture-and-identity-60s-and-70s

19   18karatreggae. *I know why Jamaicans bleach their skin.* https://www.18karatreggae.com/opinions/i-know-why-jamaicans-bleach-their-skin/#:~:text=Skin%20Bleaching%20in%20Jamaica.%20Jamaica%20has%20the%20most,ten%20use%20some%20form%20of%20skin%20lightening%20product

20   Democracy Now! (2021, September 2). *Elijah McClain Pleaded "I Can't Breathe" Before His 2019 Death. Now 3 Police, 2 Paramedics Charged.* [Video] YouTube. https://www.youtube.com/watch?v=m0cIRLQnqGA

21   *Declaration of Independence: A Transcription.* (2023, January 31). National Archives. https://www.archives.gov/founding-docs/declaration-transcript

22   Dred Scott v. Sandford. (2023, March 30). In *Wikipedia.* https://en.wikipedia.org/wiki/Dred_Scott_v._Sandford#:~:text=Dred%20Scott%20v.%20Sandford%2C%20%5Ba%5D%2060%20U.S.%20%2819,and%20privileges%20the%20Constitution%20conferred%20upon%20American%20citizens

23   Pierson, B. (2024, February 23). *Explainer: Alabama's highest court ruled frozen embryos are people. What is next?* Reuters. https://www.reuters.com/business/healthcare-pharmaceuticals/alabamas-highest-court-ruled-frozen-embryos-are-people-what-is-next-2024-02-23/#:~:text=Feb%2023%20%28Reuters%29%20-%20

The%20Alabama%20Supreme%20Court,sue%20for%20wrongful%20death%20
of%20their%20minor%20children

24 Democracy Now! (2014, December 5). *The Killing of Tamir Rice: Cleveland Police Criticized for Shooting 12-Year-Old Holding Toy Gun.* [Video]. YouTube. https://www.youtube.com/watch?v=DF25CN6CAfY

25 CNN. (2014, December 17). *Cops kill man at Walmart carrying a BB gun.* [Video]. YouTube. https://www.youtube.com/watch?v=BtPt6GrnE6s

26 Killing of John Crawford III. (2023, March 27). In *Wikipedia.* https://en.wikipedia.org/wiki/Killing_of_John_Crawford_IIII

27 BBC News. (2017, June 21). *Philando Castile death: Police footage released.* https://www.bbc.com/news/world-us-canada-40357355

28 Alfonseca Kiara. (2022, February 11). *Amir Locke's death highlights perils for Black gun owners: Advocates.* abcNews. https://abcnews.go.com/US/amir-lockes-death-highlights-perils-black-gun-owners/story?id=82774710

29 Eligon, John, Robles Frances. (2016, July 8). *Police shootings highlight unease among black gun owners.* Anchorage Daily News. https://www.adn.com/nation-world/2016/07/08/police-shootings-highlight-unease-among-black-gun-owners/

30 Oremus, Will. (2016, July 8). *Twitter exonerated this "Suspect" in the Dallas shooting. Why didn't the police clear his name?* The Slatest. https://www.slate.com/blogs/the_slatest/2016/07/08/twitter_exonerated_suspect_mark_hughes_in_the_dallas_shooting_why_haven.html

31 Lopez, German. (2016, September 21). *An open carry law didn't stop police from killing Keith Lamont Scott.* Vox. https://www.vox.com/2014/12/13/7384813/black-open-carry

32 Phalnikar S. (2020, June 12). *France grapples with racial injustice and police violence.* DW.com. https://www.dw.com/en/france-police-racism-tensions/a-53776478

33 TYTSports. (2022, March 29). *Cops racially profile Black man for wearing a coat.* [Video]. YouTube. https://www.youtube.com/watch?v=NWuWjgbIVTE

34 Channel 4 News. (2022, June 12). *Black bank manager to sue Metropolitan Police for racial discrimination after 26-month nightmare.* [Video]. YouTube. https://www.youtube.com/watch?v=1x0G4NCBTzg

35 Strudwick, M. (2023, September 28). *Moment Olympic sprinter Ricardo Dos Santos pleads 'what did I do?* Daily Mail. https://www.dailymail.co.uk/news/article-12570013/ricardo-dos-santos-police-video.html'

36 KameraOne. *Shocking police stop: World Championship sprinter handcuffed and separated from baby.* https://www.msn.com/en-us/news/world/shocking-police-

stop-world-championship-sprinter-handcuffed-and-separated-from-baby/vi-AA1hutVa#details

37   *Security Service Act 1989 - Legislation.gov.uk*. https://www.legislation.gov.uk/ukpga/1989/5/section/1

38   https://bing.com/search?q=section+one+in+UK+police+enforcement

39   Reynolds, R. (2023, October 25). *Metropolitan Police officers sacked for gross misconduct over athlete search*. Aol. https://www.aol.com/metropolitan-police-officers-sacked-gross-154546355.htmlt

40   Reynolds, R. (2023, October 25). *Metropolitan Police officers sacked for gross misconduct over athlete search*

41   Warren, J. & Campbell, A. (2023, October 25). Bianca Williams: Two Met officers sacked over athlete search gross misconduct. BBC. https://www.bbc.co.uk/news/uk-england-london-67214409

42   Prusher, I. (2015, May 4). *Why the latest protest against police brutality is happening in Israel*. Time.com. https://time.com/3845765/israel-ethiopian-police-brutality-protest/

43   Schwartz, Y. (2018, December 18). *Israeli policy keeps Black African Jews from their families*. Daily Beast. https://www.thedailybeast.com/israels-racist-policy-keeps-black-african-jews-from-their-families

44   Human Rights Watch. (2020, May 5). *China: Covid-19 Discrimination Against Africans*. https://www.hrw.org/news/2020/05/05/china-covid-19-discrimination-against-africans

45   ABC News. (2022, March 1). *Refugees of color face discrimination while fleeing Ukraine*. [Video]. YouTube. https://www.youtube.com/watch?v=rUjaoJ6mMds

46   Guardian News. (2022, February 28). *Discrimination and racism as people flee Ukraine shared on social media*. [Video]. YouTube. https://www.youtube.com/watch?v=c17tY3tgOlQ

47   Channel 4 News. (2022, March 2). *Ukraine conflict: African students fleeing war 'facing racial discrimination*. [Video]. Channel 4 News. https://www.youtube.com/watch?v=Up_V7VCsQII

48   Democracy Now! (2022, March 28). *Nonwhite refugees fleeing Ukraine war held in detention centers in Poland, Estonia, Austria*. [Video] YouTube. https://www.youtube.com/watch?v=6e1qGOqQ2YE

49   Anonymous. (No Date). *Am I not a man and a brother?* Encyclopedia.com. https://www.encyclopedia.com/history/legal-and-political-magazines/am-i-not-man-and-brother

50   Gailani, Matthew. (2023). *"I Am A Man" Dr. King and the Memphis Sanitation Workers' Strike*. Tennessee State Museum. https://tnmuseum.org/

junior-curators/posts/i-am-a-man-dr-king-and-the-memphis-sanitation-workers-strike#:~:text=The%20Civil%20Rights%20leader%2C%20Dr.%20Martin%20Luther%20King,they%20were%20fighting%20for%20equality%2C%20dignity%2C%20and%20respect

51   Signing of the United States Declaration of Independence. (2023, March 29). In *Wikipedia*. https://en.wikipedia.org/wiki/Signing_of_the_United_States_Declaration_of_Independence

52   Brown, DeNeen L. (2018, February 12). 'I Am a Man': The ugly Memphis sanitation workers' strike that led to MLK's assassination. *The Washington Post*. https://www.washingtonpost.com/news/retropolis/wp/2018/02/12/i-am-a-man-the-1968-memphis-sanitation-workers-strike-that-led-to-mlks-assassination/

53   Kiger, Patrick J. (2019, October 28). *Minimum Wage in America: A Timeline*. History. https://www.history.com/news/minimum-wage-america-timeline

54   Brown, DeNeen L. (2018, February 12). 'I Am a Man': The ugly Memphis sanitation workers' strike that led to MLK's assassination. *The Washington Post*

55   Coleman, Colette, (2020, July 21). *The 1968 Sanitation Workers' Strike That Drew MLK to Memphis.* History. https://www.history.com/news/sanitation-workers-strike-memphis

56   Brown, DeNeen L. (2018, February 12). 'I Am a Man': The ugly Memphis sanitation workers' strike that led to MLK's assassination. *The Washington Post*. https://www.washingtonpost.com/news/retropolis/wp/2018/02/12/i-am-a-man-the-1968-memphis-sanitation-workers-strike-that-led-to-mlks-assassination/

57   Brown, DeNeen L. (2018, February 12). *'I Am a Man': The ugly Memphis sanitation workers' strike that led to MLK's assassination. The Washington Post*

58   Patrick, Knox; Herbert, Tom. (2020, September 3). *Fight against racism. What is Black Lives Matter and how did it start.* The U.S. Sun. https://www.the-sun.com/news/926615/black-lives-matter-what-is-how-start/

59   Nelson, S. (2020, August 5). *Trump slams Black Lives Matter organization as 'Marxist group.' New York Post*. https://nypost.com/2020/08/05/trump-slams-black-lives-matter-organization-as-marxist-group/

60   Wilburn, J. (2023 September 24). *Republican Congressman Paul Gosar Calls for General Mark Milley to be 'Hung' in Disturbing Homophobic Newsletter*. Microsoft Start. https://www.msn.com/en-us/news/politics/republican-congressman-paul-gosar-calls-for-general-mark-milley-to-be-hung-in-disturbing-homophobic-newsletter/ar-AA1hcdSm#image=AA1eMShE|1

61   *The Arab Muslim Slave Trade Of Africans, The Untold Story*. (2012, November 15). Internet Archives. https://archive.org/stream/pdfy-ivqdcZSnaRZuiqf1/The%20Arab%20Muslim%20Slave%20Trade%20Of%20Africans,%20The%20

Untold%20Story_djvu.txt

Boddy-Evans, Alistair. (2020, August 26). *A Short History of the African Slave Trade.* https://www.thoughtco.com/african-slavery-101-44535

62   *Exploiting black labor after the abolition of slavery* (2017, February 6). The Conversation. https://theconversation.com/exploiting-black-labor-after-the-abolition-of-slavery-72482

63   Brooks, K. J. (2020, June 12). *Redlining's legacy: Maps are gone, but the problem hasn't disappeared.* CBSNews. https://www.cbsnews.com/news/redlining-what-is-history-mike-bloomberg-comments/

64   Southall, A., Bromwich, J. E. (2021, November 17). *2 Men Convicted of killing Malcolm X will be exonerated after decades. The New York Times.* https://www.nytimes.com/2021/11/17/nyregion/malcolm-x-killing-exonerated.html

65   Consulate General of Jamaica. (n.d.). *National heroes.* https://jcgtoronto.ca/national-heroes/

66   AP. (2022, October 9). *GOP Senator makes racist comment equating Black People to criminals.* Huffpost. https://www.huffpost.com/entry/gop-senator-tuberville-racist-comment-reparations_n_63433220e4b0e376dc02ec98

Chapter 1
19-Year-Old Girl for A 170lbs Bald Male

1   Pierce, H. (2017, July 10). *Black teenage woman, mistaken for machete-wielding black man, alleges police brutality.* Bakersfield.com. https://www.bakersfield.com/news/black-teenage-girl-mistaken-for-machete-wielding-black-man-alleges/article_0ae15203-8291-5774-887b-95df9acfb2a8.html

Chapter 2:
Bald or Deadlocks - It Doesn't Matter

1   CR NEWS. (2021, July 31). *Cop caught arresting the wrong man in racial profiling incident.* [Video]. UGETTube. https://ugetube.com/watch/cop-caught-arresting-the-wrong-man-in-racial-profiling-incident-nowthis_hNtWP6nXVlb4cGV.html

Chapter 3
A Minor on His Way to McDonald's

1   Freeman, J. (2021, April 5). *Peel police launch internal probe after Black teen mistakenly arrested in high-stakes takedown.* CP24News. https://www.cp24.com/news/peel-police-launch-internal-probe-after-black-teen-mistakenly-arrested-in-high-stakes-takedown-1.5375321

2   CBC News. (2022, June 15). *'We do not accept your apology,' activist tells*

Toronto's police chief after race-based data released. CBC News. https://www.cbc.ca/news/canada/toronto/toronto-police-race-based-data-use-force-strip-searches-1.6489151

Chapter 4
Black Fit the Description When the Criminal is White

1   Meara, Paul. (2022, January). *Black man suing police after He was arrested, mistaken for a White felon twice his age.* BET. https://www.bet.com/article/18vjqa/black-man-arrested-shane-lee-brown-las-vegas-mistaken-identity-lawsuit#:~:text=In%20January%202020%2C%20Shane%20Lee%20Brown%20was%20arrested,judge%20who%20ordered%20him%20freed%2C%20the%20AP%20reports

2   Ebrahimji, Alisha; Jones, Julia. (2022, January 27) *A Black man was misidentified, arrested and held for 6 days in place of a White felon twice his age.* CNN. https://www.cnn.com/2022/01/27/us/nevada-man-jailed-misidentified-lawsuit/index.html

3   Ebrahimji, Alisha; Jones, Julia. (2022, January 27) *A Black man was misidentified, arrested and held for 6 days in place of a White felon twice his age.* CNN

4   WCPO 9. (2022, February 24). *West Chester police were told a shoplifting suspect was white. They stopped a Black man.* [Video]. YouTube. https://www.youtube.com/watch?v=I-8edG3xZOU&t=116s

5   Linly, Z. (n.d.) *Black man files lawsuit accusing Ohio police officers of detaining him for a crime a White man was suspected of.* blAck Americaweb.com. https://blackamericaweb.com/2022/02/08/black-man-files-lawsuit-accusing-ohio-police-officers-of-detaining-him-for-a-crime-a-white-man-was-suspected-of/

Chapter 5
I Am Responding to Somebody Who Has A
Firearm Who Matches Your Description!

1   Rebel HQ. (2023, January 11). *AZ Cop Arrests Wrong Man Over SHOCKING Mistake.* [Video]. YouTube. https://www.youtube.com/watch?v=LdLqlugnAwE

2   Thornton, C. 'BIG CED' (2020, September 10). *Arizona police officer suspended after holding Black hotel employee at gunpoint while looking for White suspect.* Black Enterprise. https://www.blackenterprise.com/tempe-police-officer-suspended-holding-black-hotel-employee-at-gunpoint-white-suspect/

Chapter 6
You Fit the Description. You Fit the Description. You Fit the Description.

1   Imbalanced Status. (2020, September 9). *My Sgt. Say to Detain You... You Fit the Description 99%... Not Even Close.* [Video]. YouTube. https://www.youtube.com/watch?v=ydsOwV536nY

2   Rebel HQ. (2023, February 14). *LA Deputies Sued For Racial Profiling + Kidnapping Innocent.* [Video]. YouTube. Manhttps://www.youtube.com/watch?v=wJn5sZ6PFk0&t=51s; Don Andre Investigations. (2022, July 1). *California Cops Kidnap Man Eating Lunch In His Car.* [Video]. YouTube. https://www.youtube.com/watch?v=OfLl55B0wVE&t=1109s

3   Atlanta News First . (2020, June 26). *Mistaken identity leads to Black man's arrest.* [Video] YouTube. https://www.youtube.com/watch?v=FcFMW7fhl5E

Chapter 7
Are You Doing Anything Wrong?

1   KTVU Fox 2 San Francisco. (2023, March 6) *Bodycam video: Deputies detain Black mother, daughters at Castro Valley Starbucks.* [Video]. YouTube. https://www.youtube.com/watch?v=0HIe-vnBsO0

2   Guardian News. (2015, February 13). *Alabama police slam Indian grandfather into the ground, unprovoked.* https://www.youtube.com/watch?v=yNGQXeS_Xfk

3   Swaine, Jon. (2014, September, 7). *Doubts cast on witness's account of black man killed by police in Walmart.* The Guardian. https://www.theguardian.com/world/2014/sep/07/ohio-black-man-killed-by-police-walmart-doubts-cast-witnesss-account

4   KTVU Fox 2 San Francisco. (2023, March 6). *Jury awards $8.25M to Black mother, daughters handcuffed outside Castro Valley Starbucks.* [Video]. YouTube. https://www.youtube.com/watch?v=3sTh--DfYzI

5   New York Daily News. (2015, February 13). *Raw: Alabama cop charged with assault for slamming elderly man to ground.* [Video] YouTube. https://www.youtube.com/watch?v=3YL1ATsi3M8

6   Turner, S. (2021, April 9). *Indian man paid $1.75M in settlement in lawsuit over 2015 excessive force claim against former Madison police officer.* Fox 54. https://www.rocketcitynow.com/article/news/local/city-of-madison-175-million-settlement/525-8eed376a-68de-4d57-abec-20b358db68af

Chapter 8:
I Don't Know Who I Am Looking for Yet

1   Ockerman, Emma (2021, April 7). *Cops Arrested a Black Man Taking Out His Garbage While Looking For a White Suspect.* Vice News. https://www.vice.com/en/article/bvzggv/cops-arrested-a-black-man-taking-out-his-garbage-while-

looking-for-a-white-suspect

2   Good Morning America. (2021, April 8) *Body camera footage released of Black man arrested while taking out trash* 1 GMA. https://www.youtube.com/watch?v=RHoPDLl_DX4

Chapter 9:
You Stole Your Own Car!

1   The Laugh Academy. (2019, December 9). *Dave Chappelle - Calling 911.* [Video]. YouTube. https://www.youtube.com/watch?v=9xXNZPkzbTs

2   Morris, Bilal G. (2021, November 18, 2021). *Florida Black Man Says Miami PD Arrested Him For Stealing His Own Car.* Newsone. https://newsone.com/4249847/florida-black-man-says-miami-pd-arrested-him-for-stealing-his-own-car/#:~:text=On%20June%201%2C%202018%2C%20Samuel%20Scott%20Jr.%20called,police%20handcuffed%20Scott%2C%20believing%20he%20was%20the%20perpetrator.

3   Leavitt, Sarah. Morris, Erika (2022, November 5). *Black man handcuffed after car Montreal police thought was stolen ended up being his.* CBC. https://www.cbc.ca/news/canada/montreal/innocent-black-montreal-man-handcuffed-police-discriminated-against-him-1.6642194

4   Caruso-Moro, Luca. Lofaro, Joe.. (2022, November 6). *'You've humiliated me': Video shows Montreal police officers wrongly detain Black man, misplace key to handcuffs.* CTV News Montreal. https://montreal.ctvnews.ca/you-ve-humiliated-me-video-shows-montreal-police-officers-wrongly-detain-black-man-misplace-key-to-handcuffs-1.6140331

Chapter 10
Banking While Black

1   LiveNOW from FOX. (2023, Februuary 2). 'Banking While Black' grandmother sues bank for racial discrimination. [Video] YouTube. https://www.youtube.com/watch?v=s28Jxz8a94I

2   The Young Turks. (2023, February 21) *Marjorie Taylor Greene: Black People are "Lazy and Sorry."* [Video]. YouTube. https://www.youtube.com/watch?v=yN-tGXQJ7DA

3   Planas, Antonio (2022, February 3). *Black doctor sues JPMorgan Chase alleging she was refused service at Texas branch because of race.* NBC News. https://www.nbcnews.com/news/us-news/black-doctor-sues-jpmorgan-chase-alleging-was-refused-service-texas-br-rcna14753

4   CBC News: The National. (2021, April 28) *Black man refuses bank's apology fir 'degrading treatment.* CBC News. https://www.youtube.com/

watch?v=DiKXBKNR-Eg

5   Chin, Falice. (2020, October 31). *Banking barriers: How the Canadian financial sector excludes Black entrepreneurs, stifling innovation.* CBC Radio. https://www.cbc.ca/radio/costofliving/banking-while-black-1.5780927

6   Alamenciak, Tim. (2014, December 10). *Banking while black? Toronto man accuses Scotiabank of racial profiling.* Toronto Star. https://www.thestar.com/news/gta/2014/12/10/banking_while_black_toronto_man_accuses_scotiabank_of_racial_profiling.html

7   Sunshine, James. (2017, December 6). *Chase Bank reportedly has man jailed over check they issued him (VIDEO).* Huffpost. https://www.huffpost.com/entry/man-jailed-for-real-check_n_892296

Chapter 11
It Doesn't Matter Who You Are

1   Romo, Vanessa. (2023, February 4). *Yale honors the work of a 9-year-old Black girl whose neighbor reported her to police.* NPR. https://www.npr.org/2023/02/03/1154049233/yale-honors-9-year-old-black-girl-neighbor-reported-police-lanternfly#:~:text=The%20accolades%20come%20just%20three%20months%20after%20Bobbi%2C,is%20white%2C%20called%20local%20police%20on%20the%20girl

2   Department of Agriculture. *Spotted Lanternfly.* https://www.nj.gov/agriculture/divisions/pi/prog/pests-diseases/spotted-lanternfly/

3   The Associated Press. (2021, October 20). *Tiny wrists in cuffs: How police use force against children.* NPR. https://www.npr.org/2021/10/20/1047618263/tiny-wrists-in-cuffs-how-police-use-force-against-children

4   McCammon, Sarah. , Gabe, O'Connor. Brown Ashley. (2021, October 21). *Black children make up more than half of the incidents of police using force on kids.* NPR. https://www.npr.org/2021/10/21/1048130246/black-children-make-up-more-than-half-of-the-incidents-of-police-using-force-on-

5   The Young Turks. (2023, June 22). *Disturbing Bodycam Of Cops LIGHTING INTO Weeping 10-Year-Old Girl Released.* [Video]. YouTube. https://www.youtube.com/watch?v=qGgIqwOPIuE&t=37s

6   Patton, Stacy. (2014, November 26). In America, black children don't get to be children. The Washington Post. https://www.washingtonpost.com/opinions/in-america-black-children-dont-get-to-be-children/2014/11/26/a9e24756-74ee-11e4-a755-e32227229e7b_story.html

7   (2020, March 3). *Race was a factor in handcuffing of 6-year-old black girl in Mississauga school, tribunal says.* CBC News. https://www.cbc.ca/news/canada/

toronto/human-rights-tribunal-peel-police-girl-handcuffed-1.5483456

8   Natalia Goodwin. (2020, December 31) *Young Black men shaken after Ottawa police called on meeting.* CBC https://www.cbc.ca/news/canada/ottawa-black-police-mall-music-video-1.5857094

9   Morgan, Phillip Dwight. (2021, January 25). *Appalling incidents like the Keyon Harrold Jr. case happen to Black kids here too.* CBC News. https://www.cbc.ca/news/opinion/opinion-racism-black-childhood-1.5879421

10   Morgan, Phillip Dwight. (2021, January 25). *Appalling incidents like the Keyon Harrold Jr. case happen to Black kids here too.*

11   Davies, B. (2023, October) *Boy, 13, rammed off bike and surrounded by armed cops over blue and white water pistol.* Metro. https://metro.co.uk/2023/10/19/boy-13-tackled-by-police-after-water-pistol-mistaken-for-real-gun-19686499/?ico=top-stories_home_top

12   Giulia Heyward and João Costa (December 17, 2020) *Black children are 6 times more likely to be shot to death by police, study finds.* CNN. https://www.cnn.com/2020/12/17/us/black-children-police-brutality-trnd/index.html

13   MavDonald, E. (2015, June 13). *911 caller was frightened Tamir Rice might shoot him.* Cleveland.com. https://www.cleveland.com/metro/2015/06/911_caller_was_frightened_tami.html

14   Afshar, Paradise (2023, June 1). *Judge seals evidence in criminal case of White homeowner accused of shooting Black teen who went to the wrong house.* Microsoft Start. https://www.msn.com/en-ca/news/us/judge-seals-evidence-in-criminal-case-of-white-homeowner-accused-of-shooting-black-teen-who-went-to-the-wrong-house/ar-AA1c0GYq?ocid=msedgntp&cvid=85be05c8364a4c0d8a267b6a758e4064&ei=37

15   @josephmorris. (n.d.) A Kid Just Taking Out the Trash. [Video]. YouTube. https://www.youtube.com/shorts/JNKgbB3tJrI

16   The Canadian Press. (2023, August 11). *Michigan police detained a Black child who was in the 'wrong place, wrong time,' department says.* Microsoft Start. https://www.msn.com/en-ca/news/world/michigan-police-detained-a-black-child-who-was-in-the-wrong-place-wrong-time-department-says/ar-AA1fa5Ug?ocid=msedgdhp&pc=U531&cvid=9da7fb3bf4014abda8dfaab7bbb0d41b&ei=9

17   Nurse, K. (203, August 11). *Michigan police chief, mayor apologize after arrest video of 12-year-old boy goes viral.* Microsoft Start. https://www.msn.com/en-us/news/us/michigan-police-chief-mayor-apologize-after-arrest-video-of-12-year-old-boy-goes-viral/ar-AA1faCQN

18   KOIN 6 (2019, Octobe 9) Evicted DoubleTree guest files $10M racial profiling suit. [Video] YouTube. https://www.youtube.com/

watch?v=I64FB6wNlQI&t=94s

19   Griffith, Janelle. (2019, October 9). *African American guest ousted from Oregon hotel sues for $10 million.* NEWS. https://www.nbcnews.com/news/nbcblk/african-american-guest-ousted-oregon-hotel-sues-10-million-n1064361

20   Woodyard, Chris; Oliver, David. (2020, July 21). *'Do you belong here?': Lawsuits allege Hilton, other hotels discriminated against Black guests.* USA Today. https://www.usatoday.com/story/travel/hotels/2020/07/21/hilton-discrimination-lawsuits-black-guests-allege-racism-hotels/5405270002/

21   Woodyard, Chris; Oliver, David. (2020, July 21). *'Do you belong here?': Lawsuits allege Hilton, other hotels discriminated against Black guests*

22   Kansas City Star. (2022, March 28). *He was a detective with the Kansas City PD. And he still got pulled over for driving while Black.* [Video]. YouTube. https://www.youtube.com/watch?v=vYO6xZv_O5M

23   (2022, April 22). *Black Kansas City sergeant sues police after traffic stop* AP News. https://apnews.com/article/police-lawsuits-race-and-ethnicity-racial-injustice-kansas-city-cbfd8f48ab1c5417db21206f18e35978

24 Perano, Ursula (2023, March 30). *Republicans have met the enemy and his name is Alvin Bragg.* Daily Beast https://www.thedailybeast.com/republicans-have-met-the-enemy-and-his-name-is-alvin-bragg

25   Perano, Ursula (2023, March 30). *Republicans have met the enemy and his name is Alvin Bragg*

26   Palmer, Ewan. (2023, March 28). Donald Trump's bizarre Alvin Bragg baseball bat 'Threat' explanation. Newsweek. https://www.newsweek.com/donald-trump-baseball-bat-alvin-bragg-hannity-interview-1790801

27   Rupar, Aaron. [@atrupar]. (2023, March 19). Fox & Friends on Manhattan DA: "How many Black lives have you sacrificed under a higher crime city with increased murder rates to devote a limited number of resources to the priority of pursuing a weak case against Donald Trump" [Tweet]. Twitter. https://twitter.com/atrupar/status/1637444269324607489

28   Decoding Fox News [@DecodingFoxNews]. (2023, March 20). Former MTV reality star, Rachel Campos-Duffy, says that New York DA, Alvin Bragg, a Black man, must be listening to his 'master' George Soros, a Jewish man. She then ties the criminal case involving Trump into China and Hunter Biden - all in less than 1 minute. [Tweet]. Twitter. https://twitter.com/DecodingFoxNews/status/1637925978474160130

29   KMOV St. Louis. (2021, January 5). *Local police chief says he was racially profiled by officers in Alton, Illinois.* [Video]. YouTube. https://www.youtube.com/watch?v=PtmiL6JFTXQ

30   Institute for Justice. (2020, February 14). *Officers nearly beat innocent college student to death—Then claim immunity from all accountability.* [Video]. YouTube. https://www.youtube.com/watch?v=HujPlUyTXRY

31   The Telegraph. (2020, May 26). *White woman hysterically calls police to report 'African-American threatening her life.'* [Video]. YouTube. https://www.youtube.com/watch?v=2A4ugxEXkJI

32   Geigel, Natasha. (2020, August 19). *Waller County constable claims he was racially profiled during traffic stop.* Fox 26 Houston. https://www.fox26houston.com/news/waller-county-constable-claims-he-was-racially-profiled-during-traffic-stop

33   Central Park jogger case. (2023, June 9). In *Wikipedia.* https://en.wikipedia.org/wiki/Central_Park_jogger_case

34   History.com Editors. (2019, September 23). *The Central Park Five.* History. https://www.history.com/topics/1980s/central-park-five

35   Central Park jogger case. (2023, June 9) In *Wikipedia.*

36   Central Park jogger case. (2023, June 9) In *Wikipedia*

37   Central Park jogger case. (2023, June 9) In *Wikipedia.*

38   Morin, Rebecca. (2019, June 20). *'They admitted their guilt': 30 years of Trump's comments about the Central Park Five.* USA Today. https://www.usatoday.com/story/news/politics/2019/06/19/what-trump-has-said-central-park-five/1501321001/

39   Morin, Rebecca. (2019, June 20)

40   Carpenter, Mackenzie (March 29, 2003). *"Central Park jogger writes book about her life since attack; 'How the hell did I survive?'".* Pittsburgh Post-Gazette. Archived from the original on May 2, 2014

41   Relman, Eliza., & Haroun, Azmi. (2023, May 9). *The 26 women who have accused Trump of sexual misconduct.* Insider. https://www.businessinsider.com/women-accused-trump-sexual-misconduct-list-2017-12

42   Orden, Erica, & McGraw, Meridith, & Garrity, Kelly. (2023, March 30). *Trump indicted in porn star hush money payment case.* Politico. https://www.politico.com/news/2023/03/30/trump-indicted-in-porn-star-hush-money-payment-case-00089837

43   Reuters, Thomson. (2023, May 9). *Jury finds Donald Trump sexually abused and defamed columnist E. Jean Carroll.* CBC News. https://www.cbc.ca/news/world/civil-trial-trump-carroll-verdict-1.6836967

44   The Associated Press. (2023, May 2). *Woman testifies at rape trial that Donald Trump molested her on a plane in 1970s.* CBC News. https://www.cbc.ca/news/world/jessica-leeds-testifies-trump-rape-trial-1.6829645

45   Valle, L., Herb, Jeremy, et al. (2024, January). *Jury finds Trump must pay $83.3*

million to E. Jean Carroll. CNN Politics. https://www.cnn.com/politics/live-news/ trump-trial-e-jean-carroll-01-26-24/index.html

46   Eagle News. (2016, October 12). *Donald Trump - On Tape - I Grab Women By The Pussy – Election 2016.* [Video]. YouTube. https://www.youtube.com/ watch?v=qey5h-WvsVA

47   Sheth, Sonam, & Panetta, Grace. (2019, September 26). *Trump suggested the whistleblower who filed a complaint against him is guilty of treason, which is punishable by death.* Insider. https://www.businessinsider.com/trump-suggests-whistleblower-guilty-of-treason-2019-9

48   Sheth, Sonam, & Panetta, Grace. (2019, September 26). *Trump suggested the whistleblower who filed a complaint against him is guilty of treason, which is punishable by death*

49   Vice News. (2019, October 2). *Trump's long love affair with the death penalty.* [Video] YouTube. https://www.bing.com/videos/

50   Popli, Nik, & Zorthian, Julia. (2023, May 26). What happened to the Jan. 6 rioters arrested since the Capitol attack. *Time.* https://time.com/6133336/jan-6-capitol-riot-arrests-sentences/

51   Cheney, Kyle, & Gerstein, Josh. (2023, June 9). *Trump haphazardly stashed military secrets throughout his home, indictment says.* Politico. https://www.politico.com/news/2023/06/09/trump-indictment-read-00101292

52   Cheney, Kyle, & Gerstein, Josh. (2023, June 9)

53   Cheney, Kyle, & Gerstein, Josh. (2023, June 9)

54   Cheney, Kyle, & Gerstein, Josh. (2023, June 9)

55   Vice News. (2019, October 2). *Trump's long love affair with the death penalty*

56   Vice News. (2019, October 2). *Trump's long love affair with the death penalty*

57   Vice News. (2019, October 2). *Trump's long love affair with the death penalty*

58   Smith, Ben, & Tau, Byron. (2011, March 22) *Birtherism: Where it all began.* Politico. https://www.politico.com/story/2011/04/birtherism-where-it-all-began-053563

59   CNN. (2015, February 19). *Flashback: McCain tells supporter Obama is 'a decent. ... [Video]. YouTube. https://www.youtube.com/watch?v=JIjenjANqAk

60   Serwer, Adam. (2020, May 13). Birtherism of a nation. *The Atlantic.* https:// www.theatlantic.com/ideas/archive/2020/05/birtherism-and-trump/610978/

61   Smith, Ben, & Tau, Byron. (2011, March 22) *Birtherism: Where it all began*

62   Smith, Ben, & Tau, Byron. (2011, March 22) *Birtherism: Where it all began*

63   Clinton, Josh, & Roush, Carrie. (2016, August 10). *Poll: Persistent Partisan Divide Over 'Birther' Question.* NBC News. https://www.nbcnews.com/politics/2016-election/poll-persistent-partisan-divide-over-birther-question-n627446

64   Smith, Ben, & Tau, Byron. (2011, March 22) *Birtherism: Where it all began*

65   NowThisNews. (2019, May 30). *Officer pulls gun on student picking up trash outside of dorm building.* [Video]. YouTube. https://www.youtube.com/watch?v=Q9SZlypyK-4

66   Inside Edition. (2021, October 15). *Black Parking Worker says 'Mother and Son Karens' harassed him.* [Video]. YouTube. https://www.youtube.com/watch?v=xt_aSQ6-_b0

67   Roland S. Martin. (2022, August 13). *Woman calls cops on Black man standing in front of his house | 'I'd just like to see the lease'.* [Video]. YouTube. https://www.youtube.com/watch?v=IY3Au5n_oy4&t=767s

68   Krieg, Gregory. (2016, September 16). *14 of Trump's most outrageous 'birther' claims – half from after 2011.* CNN Politics. https://www.cnn.com/2016/09/09/politics/donald-trump-birther/index.html

69   SuchIsLifeVideos. (2011, April 21). *Melania Trump On Obama's Birth Certificate.* [Video] YoyTube. https://www.youtube.com/watch?v=P6i0YlHriKk

70   Associated Press. (2008, October 11). *McCain Counters Obama 'Arab' Question.* [Video]. YouTube. https://www.youtube.com/watch?v=jrnRU3ocIH4

71   CBS News. (2016, August 11). *Trump claims Obama founded ISIS.* https://www.cbsnews.com/news/trump-claims-obama-founded-isis/

72   Human rights in Islamic State-controlled territory. (2023, April 23). In *Wikipedia.* https://en.wikipedia.org/wiki/Human_rights_in_Islamic_State-controlled_territory#:~:text=under%20ISIL's%20control.-,Genocide%20and%20other%20war%20crimes,been%20recognized%20as%20a%20genocide

73   Roller, Emma. (2014, June 3). A Brief History of GOP Calls for Obama's Impeachment, From Benghazi to Bergdahl. *The Atlantic.* https://www.theatlantic.com/politics/archive/2014/06/a-brief-history-of-gop-calls-for-obamas-impeachment-from-benghazi-to-bergdahl/455544/

74   (2016, September 16). *US election: Trump accepts Barack Obama was born in US.* BBC. https://www.bbc.com/news/election-us-2016-37381452

Chapter 12
Some People Never Fit the Description

1   CNN. (2022, February 17). *Video showing how police treat Black and White teens in mall fight sparks outrage.* [Video]. YouTube. https://www.youtube.com/watch?v=dpS8-YWNadE

2   Luscombe, Richard. (2022, February 17). *Police stop brawl by letting white youth sit on sofa as Black teen is handcuffed.* The Guardian. https://www.theguardian.com/us-news/2022/feb/17/new-jersey-brawling-teenagers-black-white

3   Luscombe, Richard. (2022, February 17). *Police stop brawl by letting white youth sit on sofa as Black teen is handcuffed*

4   Freifeld, Karen, & Levine, Dan. (2016, November 18). *Trump agrees to pay $25 million to settle Trump University lawsuits.* Reuters. https://www.reuters.com/article/us-trump-lawsuit-idUSKBN13D1UI

5   Clark, Dartunorro. (2019, December 10). *Trump paid $2 million judgment for misusing his charity, New York attorney general says.* NBC. https://www.nbcnews.com/politics/politics-news/trump-pays-2-million-judgment-misusing-his-charity-new-york-n1099296

6   Trump And Our Two-Tiered Justice System | The Problem with Jon Stewart https://www.youtube.com/shorts/hR83TssFcog

7   Bernstein, Andrea, & Marritz, Ilya, & Mann, Brian (2022, December 6) *Former President Donald Trump's company is found guilty of criminal tax fraud.* NPR. https://www.npr.org/2022/12/06/1140756394/former-president-donald-trumps-company-found-guilty-criminal-tax-fraud

8   Scannell, Kara. (2023, April 19). *Former Trump Org. CFO Allen Weisselberg is released from Rikers Island jail.* CNN Politics. https://www.cnn.com/2023/04/19/politics/allen-weisselberg-released-rikers/index.html

9   BBC. (2019, December 22). *Trump impeachment: White House withheld Ukraine aid just after Zelensky call.* https://www.bbc.com/news/world-us-canada-50886437

10   Guardian US staff. (2022, February 7). *The long list of legal cases against Donald Trump.* The Guardian. https://www.theguardian.com/us-news/ng-interactive/2022/feb/07/donald-trump-list-legal-cases

11   Honderich, Holly (2023. April 5). *Donald Trump pleads not guilty to 34 felony counts in hush money case.* BBC News. https://www.bbc.com/news/world-us-canada-65182264

12   Grabenstein, H. (2023, August 15). Read the full Georgia indictment against Trump and 18 allies. PBS. https://www.pbs.org/newshour/politics/read-the-full-georgia-indictment-against-trump-and-18-allies

13   Orden, Erica, & Parnell, Wesley. (2023, April 9). *Jury finds Trump liable for sexual abuse in E. Jean Carroll case.* Politico. https://www.politico.com/news/2023/05/09/trump-e-jean-carroll-trial-verdict-00096009

14   Reuters, Thomson. (2023, June 13). *Donald Trump pleads not guilty to all 37 criminal charges in classified documents case.* CBC News. https://www.cbc.ca/news/world/trump-court-appearance-documents-1.6874391

15   Neidig, Harper. (2016, June 9). *Report: Trump has refused to pay hundreds of workers.* The Hill. https://thehill.com/blogs/ballot-box/presidential-races/282933-report-trump-has-refused-to-pay-hundreds-of-workers/

16   Forbes Breaking News. (2023, March 31). *JUST IN: NY DA Alvin Bragg Responds To GOP After Attacks Over Trump Indictment.* [Video]. YouTube. https://www.youtube.com/watch?v=gzj9zQPk3uo&t=46s

17   @CNN. *"An Outrage": Pence reacts to Trump indictment.* https://www.youtube.com/shorts/abG1WRY0C8g

18   Moore, Mark. (2023, March 20). *DeSantis blasts 'Soros-funded' DA Bragg over imminent Trump arrest.* New York Post. https://nypost.com/2023/03/20/desantis-blasts-da-bragg-as-a-soros-funded-prosecutor-in-trump-probe/

19   Brown, Hayes. (2023, March 18). *McCarthy just made it clear that he's picked Trump over the rule of law.* MSNBC. https://www.msnbc.com/opinion/msnbc-opinion/kevin-mccarthy-tweet-trump-potential-arrest-bragg-dangerous-rcna75595

20   MSNBC. (2023, April 6). *Speaker McCarthy reacts to Trump indictment: 'It's not just Republicans who view this as political.'* [Video]. YouTube. https://www.youtube.com/watch?v=4V33nhRFWzY

21   Chowdhury, Maureen, & Powell, Tori B., & Meyer, Matt. (2023, June 8). *Speaker McCarthy calls Trump indictment "grave injustice."* CNN Politics. https://www.cnn.com/politics/live-news/mar-a-lago-documents-probe-latest/h_2e0243980df2457ddcfc450b0b063a5a

22   Colson-Price, Patrick, (2023, June 21). *House Democrats chant 'shame, shame' after GOP votes to censure Rep. Adam Schiff.* USA TODAY. https://www.usatoday.com/videos/news/politics/2023/06/21/house-democrats-rally-behind-rep-adam-schiff-after-gop-censure-vote/12144330002/

23   Wong, Scott, & Stewart, Kyle. (2023, June 21). *Republicans take the rare step of censuring Rep. Adam Schiff over Trump-era probes.* NBC News. https://www.nbcnews.com/politics/congress/house-republicans-censure-rep-adam-schiff-trump-era-probes-rcna90451

24   Wong, Scott, & Stewart, Kyle. (2023, June 21). *Republicans take the rare step of censuring Rep. Adam Schiff over Trump-era probes*

25   Stieb, Matt, & Hartmann, Margaret. (2023, May 12). *Here's every single lie told by George Santos.* Intelligencer. https://nymag.com/intelligencer/article/guide-george-santos-lies.html

26   Guardian staff and agency. (2023, April 7). *Two Democrats expelled from Tennessee house over gun control protest.* https://www.theguardian.com/us-news/2023/apr/06/tennessee-gun-control-protest-house-expel-democrats

27   Schmunk, R. (2023, December 1). *George Santos expelled from U.S. Congress in wake of criminal charges, ethics disgrace.* CBC. https://www.cbc.ca/news/world/george-santos-expelled-from-house-1.7046258

28   Peller, L. (2023, November 1). *Republican-led push to expel George Santos fails in the House.* abc News. https://abcnews.go.com/Politics/ny-republicans-force-vote-push-expel-george-santos/story?id=104539525

29   PBS. (2023, June 13). *Read the full Trump indictment on mishandling of classified documents.* PBS News Hour. https://www.pbs.org/newshour/politics/read-the-full-trump-indictment-on-mishandling-of-classified-documents

30   Dale, Daniel. (2023, June 15). *Fact check: Multiple non-spies have received prison sentences under Espionage Act provision Trump is charged with violating.* CNN Politics. https://www.cnn.com/2023/06/15/politics/fact-check-espionage-act-trump-willful-retention-prison/index.html

31   WMUR-TV. (2023, June 11). *CloseUp: Pence promises overhaul of DOJ leadership.* [Video]. YouTube. https://www.youtube.com/watch?v=ImZKKB-w4eQ

32   Pilkington, Ed (2023, March 27). *Marjorie Taylor Greene led delegation to visit Capitol attack defendants in jail.* The Guardian. https://www.theguardian.com/us-news/2023/mar/27/marjorie-taylor-greene-led-delegation-to-visit-capitol-attack-defendants-in-jail

33   Neukam, Stephen. (2023, March 26). *Trump opens campaign rally with song featuring Jan. 6 defendants.* The Hill. https://thehill.com/homenews/campaign/3918877-trump-opens-campaign-rally-with-song-featuring-jan-6-defendants/

34   The Damage Report. (2023, June 13). *Kevin McCarthy's BIZARRE Defense of Trump Storing Classified Docs In His Bathroom.* [Video]. YouTube. https://www.youtube.com/watch?v=CEFZeMOKWQI

35   Forbes Breaking News. *BREAKING NEWS: Speaker Johnson Defends Blurring Faces In Jan. 6 Footage So DOJ Can't Target People.* [Video]. YouTube. https://www.youtube.com/watch?v=UFa6ezHpxxI

36   Axelrod, T. (2023, October 27). *Mike Johnson helped lead efforts to overturn the 2020 election. What that could mean for 2024.* abc News. https://abcnews.go.com/Politics/mike-johnson-led-efforts-overturn-2020-election-2024/story?id=104351307

37   Racker, Mini. (2023, June 21). Would they pardon Trump? How every GOP presidential candidate has answered. *Time.* https://time.com/6288861/donald-trump-pardon-2024-candidates-desantis-pence/

38   Ramirez, Nikki McCann. (2023, June 23). *Kevin McCarthy, who bashed Trump After Jan. 6., now backs effort to expunge impeachments.* Rolling Stone. https://www.rollingstone.com/politics/politics-news/kevin-mccarthy-backs-effort-expunge-trump-impeachments-1234777282/

39   Sigman, B. (2023, August 23) *Seven of eight Republican candidates raise hands*

to say they'd support Trump as nominee even if convicted. Microsoft Start. https://www.
msn.com/en-us/news/other/seven-of-eight-republican-candidates-raise-hands-
to-say-they-d-support-trump-as-nominee-even-if-convicted/ar-AA1fHepD

40 @Midas Touch. (n. d,) *Jamie Raskin OBLITERATES Trump on House
Floor, leaves his colleagues SPEECHLESS.* https://www.youtube.com/shorts/
c3zDm8Y8IW8

41 Marina Pitofsky. (2023, June 25). *Christie responds after being booed
while criticizing Trump: 'They need to hear the truth'.* USA TODAY. https://www.
usatoday.com/story/news/politics/2023/06/25/chris-christie-booed-donald-
trump/70354879007/

42 Commander, Anna. (2023, April 8). Greg Abbott wants to pardon Army
Sgt. convicted of killing BLM protestor. *Newsweek.* https://www.newsweek.com/
greg-abbott-wants-pardon-army-sgt-convicted-killing-blm-protestor-1793309

43 Munro, Andre.(n.d.). *Shooting of Trayvon Martin.* Britannica. https://www.
britannica.com/event/shooting-of-Trayvon-Martin

44 Commander, Anna. (2023, April 8). Greg Abbott wants to pardon Army
Sgt. convicted of killing BLM protestor. *Newsweek*

45 Etehad. M. (2022, November 8). *Upending Democracy: Texas man arrested at
the ballot box.* The Bail Project. https://bailproject.org/stories/hervis-houston/

46 (November 16, 2021). *Attorney General Ford announces guilty plea of Las Vegas
man charged with voter fraud.* https://ag.nv.gov/News/PR/2021/Attorney_General_
Ford_Announces_Guilty_Plea_of_Las_Vegas_Man_Charged_with_Voter_Fraud/

47 Siemaszko, C. (2021, June 22). *Republican official in Ohio faces charge for voting
twice in November election.* NBC News. https://www.nbcnews.com/news/us-news/
republican-official-ohio-faces-charge-voting-twice-november-election-n1271985

Chapter 13
What is the Value of a Black Life?

1 Cohen, Luc. (2023, March 12). *Former US Marine charged with manslaughter in
NYC subway choking death.* Reuters. https://www.reuters.com/world/us/former-us-
marine-surrenders-be-charged-choking-death-new-york-subway-cnn-2023-05-
12/#:~:text=According%20to%20witnesses%2C%20Neely%2C%20who%20was%20
known%20to,to%20stop%20moving%2C%20and%20was%20later%20declared%20
dead

2 ABC 7 Chicago. (2023, May 6). *Marine veteran who held man in fatal chokehold
on NYC subway 'never intended to harm' him: attorneys.* [Video]. YouTube. https://www.
youtube.com/watch?v=iaXO5x0yu-4

3 Reuters, Thomas. (2023, May 5). *Hundreds protest over Black man's killing by*

fellow passenger on NYC subway. CBC. https://www.cbc.ca/news/world/black-man-choke-death-subway-new-york-city-1.6834607

4 Reuters, Thomas. (2023, May 5). *Hundreds protest over Black man's killing by fellow passenger on NYC subway.* CBC

5 Madani, Doha. (2023, June 12). *Daniel Penny disputes he held Jordan Neely in a chokehold for 15 minutes on NYC subway.* NBC News. https://www.nbcnews.com/news/us-news/daniel-penny-disputes-held-jordan-neely-chokehold-15-minutes-nyc-subwa-rcna88916

6 Indisputable with Dr. Rashad Richey. (2023, May 8). *UPDATE: Jordan Neely's Killer Breaks Silence.* [Video]. YouTube. https://www.youtube.com/watch?v=GjeQOJjKKRU

7 Madani, Doha. (2023, June 12). *Daniel Penny disputes he held Jordan Neely in a chokehold for 15 minutes on NYC subway.* NBC

8 Statista Research Department. (2015, July 30). *Average price paid in the Thirteen Colonies for slaves from Britain's American colonies and West Africa from 1638 to 1775.* https://www.statista.com/statistics/1069716/british-american-west-african-slave-prices/

9 *Currency converter: 1270–2017.* The National Archives. https://www.nationalarchives.gov.uk/currency-converter/#currency-result

10 Reuters. (2023, June 27). *Slavery's descendants: America's family secret* NBC News. https://www.nbcnews.com/news/us-news/slaverys-descendants-americas-family-secret-rcna90826

11 Haq, S. N., Berlinger, J., John, T., Neild, B., & Xu, X. (2023, July 1). *Protests are sweeping France. Here's what you need to know.* CNN World. https://www.cnn.com/2023/06/30/europe/nanterre-france-police-protests-explainer-intl/index.htmll

12 The Breakdown. (2023, June 26). *Trump Supporters Are SO PROUD Of This Embarrassing Take.* [Video]. YouTube. https://www.youtube.com/watch?v=nmJoRyR0oRQ&t=126s

13 Martin, S. (2014, February 19). *Living Conditions Of African Americans in the 1960's.* Prezi. https://prezi.com/p1j15rv-vxzn/living-conditions-of-african-americans-in-the-1960s/

14 (2019, September 22). *African-Americans in the 1960s Essay.* IvyPanda. https://ivypanda.com/essays/african-americans-in-the-1960s/

15 Burnside, Tina. (2023, June 23). *Georgia police department under investigation for allegedly using an image of a Black man as a shooting target during a safety class.* CNN. https://www.cnn.com/2023/06/23/us/georgia-police-black-man-shooting-target/index.html

16   Indisputable with Dr. Rashad Richey. (2023, June 22). *Georgia Cops Use Only Photos Of Black Man For Target Practice.* [Video]. YouTube. https://www.youtube.com/watch?v=jOcMf_arUUI&t=19s

17   Indisputable with Dr. Rashad Richey. (2023, June 21). *WATCH: Bed, Bath & Beyond Bigotry Is Too Much For Cops To Handle.* [Video]. YouTube. https://www.youtube.com/watch?v=8qrCJuKAgVw&t=1s

18   Burnside, Tina. (2023, June 23). *Georgia police department under investigation for allegedly using an image of a Black man as a shooting target during a safety class.* CNN

19   Richardson, R. (2021, May 29). *Tulsa Race Massacre, 100 years later: Why it happened and why it's still relevant today.* News. https://www.nbcnews.com/news/nbcblk/tulsa-race-massacre-100-years-later-why-it-happened-why-n1268877

20   Getahun, H. (2023 July 9). *A reparations case brought by the 1921 Tulsa Race Massacre's centenarian survivors was dismissed with prejudice.* Insider. https://www.insider.com/judge-dismisses-reparations-case-survivors-tulsa-race-massacre-2023-7

21   Richardson, R. (2021, May 29). Tulsa Race Massacre, 100 years later: Why it happened and why it's still relevant today

22   Hassan, A., & Healy, J. (2029, June 19). America Has Tried Reparations Before. Here Is How It Went. *The New York Times.* https://www.nytimes.com/2019/06/19/us/reparations-slavery.html

23   Hassan, A., & Healy, J. (2029, June 19). *America Has Tried Reparations Before*

24   Hassan, A., & Healy, J. (2029, June 19). *America Has Tried Reparations Before*

25   Compensated emancipation. (2023, July 14). In *Wikipedia.* https://en.wikipedia.org/wiki/Compensated_emancipation

26   Compensated emancipation. (2023, July 14)

27   An Interview with Sylla, N. S., & Pigeaud, F. (2021, March 29). *How France Continues to Dominate Its Former Colonies in Africa.* Jacobin. https://jacobin.com/2021/03/africa-colonies-france-cfa-franc-currency; *Why African countries pay a colonial tax in France despite their independence?* Afrikhepri Foundation. https://afrikhepri.org/pourquoi-les-pays-africains-payent-un-impot-colonial-en-france-malgre-leur-independance/

28   Compensated emancipation. (2023, July 14). In *Wikipedia.* https://

29   Jimenez, O., & Riess, R. (2023, July 8). *Oklahoma judge dismisses Tulsa race massacre reparations case filed by last known survivors.* CNN. https://www.cnn.com/2023/07/08/us/tulsa-race-massacre-reparations-case/index.html

30   WXYZ-TV Detroit | Channel 7. (2019, August 15). Royal Oak Police apologize to black man stopped after white woman claimed. Video. YouTube. https://www.youtube.com/watch?v=yMtzluVfxVo

31   Neavling, S. (2019, August 16). *Royal Oak police disciplines an officer, apologizes for encounter with Black man.* Detroit Metro Times. https://www.metrotimes.com/news/royal-oak-police-disciplines-an-officer-apologizes-for-encounter-with-black-man-22411053

32   Hillary Chiwanza, Takudzwa. (2020, June 11). *The Hidden Holocaust: How King Leopold II Murdered 10 Million Africans.* The African Exponent. https://www.africanexponent.com/post/7586-the-hidden-holocaust-how-king-leopold-ii-murdered-10-million-africans

33   Blakemore, Erin. (2023, January 27). How the Holocaust happened in plain sight. *National Geographic.* https://www.nationalgeographic.com/history/article/holocaust-adolf-hitler-history-genocide-denial?loggedin=true&rnd=1688217195174

34   Rannard, Georgina, & Webster, Eve. (2020, June 13). *Leopold II: Belgium 'wakes up' to its bloody colonial past.* BBC News. https://www.bbc.com/news/world-europe-53017188

35   Rannard, Georgina, & Webster, Eve. (2020, June 13). *Leopold II: Belgium 'wakes up' to its bloody colonial past*

36   Rannard, Georgina, & Webster, Eve. (2020, June 13). *Leopold II: Belgium 'wakes up' to its bloody colonial past.*

37   Aguilar, Bryann. (2021, June 25). *Pastor resigns from Mississauga church over comment about 'good that was done' in residential schools.* CTV News. https://toronto.ctvnews.ca/pastor-resigns-from-mississauga-church-over-comment-about-good-that-was-done-in-residential-schools-1.5486557

38   Nsehe, Mfonobong. (2012, February 9). *The five worst leaders in Africa.* Forbes. https://www.forbes.com/sites/mfonobongnsehe/2012/02/09/the-five-worst-leaders-in-africa/?sh=baa1514dda2e

39   KTVU FOX 2 San Francisco. (2023, January 27). *Video released of Memphis police beating.* [Video]. YouTube. https://www.youtube.com/watch?v=m_4xDRXH_70

Chapter 14
Black Beauty Unveiled In a Colorless World

1   NBC News. (2023, July 13). *Rep. Crane refers to Black people as 'colored people' on House floor.* [Video]. YouTube. https://www.youtube.com/watch?v=r5DQZ54GqWY

2   Butterly, A. (2015, January 27). *Warning: Why using the term 'coloured' is offensive.* BBC News. https://www.bbc.com/news/newsbeat-30999175

3   History.com Editors. (2023, April 11). *Jim Crow Laws.* HISTORY. https://

www.history.com/topics/early-20th-century-us/jim-crow-laws

4   Wang, A. B. (2023, July 14). GOP lawmaker says he 'misspoke' in referring to 'colored people' on House floor. *The Washington Post*. https://www.washingtonpost.com/politics/2023/07/14/gop-lawmaker-says-he-misspoke-referring-colored-people-house-floor/

5   One-drop rule. (2023, June 7). In *Wikipedia*. https://en.wikipedia.org/wiki/One-drop_rule

6   Hypodescent. (2023, June 22). In *Wikipedia*. https://en.wikipedia.org/wiki/Hypodescent

7   Sally Hemings. (2023, June 25). In *Wikipedia*. https://en.wikipedia.org/wiki/Sally_Hemings

8   John Wayles. (2023, June 1). In *Wikipedia*. https://en.wikipedia.org/wiki/John_Wayles

9   Sally Hemings. (2023, June 25). In *Wikipedia*

10   Sally Hemings. (2023, June 25). In *Wikipedia*

11   Danny, Lewis. (2016, September 22). *George Washington's biracial family is getting new recognition*. Smithsonian Magazine. https://www.smithsonianmag.com/smart-news/george-washingtons-biracial-family-new-recognition-180960553/

12   Kunhardt Film Foundation. (January 4, 2021). *Jon Meacham Interview: On the Struggles that Define America*. [Video]. YouTube. https://www.youtube.com/watch?v=Xl9PQk1C9gQ&t=209s

13   MSNBC. (2023, July 30). *Congressional Black Caucus Chair: 'Black people are under attack'*. [Video]. YouTube. https://www.youtube.com/watch?v=YbBH7gpn448

14   Goodreads. https://www.goodreads.com/quotes/66880-christ-has-no-body-now-but-yours-no-hands-no

15   Andone, D. (2023, April). *Nashville school shooter fired 152 rounds during the attack, which was planned 'over a period of months,' police say*. CNN. https://www.cnn.com/2023/04/03/us/covenant-school-shooting-nashville-tennessee-monday/index.html

16   The Associated Press. (2023, March 30). *Terror of Nashville school attack captured in 911 recordings*. CBC. https://www.cbc.ca/news/world/nashville-school-shooting-911-calls-1.6796362

17   Despart, Z. (2022, July 17). *"Systemic failures" in Uvalde shooting went far beyond local police, Texas House report details*. The Texas Tribune. https://www.texastribune.org/2022/07/17/law-enforcement-failure-uvalde-shooting-investigation/

18   Gekiempis, V. (2023, May 19) *How Republicans are embracing the accused subway killer Daniel Penny*. The Guardian. https://www.theguardian.com/us-

news/2023/may/19/daniel-penny-legal-defense-fundraising

19   The Canadian Press. (2023, July 18). *In backlash over their expulsions, 2 Tennessee Democratic lawmakers raised $2M combined.* Microsoft Start. https://www.msn.com/en-ca/news/world/in-backlash-over-their-expulsions-2-tennessee-democratic-lawmakers-raised-2m-combined/ar-AA1e2cAi?ocid=msedgntp&cvid=72ed7a386fea4d1288aee62886654fea&ei=7

20   Smith, A, & Burns, D. (2023, March 31). *Trump campaign says it raised more than $4 million in the 24 hours after his indictment.* News. https://www.nbcnews.com/politics/donald-trump/trump-raised-4-million-day-indictment-rcna77699

21   Reuters. (2023, June 14). *Trump raises $7 million for 2024 campaign since federal indictment.* Reuters. https://www.reuters.com/world/us/trump-raises-7-million-2024-campaign-since-federal-indictment-2023-06-15/

22   Price, M, L, & Chandler, K. (2023, August 4). *Trump boasts at Alabama fundraiser that he needs 'one more indictment to close out this election'.* Richmond News. https://www.richmond-news.com/politics/trump-boasts-at-alabama-fundraiser-that-he-needs-one-more-indictment-to-close-out-this-election-7371753

23   Kim, S. R. & Ibssa L. (2023 August 29). *Trump campaign says it has raised more than $9 million since mug shot.* cbc news. https://abcnews.go.com/Politics/trump-campaign-raised-9-million-mug-shot/story?id=102662645

24   The Associated Press. (2023, June 15). *Ex-Starbucks manager awarded $25.6M US for firing after racially charged controversy.* CBC. https://www.cbc.ca/news/world/starbucks-jury-philadelphia-incident-1.6877402

25   Winsor, M., & McCarthy, K. (2018, April 19). *Men arrested at Starbucks were there for business meeting hoping to change 'our lives'.* abc News. https://abcnews.go.com/GMA/News/men-arrested-starbucks-business-meeting-hoping-change-lives/story?id=54578217

26   Cruz, A. (2018, May 2). *Following Starbucks Arrests, Rashon Nelson and Donte Robinson Convince Philadelphia to Set Up Charity Program.* TeenVogue. https://www.teenvogue.com/story/starbucks-arrests-rashon-nelson-donte-robinson-philadelphia-charity-program

27   Mezzacappa, D. (2022, May 23). *Philadelphia area schools among the most segregated in the country.* Chalkbeat Philadelphia. https://philadelphia.chalkbeat.org/2022/5/23/23137855/philadelphia-area-schools-among-most-segregated-country

28   History. (2023, January 1). *Rosa Parks.* https://www.history.com/topics/black-history/rosa-parks

29   National Parks Service. (2022, September 21). *The Montgomery Bus Boycott.* https://www.nps.gov/articles/montgomery-bus-boycott.htm

30   History.com Editors. (2023, January 11). *Rosa Parks.* History. https://www.history.com/topics/black-history/rosa-parks

31   Homer Plessy. (2023, October 2). In *Wikipedia.* https://en.wikipedia.org/wiki/Homer_Plessy

32   Rumble, T. (2018, March 8). *Claudette Colvin: The 15-year-old who came before Rosa Parks.* BBC News. https://www.bbc.com/news/stories-43171799

33   NewsOne Staff. (2023, February 4). Remembering Rosa Parks' Resilience And Resistance In The Face Of Racism. NewsOne. https://newsone.com/3762302/rosa-parks-bus-boycott-anniversary-facts-quotes-civil-rights-movement-remembered/

34   History.com Editors. 2023, January 10). *Montgomery Bus Boycott.* History. https://www.history.com/topics/black-history/montgomery-bus-boycott

35   Browne-Marshall, G. J. (2019, September 11). *Busing Ended 20 Years Ago. Today Our Schools Are Segregated Once Again.* Time. https://time.com/5673555/busing-school-segregation/

36   Daniels, C. M. (2023, July 26). *Alpha Phi Alpha moves 2025 convention out of Florida over 'racist' policies.* The Hill. https://thehill.com/homenews/state-watch/4121028-alpha-phi-alpha-moves-2025-convention-out-of-florida-over-racist-policies/

37   Roland S. Martin. (2023, July 7). *Alpha Phi Alpha MOVES 2025 Convention Out Of Florida Over 'RACIST' Policies | Roland Martin.* [Video]. YouTube. https://www.youtube.com/watch?v=eS7nW7MNIKE

38   Draaisma, M. (2022, March 9). *Antisemitic and anti-Black racist graffiti found at 3 York Region schools, police investigating.* CBC. https://www.cbc.ca/news/canada/toronto/newmarket-schools-antisemitic-anti-black-graffiti-york-region-police-school-board-1.6379239

39   CityNews. (2022, February 10). *Toronto Police are investigating anti-Black graffiti at Etobicoke School.* [Video]. YouTube. https://www.youtube.com/watch?v=7CW3QaQwFbU

40   Haring, B. (2019, July 27). *CNN Anchor Victor Blackwell Breaks Down On Camera After Trump Attack On His Home District.* Deadline. https://deadline.com/2019/07/cnn-victor-blackwell-emotional-elijah-cummings-trump-attack-1202655456/

41   Greene, R. (2006). *The 33 Strategies of War.* Viking

42   WatchlistTYT. (2022, October 17). *Kansas City Police Blatantly Ignore The Cries Of The Black Community.* [Video]. YouTube. https://www.youtube.com/watch?v=h_39KfDVqMk

43   Democracy Now! (2022, 18). *How Kansas City Police Ignored Warnings a*

Killer Targeted Black Women, Until One Escaped. Democracynow.org. https://www.democracynow.org/2022/10/18/missouri_police_ignored_claims_black_missing

44   Gamble, J. & Brown, J. (2022, October 19). *Black woman escaped after being 'held against her will' by a White man in Missouri, police say.* CNN. https://www.cnn.com/2022/10/18/us/missouri-reports-missing-black-women-reaj/index.html

45   Democracy Now! (2022, 18). *How Kansas City Police Ignored Warnings a Killer Targeted Black Women, Until One Escaped*

46   Corbishley. S. (2023, October 27). *Anger after £44,000 raised for Met officers sacked over search of black athletes.* Metro. https://metro.co.uk/2023/10/27/more-than-44000-raised-for-met-officers-sacked-over-search-of-black-athletes-19728577/?ico=top-stories_news_top#:~:text=The%20money%20has%20been%20pledged%20on%20a%20crowdfunding,two%20black%20Olympic%20athletes%20has%20been%20slammed%20online

47   Etehad, M. (2022, November). *Upending Democracy: Texas Man Arrested at the Ballot Box. The Bail Project.* https://bailproject.org/stories/hervis-houston/

48   Levine, S. (2021, July 9). *Texas man who waited seven hours at polls is charged with voting illegally.* The Guardian. https://www.theguardian.com/us-news/2021/jul/09/texas-voter-arrested-hervis-rogers-ken-paxton

49   Boissoneault, L. (2018, September 28). *The deadliest massacre in reconstruction-era Louisiana happened 150 years ago.* Smithsonian Magazine. https://www.smithsonianmag.com/history/story-deadliest-massacre-reconstruction-era-louisiana-180970420/

50   Opelousas massacre. (2023, December 23). In *Wikipedia.* https://en.wikipedia.org/wiki/Opelousas_massacre

51   Lewis, D. (2023, April). *The 1873 Colfax massacre set back the reconstruction era.* Smithsonian Magazine. https://www.smithsonianmag.com/smart-news/1873-colfax-massacre-crippled-reconstruction-180958746/

52   Cabral, S. (2023, July 21). *Florida's new black history curriculum 'sanitised', say critics.* BBC News. https://www.bbc.com/news/world-us-canada-66261072

53   Wilmington insurrection of 1898. (2023, October 25). In *Wikipedia.* https://en.wikipedia.org/wiki/Wilmington_insurrection_of_1898

54   Richardson, R. (2021, May 29). *Tulsa Race Massacre, 100 years later: Why it happened and why it's still relevant today*

55   SPLC. (n. d.) *Civil rights martyrs.* https://www.splcenter.org/what-we-do/civil-rights-memorial/civil-rights-martyrs

56   Tensley, B. (2021) *America's long history of Black voter suppression.* CNN Politics. https://www.cnn.com/interactive/2021/05/politics/black-voting-rights-suppression-timeline/

57   Tensley, B. (2021) *America's long history of Black voter suppression.* CNN Politics.

58   (2023, October 19). *Voting Laws Roundup: October 2023.* Brennan Center for Justice. https://www.brennancenter.org/our-work/research-reports/voting-laws-roundup-october-2023?_ga=2.143541245.99206110.1699155390-860564593.1699155390#footnote3_kciaq29

59   The independent. (2022, June 16). *Jan 6 mob threatens to hang Mike Pence during hearings.* [Video[. YouTube. https://www.youtube.com/watch?v=KCbTgDC14uY

60   Tensley, B. (2021) *America's long history of Black voter suppression.* CNN Politics

61   Mazza, E, (2023, September 7). *Mike Huckabee ripped for horrific 'Bullets' warning over 2024 election.* Huffpost. https://www.huffpost.com/entry/mike-huckabee-bullets_n_64f94986e4b02eee30c3b4c4

62   Siders, D. (2023, November 28). *Black Voters are drifting away from Democrats. Will that hurt Biden in SC?* Politico. https://www.politico.com/news/magazine/2023/11/28/black-voters-biden-2024-00128338

63   Hsieh, E. (2020, July 3). *Arab-Americans tackling anti-Blackness in the Middle East.* Middle East Eye. https://www.middleeasteye.net/news/black-lives-matter-blm-arab-americans-call-out-racism

64   Abeed. (2024, February 1). In *Wikipedia.* https://en.wikipedia.org/wiki/Abeed

65   Luck, T. (2020, June 22). *Voicing 'solidarity' against US racism, Arabs expose scourge at home.* The Christian Science Monitor. https://www.csmonitor.com/World/Middle-East/2020/0622/Voicing-solidarity-against-US-racism-Arabs-expose-scourge-at-home

66   Taylor, M. E. (2018, August 24). *The revealing story of Afro-Palestinians and how they made Jerusalem their home.* Face 2Face. https://face2faceafrica.com/article/the-revealing-story-of-afro-palestinians-and-how-they-made-jerusalem-their-home

67   Al-Azraki A. (2021, June 9). *Uncovering anti-Blackness in the Arab world The Conversation.* https://theconversation.com/uncovering-anti-blackness-in-the-arab-world-162060

68   Abbasid Caliphate. (2024, February 23). In *Wikipedia.* https://en.wikipedia.org/wiki/Abbasid_Caliphate

69   Zaaimi, S. (2024, March 24). *Black Iraqis have been invisible for a long time. Their vibrant culture and struggle must be recognized.* https://www.atlanticcouncil.org/blogs/menasource/black-iraqis-have-been-invisible-for-a-long-time-their-vibrant-culture-and-struggle-must-be-recognized/

70   Black Journals. (2023, November 16). *What it's Like To Be Black in Palestine?* (Exclusive Documentary). [Video]. You Tube. https://www.youtube.com/watch?v=B_bVnBKKxdc&t=1600s

71   Black Journals. (2023 September 26). *Blacks Beware! 10 Countries That You Never Want To Visit.* [Video]. YouTube. https://www.youtube.com/watch?v=aKXPbwOtSt8

72   Black Journals (2024 February 15). *Blacks Beware! 10 Countries That You Never Want To Visit | Part 2.* [Video]. YouTube. https://www.youtube.com/watch?v=HjykHge4DCs

73   Fawcett, E. (2023, February 1). Al Sharpton again stands at the pulpit after a death involving the police. *The New York Times.* https://www.nytimes.com/2023/02/01/us/al-sharpton-tyre-nichols-funeral.html

74   *Honour Roll 2010 to 2023.* Ontario Police Memorial Foundation. https://opmf.ca/control.php?year_range=2010

75   Iacpblog (2016, August 12). *10 Ways Community Members Can Engage with Law Enforcement.* IACP. https://www.theiacp.org/news/blog-post/10-ways-community-members-can-engage-with-law-enforcement#:~:text=1%20%231.%20Volunteer%20Citizen%20volunteers%20help%20supplement%20and,Participate%20in%20Law%20Enforcement%20Surveys%20...%20More%20items

76   Manaher, S. (2023). *Respect vs Politeness: Decoding Common Word Mix-Ups.* The Content Authority. https://thecontentauthority.com/blog/respect-vs-politeness

77   WBRC FOX6 News. 2023, December 15). *NAACP speaks in Reform on Micah Washington arrest.* [Video]. YouTube. https://www.youtube.com/watch?v=RnEjPfGbQLw

78   Brumfield, S; Raby, John; Pollard, J. (2023, December 12). *North Carolina officer who repeatedly struck woman during arrest gets 40-hour suspension.* AP. https://apnews.com/article/charlotte-north-carolina-officer-strikes-woman-e8711d6299d1dfa68fd8624b61774708

79   Indisputable. (2023, December 15). *UPDATE: Cop Who Pummeled Pinned Woman Gets 40-Hour Suspension.* [Video] YouTube. https://www.youtube.com/watch?v=VZyCFlkFuKA&t=1s

80   Brumfield, S., Raby, J., Pollard, J. (2023, December 12). *North Carolina officer who repeatedly struck woman during arrest gets 40-hour suspension.* AP. https://apnews.com/article/charlotte-north-carolina-officer-strikes-woman-e8711d6299d1dfa68fd8624b61774708

81   *Best dispensaries in Charlotte.* https://searchdispensary.com/north-carolina/charlotte

82   Dean, K. (2023, April 20). *Which cannabis-related products are legal in North Carolina? Here's what to know.* Yahoo!finance. https://finance.yahoo.com/news/cannabis-related-products-legal-north-082000185.html

83   Brumfield, S., Raby, J., Pollard, J. (2023, December 12). *North Carolina officer who repeatedly struck woman during arrest gets 40-hour suspension.* AP.

84   CBS/AP. (2015, April 20). *Spine nearly severed in police custody, but few explanations.* CBS News. https://www.cbsnews.com/news/freddie-gray-nearly-severed-spine-police-custody-few-explanations/

85   Egerton, D. R. (2018, May 17). *Vesey, Denmark.* Encyclopedia.com. https://www.encyclopedia.com/people/social-sciences-and-law/social-reformers/denmark-vesey

86   Bey, K. (2020, December 9) *Meritorious Manumission Act - Dr. Claud Anderson.* [Video] YouTube. https://www.bing.com/videos/riverview/relatedvideo?q=dr.%20claud%20anderson%20on%20Meritorious%20 20Manumission&mid=B-054F9AD668A940A4D32B054F9AD668A940A4D32&ajaxhist=0

87   Brown, A. (2021, December 14). *What Is The Meritorious Manumission Act Of 1710? How America Developed A Culture Of Snitchin' And Pro-Establishment Negro Leadership.* The Moguldom Nation. https://moguldom.com/384864/what-is-the-meritorious-manumission-act-of-1710-how-america-developed-a-culture-of-snitchin-and-pro-establishment-negro-leadership/

88   Roland S. Martin. (2020, June 8). *Best of #RMU: Check Candace Owens; BLM Vs. Trump; Jobs #s not good for us; Goodell: NFL was 'wrong'* [Video] YouTube. https://www.youtube.com/watch?v=eZ_RC6hoB4o&t=313s

89   Roland E. Martin. (2022, November 23). *Roland destroys Bill Maher; Kanye West implodes; Ginni Thomas SPEWS 'BIG LIE' | Best of #RMU.* [Video]. YouTube. https://www.youtube.com/watch?v=eXTMdTe97mM&t=4437s

90   Fabiani, A. (2022, October 5). *Why is Kanye West pro-black rights one day and desperately seeking white validation the next?* Screenshot. https://screenshot-media.com/politics/human-rights/kanye-west-white-validation/

91   Based Media (2022, October 8). *Kanye West FULL INTERVIEW with Tucker Carlson (PART 1 & 2).* [Video]. YouTube. https://www.youtube.com/watch?v=kPKCh6Z4NMI

92   Craig, B. (2023, November 5). *Kentucky historian on Cameron's response to the BVM ads: 'A hit dog will holler.'* Daily Kos. https://www.dailykos.com/stories/2023/11/5/2203846/-Kentucky-historian-on-Cameron-s-response-to-the-BVM-ads-A-hit-dog-will-holler

93   Craig, B. (2023, November 5). *Kentucky historian on Cameron's response to the BVM ads: 'A hit dog will holler.'*

94   Karson, K. (2020, August 28). *Kentucky AG Daniel Cameron pitches President Trump as 'best for this country' amid racial strife.* abc News. https://abcnews.go.com/Politics/kentucky-ag-daniel-cameron-pitches-president-trump-best/story?id=72621580

95   Bowman, B. (2023, October 18). *Kentucky's Daniel Cameron touts Trump backing in home stretch of governor's race.* NBC News. https://www.nbcnews.com/meet-the-press/meetthepressblog/kentuckys-daniel-cameron-touts-trump-backing-home-stretch-governors-ra-rcna121081

96   Craig, B. (2023, November 5). *Kentucky historian on Cameron's response to the BVM ads: 'A hit dog will holler'*

97   Dred Scott v. Sandford. (2024, January 30). In *Wikipedia.* https://en.wikipedia.org/wiki/Dred_Scott_v._Sandford

98   Roland S. Martin. (2023, October 28). *'Uncle Daniel Cameron' INSULTED By 'Skinfolk Ain't Kinfolk' Ad | Roland Martin.* [Video] YouTube. https://www.youtube.com/watch?v=ol_w6Hx5VCY&t=491s

99   Aulbach, L. (2023, Novenber 8). *Four more years: Kentucky Gov. Andy Beshear, a Democrat in a red state, wins another term.* Courier Journal. https://www.courier-journal.com/story/news/politics/elections/2023/11/07/kentucky-governor-election-2023-daniel-cameron-andy-beshear-results-reactions/71253720007/

100 Roland S. Martin. (2020, June 8). *Best of #RMU: Check Candace Owens; BLM Vs. Trump; Jobs #s not good for us; Goodell: NFL was 'wrong'* [Video] YouTube. https://www.youtube.com/watch?v=eZ_RC6hoB4o&t=313s

101 Atlanta Black Star News. (2024, January 12). *Dr. Ben Carson Tells Iowa Crowd That America's History of Slavery Is 'Nothing to be Ashamed of' As He Campaigns for Donald Trump.* https://www.msn.com/en-us/news/politics/dr-ben-carson-tells-iowa-crowd-that-americas-history-of-slavery-is-nothing-to-be-ashamed-of-as-he-campaigns-for-donald-trump/ar-AA1mRXWB

102 CBN (2014, November 21). *EXCLUSIVE: Brody File Video Exclusive: Ben Carson Compares President Obama To Vladimir Putin* [Video] YouTube. https://www.youtube.com/watch?v=QAXBsc4Z6rA

103 Cancian, D. (2020, June 8). *Everything Trump Has Said About NFL Kneeling So Far.* Newsweek 90. https://www.newsweek.com/everything-donald-trump-said-nfl-anthem-protests-1509333

104 Chung. G. (2020, June 2). *Donald Trump Poses with a Bible at Church Photo Op After Police Clear His Path Using Tear Gas.* People. https://people.com/politics/donald-trump-poses-bible-church-photo-op-after-police-clear-his-path-using-tear-gas/

105 Bobic, I. (2021, July 12). *Donald Trump Calls Jan. 6 Capitol Insurrectionists*

'Great People.' Huffpost. https://www.huffpost.com/entry/trump-january-6-great-people_n_60ec5124e4b07afbc34a05a7

106 Garrity, K. & McGraw, M. (2023, December 18). *One year of Trump's praise for authoritarians.* Politico. https://www.politico.com/news/2023/12/18/trump-praise-authoritarians-00132350

107 Holmes, K. (2022, December 4). *Trump calls for the termination of the Constitution in Truth Social post.* CNN Politics. https://www.cnn.com/2022/12/03/politics/trump-constitution-truth-social/index.html

108 Sullivan, K. & Polantz, K. (2024, January 18). *Trump again argues presidents should have immunity from prosecution even if they commit crimes.* CNN Politics. https://www.cnn.com/2024/01/18/politics/trump-presidential-immunity/index.html

109 Evans, G. (2023, June 5). *Donald Trump recorded saying he kept classified file after leaving office.* BBC News. https://www.bbc.com/news/world-us-canada-65775163

110 Bernstein, A. (2023, May 9). *Jury finds Trump liable for sexual abuse in E. Jean Carroll's civil case.* npr. https://www.npr.org/2023/05/09/1175071486/jury-finds-trump-liable-for-sexual-abuse-in-e-jean-carrolls-civil-case

111 Scannell , K. & del Valle, L. (2023, September 27) *New York judge finds Donald Trump liable for fraud.* CNN Politics. https://www.cnn.com/2023/09/26/politics/trump-organization-business-fraud/index.html

112 Frazier, K. (2024, January 12). *The violent political threats public officials are facing amid Trump's legal woes.* Politico. https://www.politico.com/news/2024/01/12/trump-legal-public-official-threats-00135084

113 Mazza, E. (2024, January 16). *Ben Carson Praises Trump With bonkers Biblical comparison. An apparent tech glitch made the exchange even more awkward.* Huffpost. https://www.huffpost.com/entry/ben-carson-trump-bible_n_65a62e04e4b07bd6950df0d5

114 Harrison, I. (2022, December 14). *The lifespan of a dollar in Black community is only 6 hours: Fact or myth?* The Moguldom Nation. https://moguldom.com/430441/the-lifespan-of-a-dollar-in-black-community-is-only-6-hours-fact-or-myth/

115 *The unsettling truth behind companies lack of support for black owned businesses.* [Video]. YouTube. https://www.youtube.com/shorts/WjColYzUswo

116 Roland S. Martin. (2024, January 13). *Roland Master Class on Tubi, Blacks gossip, and how Black-owned media gets screwed by advertisers.* [Video] You Tube. https://www.youtube.com/watch?v=I88wIuquYNw

117 Phuong, A. (2020, June 1.) *10 Organizations That Empower Black Communities In Canada.* Styledemocracy. https://www.styledemocracy.com/organizations-black-canadian-communities/#:~:text=10%20Organizations%20That%20Empower%20Black%20Communities%20In%20Canada,8%20Black%20

Women%20In%20Motion%20...%20More%20items

118 *Together, we're on a mission to empower our community.* Black ladders. https://blackladders.ca/about/

119 *Mentor Canada.* https://mentoringcanada.ca/

Chapter 15
Conclusion: Don't Blame the Stars

1 FoxNews. (2022, March 22). *Tucker: You are not allowed to ask this.* [Video] YouTube. https://www.youtube.com/watch?v=zVkS_4bIr98

2 Graziosi, G. (2023, August 24). *Why was Tucker Carlson fired from Fox News?* The Independent. https://www.independent.co.uk/news/world/americas/us-politics/why-was-tucker-carlson-fired-fox-news-b2354146.html

3 Morris, B. (2023, September 19). *Breaking Down The Stereotype: Why Are Black People So Lazy?* NewsOne. https://newsone.com/4723257/breaking-down-the-stereotype-why-are-black-people-so-lazy/

4 The view. (2022, March 3). *Tucker Calls for Judge Jackson's LSAT Scores | The View.* [Video] YouTube. https://www.youtube.com/watch?v=rdmJh6OToLw&t=14s

5 LegalEagle (March 2022). *Tucker Carlson Makes Crazy Demand of SCOTUS Nominee #Shorts.* https://www.youtube.com/shorts/p7jzYmAdf9w

6 Kilander, G. (2024, February 8). *Hillary Clinton calls Tucker Carlson Putin's 'useful idiot' ahead of controversial interview.* The Independent. https://www.msn.com/en-gb/news/world/hillary-clinton-calls-tucker-carlson-putin-s-useful-idiot-ahead-of-controversial-interview/ar-BB1hYXGk

7 Sky News Australia. (2024, February 15). *'He is a dangerous man': Vladimir Putin opens up on Tucker Carlson interview.* [Video]. YouTube. https://www.youtube.com/watch?v=dxylCxBXElg

8 Forbes Breaking News (2024, January 24). *Trump Tells Tim Scott 'You Must Really Hate' Nikki Haley After NH Primary Win—Then Scott Responds.* [Video]. YouTube. https://www.youtube.com/watch?v=mUZOiw9nK8s

9 MSNBC. (2024, February 5). *Sexyy Red fact check: Democrats made the stimulus checks happen, not Trump.* [Video] YouTube. https://www.youtube.com/watch?v=MVflkfC8AxU

10 Pramuk, J, & Higgins, T. (2020, December 24). *GOP blocks House Democrats' attempt to pass $2,000 stimulus checks.* CNBC. https://www.cnbc.com/2020/12/24/house-votes-on-2000-stimulus-checks-after-trump-supports-them.html

11 Cillizza, C. (2021, March 11). *Why Republican opposition to the Covid-19 stimulus bill looks like very bad politics.* CNN Politics. https://www.cnn.com/2021/03/11/politics/covid-19-bill-american-rescue-plan-mcconnell/index.html

12   Curse of Ham. (2024, February 5). In *Wikipedia*. https://en.wikipedia.org/ wiki/Curse_of_Ham

13   Anne Catherine Emmerich. (2024, February 9). In *Wikipedia*. https:// en.wikipedia.org/wiki/Anne_Catherine_Emmerich

14   Curse of Ham. (2024, February 5). In *Wikipedia*. https://en.wikipedia.org/ wiki/Curse_of_Ham

15   BBC. (2020, July 18). *'My Nigerian great-grandfather sold slaves'*. https://www. bbc.com/news/world-africa-53444752

16   Tutton. M. (2017, September 20). *40 million slaves in the world, finds new report.* CNN Freedom Project. https://www.cnn.com/2017/09/19/world/global-slavery-estimates-ilo/index.html

17   (2023, August 22). *African Conflicts Displace Over 40 Million People.* Africa Center for Strategic Studies. https://africacenter.org/spotlight/african-conflicts-displace-over-40-million-people/

18   OCHA. *Sudan: Ten months of conflict - Key Facts and Figures (15 February 2024).* https://www.unocha.org/publications/report/sudan/sudan-ten-months-conflict-key-facts-and-figures-15-february-2024

19   Reuters. (2023, September 6) *Who are Sudan's Rapid Support Forces?* https://www.reuters.com/world/africa/who-are-sudans-rapid-support-forces-2023-04-13/

20   *Rev. Al Sharpton to Black Trump supporters: "Have you not shame?"* @msnbc. [Video] YouTube. https://www.youtube.com/shorts/mmILonYGRJo

21   William Shakespeare's play. *Julius Caesar.* Act I, Scene II, lines 140-141

22   (2019, March 12). *The white Southerners who fought US segregation.* BBC. https://www.bbc.com/news/world-us-canada-47477354

23   Anne Braden. (2024, February 6). In *Wikipedia*. https://en.wikipedia.org/ wiki/Anne_Braden

24   John Howard Griffin. (2023, November 30). In *Wikipedia*. https:// en.wikipedia.org/wiki/John_Howard_Griffin

25   Allard K. Lowenstein. (2024, February 12). In *Wikipedia*. https:// en.wikipedia.org/wiki/Allard_K._Lowenstein

26   Mildred and Richard Loving. (2024, January 19). In *Wikipedia*. https:// en.wikipedia.org/wiki/Mildred_and_Richard_Loving

27   Category. (2024, March 1). In *Wikipedia*. https://en.wikipedia.org/wiki/ Category:White_South_African_anti-apartheid_activists

www.ingramcontent.com/pod-product-compliance
Lightning Source LLC
LaVergne TN
LVHW051050080426
835508LV00019B/1800